Term Variation in Specialised Corpora

Terminology and Lexicography Research and Practice (TLRP)

ISSN 1388-8455

Terminology and Lexicography Research and Practice aims to provide in-depth studies and background information pertaining to Lexicography and Terminology. General works include philosophical, historical, theoretical, computational and cognitive approaches. Other works focus on structures for purpose- and domain-specific compilation (LSP), dictionary design, and training. The series includes monographs, state-of-the-art volumes and course books in the English language.

For an overview of all books published in this series, please see *www.benjamins.com/catalog/tlrp*

Volume 19

Term Variation in Specialised Corpora
Characterisation, automatic discovery and applications
by Béatrice Daille

Term Variation in Specialised Corpora

Characterisation, automatic discovery and applications

Béatrice Daille
University of Nantes - LINA

John Benjamins Publishing Company
Amsterdam / Philadelphia

The paper used in this publication meets the minimum requirements of the American National Standard for Information Sciences – Permanence of Paper for Printed Library Materials, ANSI Z39.48-1984.

DOI 10.1075/tlrp.19

Cataloging-in-Publication Data available from Library of Congress.

ISBN 978 90 272 2343 2 (HB)
ISBN 978 90 272 6535 7 (E-BOOK)

John Benjamins Publishing Company · https://benjamins.com

Table of contents

Part III. Applications and tools

Part IV. Conclusions

Acknowledgements

This work could not have been completed without the help of many people. First, I am deeply indebted to my colleague and friend Professor Kyo Kageura for his constant encouragement in this project. I am also very grateful to the scientific board of *International Journal of Terminology*, Professor Marie Claude L'Homme, Professor Juan C. Sager, and two reviewers who took the time to evaluate the draft of this book and provided detailed comments that allowed me to improve and strengthen many aspects of this book.

My thanks also go to my colleagues in the field of terminology and Natural Language Processing with whom I had scientific discussions, Monique Slodzian (INALCO), Anthony Hartley (Rikkyo University), Farid Cerbah (Dassault Aviation) and my colleagues who were partners of the TTC project: Ulrich Heid (U. Stuttgart), Emmanuel Morin (U. Nantes), Helena Blancaford (Syllabs), Serge Sharoff (U. Leeds), Tatiana Gornostay (TILDE), Alexander Fraser (U. Stuttgart), Claude de Loupy (Syllabs), Andrejs Vasiljevs (TILDE), Claude Meloucham (SOGITEC). TTC was a rich and intensive project that fed this study. As the reader will see, the book is the result of research starting in 1996. It involved many colleagues and PhD students. I would like to express my appreciation to my colleagues Amir Hazem and Emmanuel Morin for the fruitful collaboration and the work done together in Chapter 7. I am very grateful to my PhD students: Elizaveta Loginova-Clouet, Rima Harastani and Emmanuel Prochasson, whose work represents a significant input to this study. A special thank to Elizaveta Loginova-Clouet without whom I would not have been able to work on Russian, and to Marion Weller and Anita Ram, NLP engineers at the University of Stuttgart, who provided German data. I am greatly indebted to the engineers who worked on the development of TermSuite, Jérôme Rocheteau, Sébastian Peña-Saldarriaga and Damien Cram.

The laboratory of Computer sciences (LINA) of the University of Nantes with which I am affiliated hosted this research and provided me with a perfect research environment. Research described in Chapters 3, 6, 9 and 10 was carried out with the support of the European Community's Seventh Framework Programme (*/*FP7/2007-2013*/*) under Grant Agreement no. 248005 for the research project TTC "Terminology, Translation and Comparable corpora" (2010–2012).

Research reported in Chapter 7 was supported by the French National Research Agency (TermITH project – "Terminologie et Indexation de Textes de spécialité en sciences Humaines" (20122016) under Grant Agreement ANR-12-CORD-0029. Research described in Chapters 6 and 10, and the development of TermSuite has been supported by ISTEX, French Excellence Initiative of Scientific and Technical Information, from 2015 to 2017.

I also have to thank Geoffrey Williams and Sandrine Henry who helped to write the English version of this book.

Finally, I would like to thank my family for their support.

Béatrice Daille
October 20, 2016

CHAPTER 1

Introduction

Terminological variation has been a very important topic in terminology, computational terminology and natural language processing for twenty years. It was approached in reference books for terminology (Sager 1990), (Cabré and Sager 1999) and (Gaudin 2003), and addressed in numerous articles published in journals (e.g. *Terminology: An International Journal of Theoretical and Practical Issues in Specialised Communication, International Journal of Corpus Linguistics, META: Translators' Journal, Cahiers de Lexicologie* or academic conference proceedings (e.g. *TIA: Terminology and Artificial Intelligence, TKE: Terminology and Knowledge Engineering, NAACL HLT: North American Chapter of the Association for Computational Linguistics: Human Language Technologies, Computerm: International Workshop on Computational Terminology, Travaux du CRTT*).

This study falls within the domain of natural language processing. Our approach is classical, in the sense that we believe that the automatic recognition of variants is not a purely engineering activity but must be based on principled linguistic and terminological approaches. By now, at the machine learning age of natural language processing, our concern with linguistically describing terminological variation may seem futile. But machine learning requires huge amounts of data that are not always available for specialised domains and language for special purpose domains. Terminological variation is a complex and heterogeneous phenomenon that is interesting to describe *per se*. Furthermore, even if machine learning approaches claim not to rely on linguistic specifications they often use linguistic features that result from them. Our conceptualisation of term variation should be useful even for machine learning approaches.

What is a variant is a vexed question. For this study, we will assume a notion of equivalence between term and variant corresponding to traditional terminology such as "referring to the same concept" or, more controversally, "related to a close concept". Clearly adequate variant recognition goes much beyond these notions since, for instance, factors of discourse, culture and professional practice are highly relevant. But natural language processing applications meet difficulties in handling such extra-linguistic contexts.

The methodology adopted is descriptive: it consists in collecting term variants for several domains and languages, analysing them and classifying them so as to identify typical terminological processes beyond their creation. Our specification of terminological variants is orthography- and grammar-based and exploits surface linguistic representations. Some semantics of term variants were addressed but only if they could be inferred from surface linguistics. So we fully acknowledge the rather limited semantic and conceptual analysis of this study. In addition, it is a fully synchronic study: we do not tackle diachronic variation and concept evolution across times and cultures.

This study fits in with multilingual trends in as much as describing terminological variation as detecting it. We deal with five languages: French, English, German, Spanish and Russian. We assume that these languages are subject to the same processes of variation and can be formally described. Our multilingual framework leads us to discover common characteristics in several languages. Hence the importance of morphology in our study which has been often neglected in term variation recognition. In order to compare term variants across languages, we look at terms of the same concept found in several languages belonging to different groups of Indo-European origin. Obviously, it is an ideal framework because many terms have no translation, and concepts are not always shared across languages. We met conceptual variation between languages, in the sense that similar surface phenomena conceal concept variation. Conceptual variation is not in the scope of this study and if we met it while looking for variants, we neither describe nor theorise about it.

Table 1.1 Example of variants of the term (AGR) Fr: *produit forestier* 'forest product'.

1	*pro-duit forestier*	'forest pro-duct'
2	*produit fo-restier*	'fo-rest product'
3	*produit forestier*	'forest product'
4	*produits forestiers*	'forest products'
5	*produit de la forêt*	'product of the forest'
6	*produit d'origine forestière*	'forest-origin product'
7	*sous-produit forestier*	'forest by-product'
8	*produit agroforestier*	'agroforest product'
9	*production forestière*	'forest production'
10	*produit alimentaire forestier*	'forest food product'
11	*produit alimentaire de la forêt*	'product of food from the forest'
12	*produit fini d'origine forestière*	'forest-origin finished product'
13	*produit non forestier*	'non-forest product'
14	*non-produit forestier*	'forest non-product'
15	*produit ligneux non forestier*	'non-forest timber product'
16	*produits halieutique et forestier*	'forest and fish products'
17	*produit agricole ou forestier*	'forest or crop product'
18	*produits agricole et forestier*	'forest and crop products'
19	*le produit et le service forestiers*	'the forest service and product'
20	*produits agricoles, halieutiques et forestiers*	'forest, fish and crop products'

In the context of this study, the conceptualisation of term variants is not based on a single language but on any of our five languages. We attempt to be as exhaustive as possible and to systematise the linguistic description of terminological variation across languages for their linguistic processing. But of course, some variants may have been omitted. We also know in advance that exhaustivity is hardly reachable when dealing with language. We do not propose a new linguistic theory about term variation; on the contrary we refer to linguistic works as much as possible and take from them what could be useful to automatically identify variation in texts. So, what is offered below is a contribution to multilingual variant recognition from specifications to the design of a multilingual system.

1.1 Preliminary example

In order to illustrate the theme of this study dedicated to variants of terms and the scale of terminological variation in specialised domains, Table 1.1 compiles some variants of the term Fr: *produit forestier* 'forest product' automatically identified in a French corpus of texts in the domain of agriculture.

Examples 1 and 2 are graphical variants, the components of the term have been split for a line feed and were then recomposed by the program, but keeping the word break location. Examples 3 and 4 are respectively the singular and plural inflections of the term. Examples 5 and 6 are denominative variants of exemplification of the term; variants 5 and 6 are more explicit than the term, and variant 6 is even more explicit than variant 5. The term and the denominative variants 5 and 6 produce conceptual variants shown by variants 7 to 15. Variants 7 to 12 are conceptual variants of expansion which are formed by: a prefix for variant 7, a morphological component for variant 8, a derivational suffix for variant 9, or an adjective for variants 10 to 12. Variants of expansion 13 to 14 are two antonyms of the term; antonym 13 also has a conceptual variant in number 15. Finally, variants 16 to 20 are linguistic variants of coordination and enumeration.

For all of the variants of Table 1.1, the form of the entry term is altered by the insertion of a character, a morphological component or a word. There are other variants that we have not included in Table 1.1. They do not alter the form of the entry term. They are obtained by expansion of the term, either to the left, such as *produit forestier fini* 'finished forest product', or to the right, such as *développement de produits forestiers* 'development of forest products'. In this study, we are interested in variants that refer to the same concept pointed out by a term, such as variants 1 to 6 and 16 to 20, or that show a conceptual difference with the term, such as variants 7 to 15 and all variants of expansion. This first example is in French, and French will be the main language illustrated, but as we already explained, our study deals with five languages.

1.2 Variants and terminological analysis

We begin by clarifying the position of term variation in the framework of two theories of terminology. Then, we stress its central role in the mechanism of neonymy.

Variants and theories of terminology

The notion of "term variant" depends strongly on the definition of "term". Different theories will treat the notion from different angles (L'Homme 2005).

The prescriptive tradition of terminology, which used to be most typically represented by the Vienna school and the General Theory of the Terminology (GTT) introduced by Wüster (1968), adopts a conceptual or an onomasiologic approach (in Greek *onoma* 'noun') that emphasises the rigidity of the forms of terms. The conceptual approach supposes the presence of the concept. The terminological analysis aims to discover linguistic forms useful for labelling the concept, rather than for electing one that will be considered the standard designation for that concept. GTT therefore recognises implicitly the existence of variants because normalisation is necessary, but it does not look for detecting, nor for compiling these variants. The linguistic forms considered as variants are necessarily related to a term. The prototypical examples of variants admitted by GTT are synonyms, acronyms and abbreviations. These are included in terminological records.

New approaches to terminology have risen since the 1990, many of them adopt an opposing approach, i.e. a semasiological approach to the term. The contextual or semasiological approach (in Greek *sêma* 'sign') studies the linguistic forms in order to identify the concepts. The linguistic forms are studied in specialised texts. Therefore for Kocourek (1991: 72), the term is an essential component of specialised texts and its analysis in texts consolides the terminological knowledge of the domain:

> Le contexte du terme met en évidence des propriétés terminologiques graphiques, phoniques et grammaticales, telles que l'orthographe, la prononciation, le genre, le pluriel, le comportement dans les textes des syntagmes lexicaux du type langue de spécialité (nombre, article du nom modificateur). Émergent, ou apparaissent plus clairement, les problèmes syntactico-sémantiques, de pluralité et de généricité par exemple.[1]

1. "The context of the term clarifies graphic, phonic and grammatical properties of terminology, such as orthography, gender, plural, behaviour in texts of lexical syntagma of the type of specialised language (number, modifier article of the noun). The semantic and syntactic problems arise or appear more clearly from plurality and genericity, for instance."

Textual Terminology (Bourigault and Slodzian 1999) considers texts of specialised domains as authentic terminological resources. The term is a lexical unit that is defined by its linguistics properties and according to the place it occupies in a corpus (Bourigault and Slodzian 1999) or, generally, in the discourse (Gaudin 2003). The term is subject to the linguistic variations found in all lexical units in the discourse such as inflection, modification or coordination.

In spite of their differences, the two approaches recognise the existence of term variants: conceptual variants for the conceptual approach, and linguistic variants for the contextual approach. Our study of term variation adopts a semasiological approach. All term variants will be linguistic, but some of them will have further properties. We will distinguish denominative variants offering alternative forms to name the concept, and conceptual variants, i.e. those conceptually related to the term.

Variants and neonymy

The variants of a term make up a bank of neonyms. The four mechanisms of neonymy identified by Cabré (1998: 256) are:

1. "neonymism of form": formed by derivation, compounding, syntagmatism and process of reduction or brachygraphy (initials, acronyms, abbreviation);
2. "neonymism of function": lexicalisation of an inflected form, conversion;
3. "semantic neonymism": expansion, restriction or modification of the content of the base form;
4. "borrowing" and "loan" from other languages.

In addition, there are also mechanisms of term variation that we will detail and exemplify in Chapter 3.

Term variation is a mark of the systemic instability that characterises neologisms. The variants that are often used are lexicalised over time and recorded in specialised dictionaries (Delpierre 2007). Dury (2007), in her study on clues to diachronic evolution in dictionaries, confirms the emerging of variants of terms as sub-entries of a term, as the variant *carbon dioxide* that appears as sub-entry of *carbon*, or the change of state of sub-entry to that entry in the dictionary, as *carbon dating*. Jacquemin (2001: 3) remarks that:

> Term fluidity is another important aspect of the evolution of terms. Denotations, spellings, syntactic properties, and usages of terms are continually evolving.

Similarly to Cabré (1998) for neonyms, we will define the mechanisms of formation of variants of terms, which are specific to the variant category. Although the mechanisms and the linguistic operations that implement these mechanisms are multiple, we will apply them without distinction to single terms and to complex terms, regardless whether they are morphologically or syntactically built. Our linguistic specification of variants treating morphology and syntax as equal, guarantees a language-independent analysis of term variants across languages.

1.3 The automatic detection of variants

The automatic detection of term variants has been the subject of numerous studies within the field of Natural Language Processing (NLP). There are two main streams in NLP. The first applies symbolic approaches that aim to model language before elaborating methods (Jurafsky and Martin 2009); the second advocates empirical approaches that build models from data (Manning and Schütze 1999). Up to now, the detection of variants has stemmed mainly from the first. Modellings were proposed and implemented in order to detect variants of a specific language, such as Takeuchi et al. (2004) for Japanese, or variants of a category, such as Hamon and Nazarenko (2001) for the detection of synonymic variants for French, or variants which were given an application, such as Jacquemin (2001) for automatic indexing. The second stream was been omitted, here, because of the relatively low frequency of the variant. Variants have many forms, but each form has very few occurrences. Thus, quantitative methods that automatically detect regular and frequent patterns in data fit poorly for variant discovery, at least for some categories of variants.

Our specification of term variants lists many linguistic operations used for the production of variants. There will be as many methods of detection. Indeed, up until now, linguists and terminologists looking for term variants in text had to do so semi-automatically. We aim to play the role of a variant-hunter using a simple, language-independent and user-friendly method for evaluating its benefits and its shortcomings in line with our specifications. We will use comparable specialised corpora available in several languages and domains. But for an extensive discovery of variants, many methods are required that are difficult to aggregate, however experienced one may be. We will review the main methods to detect term variants. We will complete our specification of term variants by describing occurrence properties that will direct us toward the method to be applied. We will pursue our variant detection by firstly applying a symbolic approach that will rely upon our specifications, and then an empirical method. We will adopt a multilingual and multi-domain framework for both investigations. Finally, we will describe TermSuite: a multilingually designed tool to provide effective procedures for mapping terms and variants capable of accomodating new languages without major upheaval.

1.4 Variants and applications

Bourigault and Slodzian (1999) claim that terminology cannot be apprehended without addressing the purposes of its applications. The notion of term is always coloured by the specialist approach. Estopà Bagot (2001) has shown that in the health domain, terminological units differ according to professional usage. Differences mostly arise from the quantity of selected terms, the grammatical categories of terms and complex term patterns. The notion of variants of terms is also dependent on the domain of application, as shown in our article (Daille 2005).

We have designed the specification of variants regardless of any applicative constraints as our goal was to reach a complete census of variants. As for an application, this typology should be restricted to certain categories of variants. For example, in translation, the majority of linguistic variants obtained by coordination do not pose any problem of translation, and thus do not need to be detected. On the contrary, for controlled indexation, for which the objective is the recognition of occurrences of terms of a thesaurus, the variants obtained by coordination have to be located. Furthermore, the typology will be approximated or generalised depending on the method employed.

In Daille (2005), we examined four applications that process term variants: terminology acquisition, machine-aided text indexing, scientific and technological watch, and computer-assisted translation. If we argued that the identification of term variants benefits terminology acquisition, we did not demonstrate it. This study and our experiments will confirm that the recognition of variants generally improves results of terminology acquisition, but that the improvement varies by language and specialised domain. This application-oriented evaluation will be preceded by a state-of-the-art terminology acquisition methods.

1.5 Typographical conventions

We apply the following typographical conventions, reduced to the minimum so as not to unnecessarily overload the reading. The main concepts are indicated using double inverted commas. The linguistic examples appear in italics and their English translation, when necessary, follows inside inverted commas. Discourse categories belong to grammatical labelling categories defined by Multext. Capital letters are used for grammatical categories such as N for noun, V for verb, A for adjective, P for preposition. They can be followed by a semicolon and lower-case letters specifying inflexion at a given position, such as for the noun: c for common at first position, m for masculine at second position (N:cm). Encoding is explained in Appendix B.

The capital letter E is used for roots of compounds. Citation forms are most of the times lemmas of lexical units but when lemmas for complex terms look ungrammatical, we use a corrected lemma form. For morphological concatenation, when necessary, the sign | is used in the linguistic examples and the sign + in the patterns. The linguistic elements shared by the term and the variant are numbered with the same subscripts. For example, the variant rule: N_1+N_2 (term) → N_2PN_1 (variant), the lemma N_1 of the term and the variant are identical (and the same applies for N_2).

PART I

Characterisation

CHAPTER 2

Definitions

Studying the variants of terms firstly requires us to introduce their linguistics and terminological foundations in order to better grasp the complexity and the diversity of the phenomenon. The first necessary definition is that of the term itself, "a unit that is defined in specialised texts"[1] (Kocourek 1991: 180). We will present the linguistic mechanisms that lead to the formation of a variant: derivation, compounding and borrowing. As the variant is defined by its reference to a term, we will provide an overview of the main term patterns and their statistics. Lastly, we will define the main categories of term variants: denominative variants and conceptual variants. While defining and characterising the basic concepts of this study, we will also emphasise their shallow borders. Whatever the legitimacy of these concepts, boundaries blurred between a term and a variant, between a denominative variant and a conceptual variant. As a conclusion, we will justify our approach to the analysis of the term variants which is intended to be fully comprehensive and not limited to the sole ontological framework.

2.1 Term

Terms generally have three dimensions: a linguistic form, a denotative function to a specific class of mental or real-world objects (Cabré and Sager 1999), and a domain (Otman 1996). L'Homme (2004: 22) suggests that the term is a lexical unit whose meaning is determined within a specialised domain. The linguistic form of the term may be affected by the domain as well as the target application. According to the "Communicative theory of terminology" (Cabré 1999, 2000), the term must satisfy the requirement of the user's needs.

The underlying premise of Wüster's General Theory of Terminology is that terms are labels for clearly defined concepts. As such, terms should follow the four principles identified in Bowker and Hawkins (2006: 83):

1. "Une unité définie dans les textes de spécialités."

> *Monosemy and Mononymy:*
> a term refers to a single concept, and a concept is designated by only one term;
> *Linguistic accuracy:*
> a term conforms to the morphological, syntactic, orthographical and phonotactic conventions of the language in question;
> *Transparency:*
> a term is self-evident and reflects the essential characteristics of the concept it designates;
> *Conciseness:*
> a term is concise and in keeping with the principle of linguistic economy.

Otman (1996: 15) indicates that the properties of monosemy and mononymy are contested, and therefore questioned by everyday terminological practice. Homonymy and synonymy of terms are frequent phenomena in texts and are at the heart of terminological variation. Monosemy and mononymy can also be in conflict with transparency and conciseness. Compounding, whether morphological or syntagmatic, remains one of the privileged linguistic processes for neonyms. Compounding is interpreted by Lerat (1995: 70) as a way of condensing information in a motivated form rather than an entirely explicit form. This minimalism might disturb the interpretation of a term and cause an ambiguity of the term's designation value. Does the syntagmatic compound (AGR) Fr: *farine animale* 'animal flour' mean flour for animals or flour made from animal waste? Here as well, variants can play an important role of disambiguation by making a too minimal term clearer.

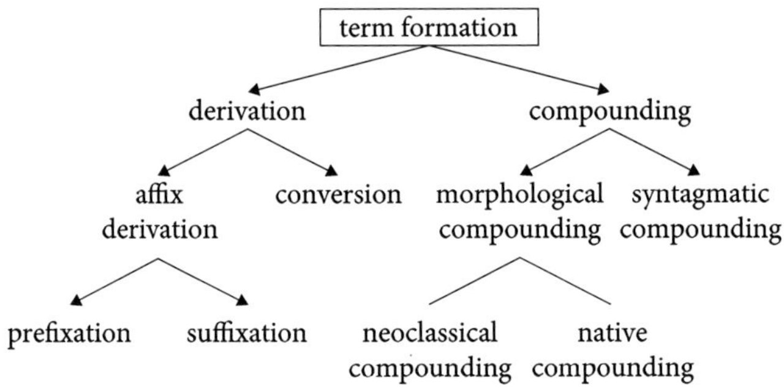

Figure 2.1 A detailed representation of the mechanisms of neonymy.

A term can be simple or complex. ISO 1087 defines simple terms as terms formed with one stem form, with or without affixes, and complex terms as terms formed by one or several stem forms to which several forms can be added. The root is a lexeme, also called a lexical morpheme, or a neoclassical form, also called a "Greek or Latin form". For example, (EOL) Fr: *rotor,* (MOB) En: *packet* are simple terms; (EOL) Fr: *pale de rotor* 'rotor blade' and En: *aerogenerator,* with the neoclassical form *aero,* (MOB) En: *frequency band, multiplexing,* with the neoclassical form *multi, broadband* are complex terms.

The linguistic mechanisms for creating terms are similar to those applied to general language and are described in lexicology (Cabré 1998; Lerat 1995). The two main mechanisms of the formation of neologisms in general language are "derivation" and "compounding". Concerning the formation of new terms or neonyms, Cabré (1998: 256) pinpoints the linguistic processes of derivation, compounding and syntagmatic formation. She distinguishes two types of composition of derivation: morphological and syntagmatic compounding. Figure 2.1 summarises the linguistic mechanisms of term formation: derivation and compounding (illustrated above and detailed in Sections 2.2 and 2.3).

Mechanisms			Term	Neonym
Prefixation	(EOL)	Fr	*rotor*	*birotor*
Suffixation	(MOB)	En	*connexion*	*connectivity*
Conversion	(MOB)	Fr	*exécutable/A*	*exécutable/N*
Neoclassical compounding	(MOB)	En	*location*	*geolocation*
Native compounding	(MOB)	En	*band*	*broadband*
Syntagmatic compounding	(MOB)	En	*interface*	*user interface*

Derivation and compounding processes are two vital processes of neonymy. The privileged compounding type, whether it is morphological or syntagmatic, depends on the language, and sometimes on a specialised domain. Therefore, in general, Romance languages adopt syntagmatic compounding, and German and Japanese adopt morphological compounding. In French, however, although syntagmatic compounding is dominant, the medical domain adopts morphological compounding more easily than other domains.

The distinction between simple and complex terms is a linguistic definition, which can create difficulties for NLP. The analysis techniques of terms in a corpus requires operational definitions which should only be approximate interpretations of linguistic definitions. L'Homme (2004: 59) defines simple terms as lexical units composed of one graphic unit, called single-word terms (SWT), and complex terms constituted of graphic entities, separated by a space or diacritical signs such as hyphen or apostrophe, called multi-word terms (MWT). Even if this definition excludes neoclassical compounds, it is operational in Romance languages where syntagmatic compounds dominate. However, it causes problems for Germanic languages, especially German, because the majority of German complex terms are morphological compounds. In the computer science field, the term *système-expert* is a MWT in French and *Expertensystem* is a SWT in German.

2.2 Derivation

In linguistics, derivation is defined as an operation which creates a new lexical unit (a derived word) from one existing word through modification processes (Lehmann and Martin-Berthet 2008: 147). Let us cite some of them:

1. "Affixation" groups together "prefixation" *histoire* 'history' / *préhistoire* 'prehistory', "suffixation" *manger* 'to eat' / *mangeable* 'edible', or "circuminflection" De: *ge ... t gesagt* 'said'. Affixation keeps the combination order of the affixes and the base, called "morphotactics". The classes of prefixes, suffixes and circumflexes are disjointed. Prefixation and suffixation, when they are applied simultaneously to a word, are called "parasynthetic derivation" (Lehmann and Martin-Berthet 2008), Fr: *câble* N / *encablure* N with no trace of the following forms in French: **encâble, *cablure, *encabler);*
2. "Conversion" (also called "zero-derivation", "non-affixal derivation", "recategorisation" (Neveu 2004) or "improper derivation") consists in changing the grammatical category of the word without affixation: *linguistique* 'linguistics' N / *linguistique* 'linguistic' A. Conversion may include inflection and the dropping of inflectional marks En: *telephone* N / *to telephone* V;
3. "Back-affixation" (also called "regressive derivation") forms a new word by removing an affix: Fr: *embranchement N/embrancher* V.

Derivation cannot be identified solely based on concatenation. Derivation can produce a change of the stem or the affix, according to a phonetic or an orthographic context called "allomorphy": Fr: *misère, able → misérable.* Some suffixes are specific to a specialised domain. In chemistry, the suffixes Fr/En: *-ate* identifies a salt En: *sulphate* Fr: *sulfate;* Fr/En: *-ase* identifies an enzyme *oxydase; -ol* identifies an alcohol En: *phenol* Fr: *phénol;* Fr/En: *-ose* identifies a sugar Fr/En: *glucose.*

The words derived from the same base form a "derivative paradigm": Fr: *compétition, compétiteur, compétitif.* The derivative paradigm of one base is characteristic of a term, and L'Homme (2004) cites two paradigms of *fraise* 'strawberry' in the domain of agriculture, *fraise, fraisier, fraiseraie* 'strawberry, strawberry plant, strawberry field'; in the domain of equipment, *fraise, fraiser, fraisage, fraiseuse* 'mill, to mill, milling, milling machine'.

2.3 Compounding

Some typical definitions of compounding are:

> Combining two or more otherwise free morphemes or series of morphemes (= words) to form a compound. (Bussmann 1996: 84)

> A compound lexeme (or simply a compound) can thus be defined as a lexeme containing two or more potential stems. (Bauer 2003: 28)

> A lexical unit made up of two or more elements, each of which can function as a lexeme independent of the other(s) in other contexts, and which shows some phonetic and/or grammatical isolation from normal syntactic usage. (Bauer 2001: 695)

The common element of these definitions is that a compound is made of two lexemes. But Benveniste (1974: 171) enlarges this definition:

> There is compounding when two forms are conjoined in a new lexical unit with constant and unique meaning. These forms are Greek or Latin stems, Fr: *centimètre, palmipède, télégraphe* or native words, Fr: *portefeuille, orfèvre, betterave, marchepied, averse, entresol.*

Benveniste's definition introduced morphological compounds split between neoclassical and native compounds. He adopts the term "synapsy" for syntagmatic compounds. Syntagmatic compounds are compounds in which the elements are separated by a blank space while having one meaning (EOL) Fr: *parc éolien* wind park . Morphological compound are written as single words, possibly including a hyphen (EOL) De: *Windpark* 'wind park'. Semantically, morphological and syntagmatic compounds are units of the same level, because both refer to single concepts.

Compounds can be distinguished by their endocentric or coordinated semantic nature. An endocentric compound has a dependency relation composed of a head and a modifier, called by Bauer and Renouf (2001) the "headedness rule". The grammatical and syntactic properties of the compound – its grammatical category and inflections – are those of the head. Several orders can be used in compounding:

1. left-headed, adopted by most syntagmatic compounds;
2. right-headed, shared by many morphological compounds, (EOL) Es: *mecánico* 'mechanics', *electromecánico* 'electromechanics', and by centripedal languages such as German: (Environment) De: *Wasser* 'water', *Grundwasser* 'groundwater;
3. head-head or compounds of coordinates where the branching is not allowed (Computer science) Fr: *entrée-sortie* N 'input-output', (EOL) Es: *èolico-solar*/A 'wind-solar'.

Compound order is semantically determined in the case of endocentric compounds. It generally concerns a relation of specification of the head, and that could be repeated with a new branching on the newly constructed compound. We can see other semantic features such as direction or cause and effect: in the medical domain, a compound such as *craniocaudal* indicates a movement of the point close to the head, *cranio,* to a point close to the tail, *caudal,* while *caudalcranio* indicates the opposite direction (Bowker and Hawkins 2006: 90).

2.3.1 Morphological compounds

Following Namer (2007), we consider two types of morphological compounds: neoclassical compounds and native compounds. The lexical constituents of compounds are nouns, adjectives or verbs.

Neoclassical compounds

The term "neoclassical compound" was introduced by Bauer (2003). The neoclassical compound consists of at least one neoclassical element of Greek or Latin etymological origin such as *patho, bio, logy.* We therefore consider that neoclassical compounds are heterogeneous compounds integrating either a lexical unit and a neoclassical element such as Fr: *mobilomane* made of the French noun *mobile* and the Greek element *man,* or the combination of two or more classical elements of various origins. Unlike the native compounds, the neoclassical elements are not language independent. They are always combined with other elements, for example, the stem *patho* is used for establishing a compound, such as Fr: *pathologie* (Amiot and Dal 2008). Each language phonetically adapts neoclassical stems before integrating them into a compound (Ludeling 2012). For example, the Greek stem *pathos* produces the neoclassical elements in French *pathie* and in English *pathy.* Neoclassical elements can appear in different positions of the compound:

1. at initial position: *homo-*, Fr: *homomorphique* 'homomorphic';
2. at final position: *-cide,* Fr: *génocide* 'genocide'.

Here are some examples:

De: *magnetisch* A 'magnetic' → <u>*elektro*</u>|*magnetisch* A/CE+A 'electromagnetic'
Several neoclassical elements can be combined at initial position like *histopathologie.*

In some phonological contexts, a linking vowel can be inserted between the first and the second element, and its form depends on the origin of the second element: *o* for a Greek element, Fr: *granulothérapie,* and *i* for a Latin element, Fr: *spermicide.* According to Amiot and Dal (2007), vowel linking is one feature of the definition of the neoclassical compound, as well as the association of an element of Latin or

Greek origin, the non-autonomy of the neoclassical element, and the attachment of the compound to a specialised domain.

Native compounds
"Native compounds" are also called ordinary compounds by Amiot and Dal (2008). They are composed of lexical elements of the language they belong to. The lexical elements are autonomous and occur freely in a text. In highly analytical languages such as English or French, compound parts are just concatenated (by juxtaposition or hyphenation): Fr: *kilowatt-heure* 'kilowatt-hour', En: *parrotfish.* In languages with a rich morphology (German, Swedish, Greek, Russian, etc.), the compound parts are also concatenated, De: *Windenergie* 'wind power' which is the concatenation of *Wind* 'wind' and *Energie* 'power', but some transformations are possible at the boundaries of the compound parts. The word inflection can be omitted, and/or a "linking morpheme" can be inserted. In German, a linking morpheme is inserted when the first element is a noun. Linking morphemes are:

1. *s* preceded operationally by *e*.
   (EOL) De: *Korrosionsschultz* 'protection against corrosion', the concatenation of *Korrosion* 'corrosion', of the linking morpheme *-s-* and of *schultz* 'protection';
   (EOL) De: *Meresstrom* 'ocean current';
2. *n* preceded operationally by *e* and followed operationally by *s*
   (Medicine) De: *Augenmuskel* 'ocular muscle'.

The elements of some native compounds may be not autonomous in a specialised domain, i.e. they occur only as elements of syntagmatic compounds.

(CAN) En: *outpatient visit* with *outpatient* occurring only with *visit*

Furthermore, some elements may be in inflected when they occur in native compounds but never when they are used as autonomous units:

(EOL) Ru: vodosnabženie 'water supply' voda 'water' + snabženie 'supply'

Gelbukh and Sidorov (2003) observed this phenomenon in languages with a tendency for synthetism having a rich morphology, such as German, Greek, and Russian.

Border between neoclassical and native compounds
The distinction between neoclassical and native compounds is found in the origin as well as the degree of autonomy of their elements. It is sometimes difficult to define whether a lexical element is independent or not because of the processes of grammaticalisation and lexicalisation continuously present in languages. As for the origin of the constituent, two phenomena cause problems during the analysis:

1. The shortened lexeme produces an ambiguous form: Fr: *télécommande* 'remote-control', *télé* can be analysed as a neoclassical element or as an apocope of Fr: *télévision* 'tv' (Namer 2009: 319);
2. The shortened lexeme provokes the insertion of one of the two liaison vowels of neoclassical compounding. This appearance is always explained by a phonological context, but the introduction of *o* or *i* is not dictated by the origin of the second constituent. The shortened lexeme, the introduction of the liaison vowel and the right-headed order lead to a compound which looks like a neoclassical compound without being one. As neoclassical compounding has a very long tradition in medicine and other health sciences, compounds built with a loan neoclassical construction usually gain in terminological legitimacy. For example, the compound Fr: *hormonodépendance* is built from the lexeme *hormone; larviforme* 'larviform' comes from *larve* 'larva'. This type of neoclassical compounding is called "hidden compounding" by Fradin (2003: 53).

Thus, the difficulty of judging the autonomous character of elements comes from two main causes: the variant forms of an element and the doubt about its affiliation to the language.

2.3.2 Border between derivation and compounding

Compounding shares some properties with derivation. So that the border between derivation and the compounding is still not clearly defined. Some transitional cases are attested. Therefore, En: *work* is an independent lexeme which may appear as a compound part (*workflow, artwork*). Compounding with *work* as second element was so productive that in some cases it now can be seen as a suffix (*wirework, woolwork* meaning "decoration", "ornamentation" (Collins)).

Prefixed words cannot be called compounds in the strict sense of the term because prefixes are not independent lexical units. However some prefixes are very close to the neoclassical roots, e.g. comparing the prefix *bi-* with the neoclassical root *uni-*, according to Béchade (1992). The difference lies in their origin (neoclassical roots come from Latin or Greek content words, whereas prefixes come from function words) and the period when they entered into usage (prefixes entered earlier). Lehmann and Martin-Berthet (2008) analyse the element Fr: *télé* as a neoclassical stem in *téléphone* and as a prefix in Fr: *télésurveillance*. Such neoclassical prefixes may have native equivalents in other languages: En: *sub-* (subsystem) is equivalent of Ru: под- (подсистема). It is also difficult to tell derivation from morphological compounding when the term is morphologically constructed with the elements of Greek or Latin origin situated in initial position, e.g. prefixes like *multi-* and *poly-*.

Prefixation and compounding are close: "Prefixation as well as compounding are used to lexically condense a syntagm"[2] (Lehmann and Martin-Berthet 2008: 168).

2.3.3 Syntagmatic compounds

Benveniste (1966: 172) named syntagmatic compounds "synapses":

> A synapse is made of an entire group of lexemes that are related by various steps, forming a constant and specific designation. We find the initial nucleus in words which are already long established, e.g. *pomme de terre* 'potato', *robe de chambre* 'dressing gown', *clair de lune* 'moonlight', *plat à barbe* 'beard dish'. A new and important situation has arisen in that this type of compound takes considerable extensions today, and this causes an unlimited productivity: it will be the base formation in technical nomenclatures.

In French, synapses are characterised by the following features:

1. the syntactic nature (not morphological) of the relation between the components;
2. the usage of junctors for this effect, especially the *de* and *à* prepositions;
3. the left-headed order;
4. their full lexical form and the free choice for every substantive or adjective;
5. the absence of any article in front of the head;
6. the possibility of expansion for one or other member;
7. the single and constant character of the signified.

This definition is interesting because it is the first time that the extreme productivity of the forms N P N and N A in French technical nomenclatures has been taken into account. This productivity will be confirmed by the studies of the LADL on the DELAC dictionary of French compounds. Gross (1988) observed that the majority of the compound nouns belong to nominal groups to be lexicalised.

The syntagmatic compounds "contribute to the building of terminological systems" (Sager 1990: 77). According to Estopà Bagot (2001), who called them "nominal multiword terms",[3] they are the most prototypical and the most frequent units in specialised texts.

---

2. La préfixation apparaît ainsi comme la condensation lexicale d'un syntagme, de même que la composition.

3. "Unités terminologiques nominales polylexicales".

Complex terms are motivated combinations that meet the requirement of transparency and so clearly convey the concept they designate. The requirement of transparency argues in favor of compositional semantics for complex terms. Compositionality means that the whole meaning can be deduced from the meaning of its components and the syntactic rule by which they are combined (Parnee et al. 1990). Some complex terms, either morphological or syntagmatic, indeed are compositional:

(EOL) De: *Blindleistungsbedarf* 'reactive power requirement' = *Blindleistung* 'reactive power' + *Bedarf* 'requirement'.

Often the whole meaning cannot be totally restored, however it can be predicted to some extent ("weak compositionality" according to Pirelli et al. (2010)):

(Psychology) De: *Trotzkopf* 'stubborn person' = *trotz=* 'despite' + *Kopf* 'head, mind'.

Pirelli et al. (2010) claim that the most productive compounds are compositional (at least weak compositional) constructions. Only a few complex terms are semantically opaque. For example, De: *Trotzkopf* has the equivalent En: *pighead,* which is also a compound, but idiomatic. Compositionality of complex terms is a key element of variant production. Compositional compounds are more able to accept variants than idiomatic fixed-phases.

Nevertheless, transparency often clashes with conciseness. During the denomination process that we will present in Chapter 3, denominations of complex terms result from simplification processes that break the direct left-headed order of the term components which make it difficult for non-experts to build the meaning from the parts. The compositionality of complex terms remains a useful hypothesis for the detection of denominative variants that we will exploit in Chapter 8.

2.3.4 Border between morphological and syntagmatic compounds

We differentiated between morphological and syntagmatic compounds, but we classified both of them as compounds in order to stress that mono- and multi-word terms are terminologically equivalent, as they all refer to a single concept. Thus, a concept will be incarnated by terms of various types in different languages: a syntagmatic compound (Sport) Fr: *cheval de course* 'racehorse' is translated by a single word Es: *corcel* (example given by Léon (2004)), the majority of German morphological compounds are translated in French as syntagmatic compounds, (EOL) De: *Rotorblatt* 'rotorblade' → Fr: *pale de rotor).* The border between morphological and syntagmatic compounds is emphasised by graphical variation: the optionality of the segmentation sign for the morphological compound, (MOB) *intercarreer / inter-carrier,* and the substitution of segmentation signs by spaces, (MOB) *ip-network / ip network.* Furthermore, some formations are at the boundary between closed compounds and purely syntactic constructions. This kind of compounds are called "verbal compound" (Roeper and Siegel 1978). For instance, (Medecine) En: *anthracycline-based* can be paraphrased as *something (usually a therapy) based on anthracycline.* Bauer (1983) does not agree on their compound status and qualifies them as "complex words", while Melloni and Bisetto (2010) introduce a specific category, the "parasynthetic compounds".

2.4 Borrowing

Borrowing refers to the result of the transfer of a linguistic phenomenon from one language for use in another. It is characterised by a source language, a target language and a category. Borrowing from English is common in scientific domains. The borrowing categories are as numerous as the linguistic phenomena of a language (Haugen 1950; Colpron 1965; Pageau 2003). Lexical borrowing concerns simple or complex terms and is carried out:

1. Entirely when the source term is taken as such to the target language, such as (EOL) *rotor,* with a possible phonetic adaptation;
2. Partly (or in a hybrid manner) when only one element of the source term is adapted in the target language. This element is a morpheme of the simple term or an element or a lexeme of the complex term, such as (EOL) De: *Repowering-Leitfaden* 'assistance for energy reconnection', (TEL) Ru: ip-адрес 'ip address';
3. By assimilation (or reformulation) when the source term is replaced by a term in the target language by word-for-word translation. For a simple term, the choice of a term in the target language may lead to the adding of a new sense for an existing word, (Computer) *souris* 'mouse'. For a complex term, the structure of the source complex term may be either transferred as such in the target language, (DIA) Fr: *hormono-dépendance* 'hormono-dependent', where the right-headed order is kept from English, or adapted to the structure of the compound in the target language that is deemed to be equivalent of the source language, such as (SAT) En: N N *grid reflector* and (SAT) Fr: N P N *réflecteur à grille.*

The corpus study of Pageau (2003) dealing with the borrowing from English to French in the molecular biology domain stresses that most common borrowings are graphical borrowings, i.e. 75% are abbreviations, followed by 21% lexical borrowing.

Lexical borrowing can engender an additional compound category: "loan compounds". Loan compounds can be totally English, such as (EOL) De: *Repowering,* or partially, such as (EOL) De: *Repowering-Leitfaden* 'repowering guideline'. They can be adapted phonetically and graphically for languages that are written with other alphabets: (EOL) Ru: прайс-лист 'price-list', where прайс is the English word *price* transliterated into Cyrillic. This kind of compounding is close to the neoclassical one, but the loan elements from modern languages are more easily identified and are generally attached to the second root by a hyphen and not by a linking morpheme.

2.5 Term patterns

Terms as lexical units have a grammatical category. In addition, complex terms, either morphological or syntactic compounds, adopt a morpho-syntactic structure expressed by grammatical categories, i.e. patterns. Terms can be classified according to patterns some of which are the foundations of specialised dictionaries. Dominant patterns are nouns and nominal multi-word terms whose patterns are defined in a language.

Estopà Bagot (2001) recommends enlarging grammatical categories commonly restricted to the noun, to adjectives, adverbs and verbs, both for simple and complex terms. However her study of terms shows that nominal terms are used by 80% in some professional activities. For our study of term variants, we take into account only nouns, with the only exception of simple terms that are either nouns or adjectives.

Table 2.1 Simple terms of noun category.

	Multext category	**Example**	**English translation**
En	N:cms	*blade*	
Es	N:cms	*rotor*	*rotor/N*
Fr	N:cfs	*pale*	*blade/N*
De	N:cms	*Windpark*	*wind farm/N N*
Ru	N:cfsn	лопасть	*blade/N*

Table 2.2 Simple terms of adjective category.

	Multext category	**Example**	**English translation**	**Comment**
En	A:f--s	*renewable*		epithetic
	A:f--s	*electrical*		relational
Fr	A:f--s	*renouvelable*	*renewable/A*	epithetic with inflected forms *-s*
	A:f-ms	*éolien*	*wind/N*	relational with inflected forms *-s -ne, -nes*
De	A:f	*erneuerbar*	*renewable/A*	epithetic with inflected forms *-e, -es, -en, -er, -em*
	A:f	*atomar*	*atomic*	relational with inflected forms *-e, -es, -en, -er, -em*
Ru	A:f-msn	возобновляемый	*renewable/A*	
Es	A:f--s	*renovable*	*renewable/A*	
	A:f-ms	*eólico*	*wind/N*	

2.5.1 Simple term patterns

A simple term is a noun or an adjective. For adjective, we distinguish between epithetic, such as *important* 'significant' and relational, such as *laitier* 'dairy'. Relational adjectives have a strong naming function and a potential as subclassifiers acknowledged by linguists (Levy 1978; Bosredon 1989 and 1991) and are used in a privileged way in scientific domains. They belong to romance languages and English, but are less frequent in that language. Relational adjectives are built from nouns with suffixes of denominative adjectivation such as En: *-al* or *-ic*, Fr: *-ique*, Es: *-ico*.

Noun examples are given in Table 2.1 and adjective examples are in Table 2.2. We use as citation form singular and nominative for nouns and singular and masculine for adjectives.

2.5.2 Morphological compound patterns

We distinguish three types of compounds: neoclassical, native and loan compounds. Neoclassical compounding applies one of the following patterns with CE as neoclassical stem and NE as native stem:

1. CE+CE such as *hydropathy* where *hydro-* and *-pathy* are two neoclassical stems;
2. CE+N such as *aerogenerator* where *aero-* is a neoclassical stem and *generator* is a lexical element belonging to the native language;
3. NE+N such as *céréaliculture* 'cereal cultivation' where *céréali* 'cereal' is a native stem and *culture* 'cultivation' is a word in the native language.

Table 2.3 Neoclassical compounds (EOL).

	Element category	Example	English translation
En	N/CE+N	*electro|magnet*	
Fr	N:cms/CE+N	*aéro|générateur*	'aerogenerator/N'
	N:cms/CE+CE	*hydro|carbure*	'hydrocarbon'
De	N:cms/NE+N	*Solar|strom*	'solar electricity'
	N:cfs/CE+CE	*hydro|phoby*	'hydrophoby'
Ru	N:cmsn/CE+N	анемо|метр	'anemometer'
Es	N:cfs/CE+CE	*anemo|grafía*	'anemography/N'
	N:cfs/CE+N	*aero|dinámica*	'aerodynamics/N

Table 2.4 Native compound patterns (EOL).

	Element category	Example	English translation
En	N/N+N	*wind|mill*	
Fr	N:cms/V-N	*chauffe-eau*	'water heater
De	N:cfs/N+N	*Strom|einspeisung*	'power input'
Ru	N:cfsn/N+N	ветро|турбина	'wind turbine'

Native and loan compound patterns are described similarly to syntagmatic compound according to the morpho-syntactic categories of their elements.

Compound patterns from different subfamilies of languages, illustrating their multilingual construction, are given in Tables 2.3 and 2.4.

2.5.3 Syntagmatic compound patterns

Syntagmatic compounds are mainly nominal compounds. However, we present here an adverbial compound, dominant in specialised language. We concentrate on terms of length 2 or 3, and show some examples of terms of length of more than 3. A MWT of length 2 is typically a nominal compound composed of a syntagmatic head, the noun, and is accompanied by its dependant that is either an argument if the head noun is predicative, or a modifier, regardless of the nature of the noun. The head noun, like its dependant, can be itself a compound. To facilitate the presentation of patterns, we calculate the length by considering the number of full lexical forms of the compound that are separated by spaces. We neither consider idiomatic expressions that might reduce the length, nor compounds that might augment the length. Therefore, a MWT of length 2 can be considered as a term of length 3 if one of its lexical elements is a morphological compound, such as *aérogénérateur caréné* 'ducted turbine', or a syntagmatic compound combined by a hyphen *coût-efficacité* 'cost effectiveness'. Symmetrically, a MWT of length 3 including three lexemes can be considered as a term of length 2 if it admits only one dependency of level 1, and if the noun of the modifier is itself a compound noun, such as *éolienne face au vent* 'upwind windmill' where *face à* 'in front of' is a syntagmatic compound preposition.

Table 2.5 Syntagmatic compound patterns of noun category of length 2 (EOL).

	Pattern	Example	English translation
En	N N	*rotor blade*	
	A N	*renewable energy*	
	V:mp N	*installed power*	
	V:mg N	*trailing edge*	
	N P N	*angle of attack*	
Fr	N A	*énergie renouvelable*	'renewable energy'
	N V:mp	*aérogénérateur caréné*	'shrouded turbine
	N V:mg	*contact glissant*	'sliding contact'
	N N	*parc offshore*	'offshore park'
	N P N	*caisse de résonance*	'sounding-box'
	N P D N	*vitesse du vent*	'speed of the wind'
	A N	*petite antenne*	'small antenna'
De	A N	*fossiler Energieträger*	'fossil energy source'
	N P N	*Netzintegration von Windenergie*	'grid integration of wind energy
	N T:---g N:c--g	*Ausbau des Stromnetzes*	'expansion of the electricity network'
Ru	A N	метеорологическая станция	'meteorological station'
	N N:cm-g	выработка энергии	'energy production'
	N N:cm	управление электропотреблением	'load management'
Es	N A	*energía eólica*	'wind energy'
	N V:mp	*aerogenerador carenado*	'shrouded wind turbine'
	N N	*efecto invernadero*	'greenhouse effect'
	N P N	*fuente de energía*	'energy source'
	N P D N	*velocidad del viento*	'wind speed'

We show the main patterns of syntagmatic compounds of length 2 in Table 2.5 and of length 3 in Table 2.6. Some remarks:

1. Some terms do not accept many inflections or they have a privileged inflection: (EOL) De: A N *erneuerbare Energien* 'renewable energy' is always plural.
2. For N P D N pattern, the definite article (T:d) is mainly used in Romance languages:

   Fr: *T:dms: le, T:dfs: la, T:d-p: les,*
   Es: *T:dms: el, T:dfs: la, T:dmp: los, T:dmp: las,*
   as well as the indefinite article contracted with prepositions:
   Fr: de: *P+T:ms: du, P+T:-p: des* and *à*: *P+T:ms: au, P+T:-p: aux,*
   Es: de: *P+T:ms: del.*

   The indefinite article is used in a marginal way.

3. We have distinguished N A, N V:mp and N:Vmg patterns. N A pattern is similar to the compound terms made from a qualitative adjective such as Fr: *fort* 'strong' in Fr: *vent fort* 'strong wind' and the one made from a relational adjective Fr: *gyroscopique* 'gyroscopic in *effet gyroscopique* 'gyroscopic effect'. The patterns N V:mp and N:Vmg include respectively adjectival past participle and present participle such as Fr: *installée* 'installed', past participle of the verb *installer* 'install' in Fr: *puissance installée* 'installed capacity', and *glissant* 'sliding', present participle of the verb *glisser* 'to slide along' in *contact glissant* 'sliding contact'.
4. Among the patterns of length 3, some are particularly significant, for example, the patterns N P A N or N P N A for the Romance languages. The prepositional groups P A N or P N A occupy an attributive position but are still invariable. The preposition and the noun are generally fixed to each other; only small numbers of adjective are used with a given preposition and noun. These prepositional groups are derived from sentences of form N *être* 'be' P X and accept therefore the following restructurings:

   N_1 P A N_2(SAT) Fr: *connexion à haute vitesse* 'high-speed connection'
   N_1 *être* 'be' P A N_2: *connexion est à haute vitesse* 'connection is high speed'
   D:d A N_2 *de le* N_1: *la haute vitesse de la connexion* 'the high speed of the connection'

5. From the length 3, the pattern sequences become ambiguous: a sequence such as N P N A produces two interpretations of dependence:

   N_1 P N_2 A where the adjective relies on the head noun (N_1)
   (CAN) Fr: *mastectomie de rattrapage totale* 'total salvage mammectomy'
   N_1 P N_2 A where the adjective relies on the noun of the expansion (N_2)
   (EOL) Fr: *axe de rotation horizontale* 'horizontal axis of rotation'

   and many syntagmatic cut-outs if we consider that the fixed character is possible in some elements:

   N P (N A): *axe de rotation horizontale* 'horizontal axis of rotation'
   N (P N A): *éolienne à pas fixe* 'fixed-pitch wind' where *à pas fixe* 'fixed-pitch' is an adverbial modifier that is invariable in number
   N (N P) D N: *éolienne face au vent* 'upwind windmill' where *face à* 'upwind' is a compound preposition
   (N P N) A: *mise en forme cartographique* 'cartographic formatting' where *mise en forme* 'formatting' is a idiomatic compound noun.

   This problem is even more problematic in English where there is no inflection that is helpful to disambiguate.

Table 2.6 Syntagmatic compound patterns of noun category of length 3 and more (EOL).

	Patron	Example	English translation
En	N N N	*wind power plant*	
	A N N	*offshore wind park*	
	V:mp N N	*land-based wind energy*	
	A A N	*large offshore wind*	
Fr	N A A	*parc éolien terrestre*	'onshore wind farm'
	N R A	*zone non volcanique*	'non volcanic zone'
	N N P N	*éolienne face au vent*	'upwind turbine'
	N P N P N	*induit à cage d'écureuil*	'squirrel cage induction generator'
	N A P D N	*cisaillement horizontal du vent*	'horizontal wind shear'
	N P A N	*éolienne de grande taille*	'large wind turbine'
	N P N A	*éolienne à pas fixe*	'fixed-pitched rotor'
Es	N A A	*energía eólica terrestre*	'land-based wind energy'
	N P N N	*gas de efecto invernadero*	'greenhouse gas'
	N P D N P N	*recursos para la producción de energía*	'energy production resource'
	N P N A	*coeficiente de velocidad periférica*	'tip-speed ratio'

Of course, longer terms exist, up to four, five or more lexical forms, for instance:

N A V:mp A: (SAT) Fr: *puissance isotrope rayonnée équivalente (PIRE)* 'equivalent isotropically radiated power (EIRP)'
N A P D N A: (AGR) Fr: *produit issu de l'agriculture biologique* 'product of organic agriculture' where *issu de* 'derived from' is a compound preposition
N P N P N P N A: (Computer science) Fr: *système de gestion de base de données relationnelles (SGBDR)* 'relational database management system (RDBMS)'

From the terminological point of view, the processes of syntagmatic and morphological denominations are recurrent and thus, up to five iterations could be produced. In spite of that, the longer the term, the less it fits the criterion of minimality (cf. Section 2.1).

2.5.4 Frequency of term patterns

The representativeness of simple and complex terms depends on the kind of lexical resources in which they are found: e.g. terminological lexicon, thesaurus, terminological database; its use: e.g. translation, indexation; its number of languages and its mono- or multi-domains. Moreover, simple and complex terms are distinguished by graphical criteria, so morphological compounds are counted as single-word terms. These numbers have to be taken with caution. They are reliable only for romance language where the syntagmatic compounding is the predominant pattern. Royauté (1999: 54) studied four lexical resources of various domains and counted the ratio of syntagmatic compounds in English:

Table 2.7 Representativeness of term patterns in Terminalf (EOL) for En, Es and Fr.

	En	Es	Fr
Simple terms			
N	14	15 16	
Complex terms			
Morphological compounds			
Neoclassical compounds	2	3	3
Syntagmatic compounds			
Length 2			
A N	9	–	–
N A	–	16	14
N N	32	4	7
N P N	–	30	29
Length 3			
A N N	7	–	
N A A	–	1	
N A N	2	–	
N A P N	–	2	2
N N N	10	–	
N N P N	–	–	1
N P A N	1	–	2
N P N A	–	9	4
N P N P N	–	1	2
Length 4			
A N N N	3		
N A P A	–	2	
N N P A N	1		
N P N A A	–	–	1
N P N A P N	–	1	
N P N P N N	1		
N P N P N P N			1
Length 5			
A N AN N	1		
Total	**83**	**84**	**82**

Domain	Type of resource	Name	Size	%
multidomain	documentary database	PASCAL (INIST)	72 213	74%
metallurgy	terminological lexicon	METAL	6 620	79%
agriculture	trilingual thesaurus Fr-En-Es	AGROVOC (FAO)	15 470	54%
physics	thesaurus	FIZ	22 401	72%

From the quantitative point of view, term patterns of lengths 2 and 3 are the most represented in the texts and in terminological data banks. In Japanese, Kageura (2012: 36) studied the terminologies of six domains. He noted that from around 70% to over 80% of terms were complex, and that in all six domains, terms consisting of two Japanese morphemes are dominant, close to 60%.

Many terminological dictionaries are available on the Web. The portal of the University of Vaasa in Finland has listed some of them.[4] We have studied the distribution of term patterns of the wind energy domain, provided by Terminalf[5] in English, Spanish and French. Table 2.7 shows numbers of each patterns. For this multi-language lexicon, interlingual numbers are the same with 22% of single-word terms and 78% of multi-word terms. Syntagmatic compounds of length 2 are used for 60% in French and Spanish, 50% in English; those of length 3 for 14% in Spanish and French, and 23% in English. Syntagmatic compounds of length superior to 3 are marginal.

2.6 Term variants

Term is defined according to its place in a corpus (Bourigault and Slodzian 1999), or generally speaking, in discourse (Gaudin 2003). A term is a lexical unit and it can be realised as such in discourse with various forms that could lead to neonyms. The terminological analysis is therefore based upon a lexical stock (Gaudin 2003) related to the set of these forms. We call them "variants". The phenomenon of variation is applied to simple and complex terms, and includes all parts of speech.

2.6.1 The definition of variant

Daille et al. (1996: 201) give the following definition for term variant:

> A variant of a term is an utterance which is semantically and conceptually related to an original term.

4. http://www.uva.fi/en/sites/terminology/

5. http://terminalf.scicog.fr

There are three important points in this definition: **utterance:** a variant of a term is an attested form encountered in a text; **original term:** a variant is defined with respect to an authorised term either listed in a thesaurus or in a terminological resource; **semantically and conceptually related:** a variant can be a synonym of the term, called a denominative variant, or reflect a semantic distance from the term. The semantic distance can be the motivation for a new naming. In this case, the variant is itself a term related to the original term thanks to a conceptual or semantic relation. We call this second type of variant, a conceptual variant. This definition distinguishes two main categories of variants, denominative and conceptual, that will be related to the intracategorial level, e.g. their information content regarding the concept, or to the intercategorial level, e.g. the links with the other concepts of the domain (Temmerman 2000).

2.6.2 Denominative variants

Denominative variants reflect a synonymy relation. The General Theory of Terminology advocates to use one term for one concept, and thus to identify a strongly preferred linguistic form for a concept. Synonym forms should not exist. In real-life terminology work, as for terminology-resource building for a professional activity, synonymous variants are common. Such variants are exact synonyms or approximate synonyms. Approximate synonyms show a difference between synonyms concerning term characteristics that do not define the concept, such as the language register, time and location. Freixa (2006: 52) names these approximate synonyms, "denominative variants". Denominative variants are lexicalised forms, representing the same concept, but adopting different lexical forms according to different contexts. The use of denominative variants is known and attested in specialised domains. Denominative variants are either lexicalisable forms or paraphrases referring to the same concept. Lexicalisable forms are obtained through simplification processes to meet conciseness. For example, (MED) *histamine flare test* → *histamine test.* Paraphrases are generated to make explicit complex terms which lose their transparency and become ambiguous in context. For example, GR) Fr: *protéine végétale* 'plant protein' → *protéine d'origine végétale* 'protein from plant'.

2.6.3 Conceptual variants

Between the conceptual variant and the term, there is a semantic gap. Conceptual variants are either lexicalisable forms created to sharpen the concept or lexicalised forms invoked to generalise it. Lexicalisable forms result from expansion processes, such as (MED) *blood cell* → *blood cell line.* Invoked lexicalised forms are expansion ellipsis, such as (MED) *blood cell* → *cell.* Conceptual or semantic differences can be characterised by conceptual or semantic relations. From the lexical semantic relations studied by Cruse (1995) for general language, L'Homme (2004: 91–100) keeps the relations of synonymy, antonymy, taxonomy and meronymy for specialised domains. Among the conceptual relations, hierarchical relations are used to build taxonomies using partitive and generic relations. But there are other relations, the so-called "complex relations" of Sager (1990: 34) which are domain and application dependent. Examples of such complex relations are:

causality: fallout is *caused by* nuclear explosion
location: coal-mine is *a place for* coal-mining

Mechanisms that produce denominative and conceptual variants are described in Chapter 3. Semantic and conceptual relations involving conceptual variants are detailed in Chapter 4.

2.7 Border between terms and variants

We have introduced simple and complex terms with their grammatical patterns, exemplified in several languages. We have defined variants that should be distinguished from terms. But when variants adopt term grammatical patterns, it is virtually impossible to decide which are terms and which are variants without considering the contexts in which terms and variants occur (and, in some cases, even contexts do not help distinguish them). A complex term such as (EOL) Fr: *énergie éolienne* 'wind power' can be a variant of the simple term (EOL) Fr: *énergie* 'energy', or *énergie* 'energy' can be inversely a variant of the complex term *énergie éolienne* 'wind power'. This problem is emphasised by the fact that many neonymy and variation production mechanisms are shared. The present study takes the view that the majority of variants are likely to be terms.

This chapter recalled the main linguistic and terminological concepts of this study. We introduced the notions of term and variant, and stressed the fuzzy borders between prefixation, morphological and syntactic compounds. Variants are created according to complex processes that we will model in the ensuing chapter. Chapter 3 is dedicated to the linguistic specifications of term variation and the identification of the main mechanisms involved in their production.

CHAPTER 3

Conceptualisation of terminological variants

Terminological variation is a complex phenomenon that involves competing processes of denomination of specialised concepts and their insertion in the domain terminology. These processes lead to two categories of variants: denominative and conceptual variants. Term variants are also functional elements at the discourse level. When terms are used in discourse, they are subject to variations that may be neutral from the terminological point of view. Therefore, we introduce a third category of variants: linguistic variants. We single out the main mechanisms and linguistic operations that lead to variants and detail their application to each category of variants. We stress the undifferentiated use of morphology and syntax by such mechanisms.

Many studies on terms adopted an analytic point of view supported by the idea that complex terms are variants of simple terms, i.e. the head of complex term, representing the general class, and the expansion by an adjectival or a noun complement, indicating a specific characteristic, for instance (Bourigault 1994: 27). This choice is based on a ontological view, basing hierarchies of concept classes on terms. While this view might be a reasonable option, I think it must be enlarged for a broad study of variations. Complex terms offer a larger spectre of variants than simple terms. The present study starts from simple and complex terms, examining variants from the whole range of term patterns and detailing the variety of linguistic mechanisms that come into play.

In addition to the three main variant categories we add the "register variant", for which the process of generation answers a communicative need and which borrows a subset of mechanisms from the denominative and conceptual variants.

Some mechanisms are specific to one category of variants, some linguistic operations characterise one mechanism. This classification results from our analysis and may be challlenged. At the conclusion of this classification, we discuss alternative choices. As mentioned in the introduction, our study of variants is synchronic. We observe term variants in several specialised domain corpora compiled over a short period of time and in five languages. All the examples of variants are samples collected from these corpora. They attest a "real language usage" (Temmerman 2000: 32). Mechanisms and linguistics operations are observed separately. From the diachronic point of view, some mechanisms precede. For example, the simplification mechanism observed for denominative variants can only occur on conceptual variants as it has been shown by work about term necrology by Dury and Drouin (2010) and by experimental studies on corpora by Haralambous and Lavagnino (2011). As our classification is mainly dedicated to design automatic treatments for variant recognition, the diachronic dimension is not taken into account.

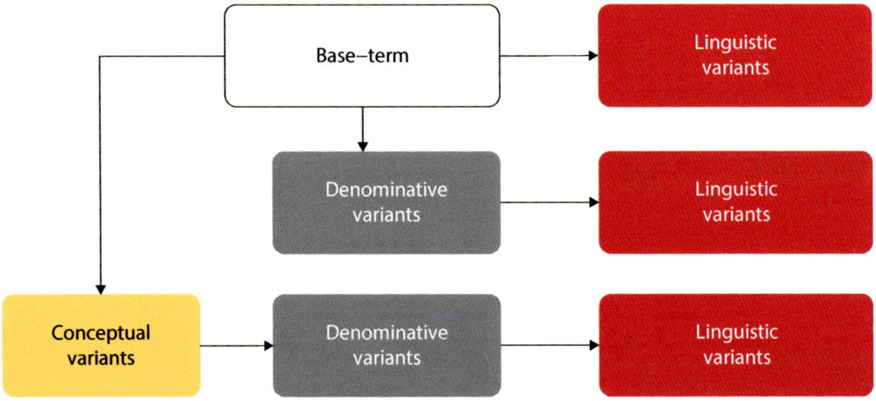

Figure 3.1 Relationships between categories of variants.

3.1 Description of variants

First, we recall the categories of variants and their relationships. A variant is the result of an operation on the term. We describe this operation linguistically rather than with an editing operation. Later on, we will formulate the properties of the utterances of a variant.

3.1.1 Organisation of variants

In Section 2.6, we defined terminological variation and recalled the two main categories of variants: denominative and conceptual. To these acknowledged categories, we add linguistic variants. Linguistic variants have surface forms that differ from those of the terms but do not lead to the creation of new lexical units in the specialised domain. Linguistic variants are not suitable for being concurrent denominations nor neonyms. They are terminologically neutral.

To summarise, a term that is employed in a document sways constantly on a triple scale corresponding to our three main categories of variants:

Denominative variants:
to respond to the properties of transparency and of minimality of the denominative core of the term;

Conceptual variants:
to anchor the term in the system of knowledge instantiated in the text;

Linguistic variants:
to link the term into the language system only.

Denominative and linguistic variants always refer to the same concept. Denominative variants are potential terms of the specialised domains while linguistic variants are only synonymic forms in context. All conceptual variants are part of the terminology of the specialised domain. Figure 3.1 clarifies the relationships between the three categories of variants. All of them are optional. Conceptual variants as potential neonyms may have denominative and linguistic variants. Denominative variants themselves may have linguistic variants. Variants of register that we will introduce later in this chapter are not included in Figure 3.1. These variants are marginal compared to the first three categories as the communicative situation prioritises the selection of terms over the creation of specific variants.

Even if our goal is not to qualify the causes of term variation, our categories of variants can be paired with Freixa's categories of causes of denominative variations (Freixa 2006):

Conceptual ↔ "Cognitive", caused by different conceptualisations or motivations;

Linguistic ↔ "Discursive", caused by stylistic and expressive needs of the authors;

Register ↔ "Functional", caused by the communicative register.

The "dialectal" and "interlinguistic" causes identified by Freixa (2006) may lead to the creation of additional categories of variants. Nevertheless, as dialectal and interlinguistic variants are spread over denominative, conceptual and linguistic variants, we have decided not to distinguish them. On the contrary, Freixa (2006) considered the linguistic variants among denominative variants. We made a different choice by splitting the two categories. Our linguistics variants are not generated with the purpose to act as a competing form of the term.

3.1.2 Mechanisms and linguistic operations

In Daille (2005), we presented four typologies of variants elaborated for application-oriented terminology engineering. Transformation of the term that leads to the variant creation is described either by linguistic operations, editing operations or a mix of the two:

1. linguistic operations: terminology extraction, controlled indexing used for information retrieval;
2. editing operation: science and technology watch;
3. linguistic and editing operations: controled indexing for computer-assisted manual translation.

Editing operations have been introduced for the document revision process by Faigley (2001). There are four processes: addition, deletion, substitution and permutation, each working at word level. Permutation is often associated with the processes of addition and deletion. In the context of document revision, the editing unit is the word.

To express editing operations for variants, it is necessary to access additional segmentations at the letter, morpheme and sentence segment levels. Editing units vary according to the linguistic operation, and the type of lexical items since there are important differences between simple and complex terms. The editing unit would typically proceed by letter for spelling, by morpheme for derivation, by word or sentence segment for syntactic operations. Letter and morpheme editing units apply for simple terms. All editing units apply for complex terms and generate competing descriptions of the change. Furthermore, the generation of variants of complex terms result from the application of several editing operations. As an example, the variant (DIA) Fr: *insulino-dépendance* 'insulin dependency' of the term *dépendance à l' insuline* 'dependency with insulin' can be formulated with the following sequence of editing operations: substitution at the letter level: *e* by *o* on the term component *insuline,* deletion of the functional words *à* and *l,* permutation of the *insulino* and *dépendance,* and lastly, substitution of the morpheme *insulino* with *insuline.* Describing the formation of a variant using linguistic operations is more concise and precise than using editing operations. Thus, we decide to explain the formation of variants through linguistic operations. Editing operations will be used to build the generic grammar for variant recognition in Chapter 9.

Variants are the outcome of a linguistic operation described by orthography and grammar according to syntagmatic and paradigmatic relations. The main operations lead to the creation of terms described in Chapter 2 such as derivation or composition, and regular combinatorial syntactic operations such as modification or coordination. Reversed operations of derivation and composition have been introduced to properly qualify the dynamics of terminological denomination processes. We also define general mechanisms gathering several linguistic operations leading to the creation of denominative and conceptual variants. As a matter of choice, mechanisms are defined to apply only to a variant category. On the contrary, only a few linguistic operations apply to a variant category. Several linguistic operations are share by several mechanisms.

Many linguistic operations only apply to complex terms, and some of them are further restricted either to morphological or syntagmatic compounds. For example, lexical reduction and initialism only apply to syntagmatic compounds. The composition of linguistic operations is possible since a denominative variant accepts linguistic variants, and since a conceptual variant accepts denominative variants. We will mainly focus on variants that are the outcome of a linguistic operation. But for a few remarkable cases, we will introduce variants resulting from more than one linguistic operation.

3.1.3 Properties of variants

A variant is characterised by the following properties:

1. a variant always involves at least one term;
2. a variant is obtained by applying at least one linguistic operation which belongs to a mechanism for denominative and conceptual variants;
3. a term can produce several variants;
4. the number or utterances of the term in a text is slightly superior to the number of utterances of the variant. Equality of utterance numbers may be encountered for graphical and denominative variants.

Furthermore, property 4 should be qualified when the term belongs to a reference terminology, as a denominative variant could be preferred in the corpus.

We now present our classification of variants according to their category. We begin by terminological variants, first denomivative and then conceptual variants, and end by linguistic variants.

3.2 Denominative variants

A term is a lexical unit whose objective is to represent knowledge within a domain. The denomination of the term is an active process that sways constantly between the incompatible properties of transparency and minimality.

There are several mechanisms leading for creating denominative variants. Firstly, synonymic substitution which affect lexical content. Secondly, simplification and exemplification which modify term patterns and, remove and add term components respectively. Simplification either compacts or deletes components of the complex term. Conversely, exemplification decompacts or adds components to the term. All mechanisms apply without modifying the conceptual reference. Among them all, term simplification, which increases term conciseness is undoubtedly favoured for the production of concurrent term denominations that may replace terms. Synonymic substitution and exemplification apply to simple and complex terms. Compression and reduction apply to complex terms. Lastly, long complex terms of patterns of length 3 and more have competing patterns.

3.2.1 Synonymic substitution

Synonymic substitution applies to simple terms or one of the components of complex terms. Morphemes, functional words or lexical elements are substituted, keeping the term pattern unchanged. It implies that a component is substituted by a component of the same linguistic nature: a morpheme by a morpheme, a functional word by a functional word, a lexeme by a lexeme. The main linguistic operations are derivation and compounding.

We only consider synonymic substitution that do not attest any morphological or syntactic relations with the substituted component.

Morpheme

For some derivative operations, several affixes produce allomorphic variants. For example:

> (decision-making process) Fr: *-eur/-aire* for nouns: *décideur* 'decision taker' ↔ *décisionnaire* 'decision maker'
> (decision-making process) Fr: *-el/-aire* for adjectives: *processus décisionnel* 'decision-taking process' ↔ *processus décisionnaire* 'decision-making process'

Other denominal substitutions would be theoretically possible with the suffixes:

> Fr: *-if/-oire/-el: décisionnel* ↔ *décisif* ↔ *décisoire* 'decision-making'
> (EOL) En: suffix of denominative adjectivation *-ic/-ical: electric/A* ↔ *electrical* /A

Functional word
In the syntagmatic compound of N P N pattern, variations of preposition are possible, either to clarify the semantics of the relation which is often neutral such as the case of the preposition Fr: *de,* or in the case of a semantic paradigm of locative type, for example:

(AGR) Fr: *chromatographie en colonne* ↔ *chromatographie sur colonne* 'column chromatography'
(EOL) Es: *enfriamiento del aire* ↔ *enfriamiento por aire* 'windchill'

Lexical component
Synonymic lexical substitution applies to simple and complex terms. In the case of simple terms, two or more lexemes are in competition. As for complex terms, one of the components of the term is substituted by one of its synonyms in the same language without changing the compound pattern. Substitution of lexical components applies to morphological and syntagmatic compounds.

Allomorphies are found in neoclassical compounds both in the neoclassical and the lexical elements. Those on neoclassical elements adapt to the language. For example, the neoclassical element *neuro* has two forms in French *neuro* in (Nervous system) *neurologie* 'neurology' and *nevro* in (Epidermis and dermis) *nevrodermite* 'neurodermatitis'.

Substitution of lexical elements occurs inside neoclassical or native compounds:

(EOL) De: *Rotorblattprofil* 'blade profile' ↔ *Flügelprofil* 'wing profile' where *Rotorblatt* 'rotor blade' is substituted by a synonym of blade *Flügel* 'wing'
(EOL) Es: *aerogenerador* 'aerogenerator' ↔ *aeroturbina* 'wind turbine'

Lexeme substitution inside a syntagmatic compound applies equally to the head noun or its dependant:

(EOL) En: *wind energy* ↔ *wind power*
(EOL) Fr: *énergie éolienne* 'wind energy' ↔ *courant éolien* 'wind power'
(MED) Fr: *parenthèse thérapeutique* 'therapeutic range' ↔ *fenêtre thérapeutique* 'therapeutic window'

This type of synonymic variation had been studied by Hamon and Nazarenko (2001). They also wrote about the possibility of double substitution of a term with N P N pattern such as:

(Electricity) Fr: *liaison d'alimentation* 'feed connection' ↔ *ligne de distribution* 'distribution line'.

3.2.2 Simplification

Contrary to synonymic substitution which keeps the term pattern but changes the lexical context, simplification reduces the initial structure of the term. Variants become monolithic in order to answer to the criterion of minimality. Thus, the term structure is not preserved.

We distinguish two main mechanisms: compression and reduction. Compression keeps all lexical components of the terms but shifts a component type into another of shorter form that often leads to the adoption of a more concise term structure. For example, a lexical unit of a syntagmatic compound will be replaced by a pseudo-neoclassical element leading to a morphological compound. Reduction removes one of the lexical constituents of the complex term. If removing is possible, it is because its reduced form refers to the same concept. We distinguish morphological and lexical reduction. The difference lies in the linguistic type of deleted constituents. Thus, we extend lexical reduction of syntagmatic compounds studied by Collet (1997), Jacques (2005), and Haralambous and Lavagnino (2011) to morphological compounds.

Moreover, we take Collet's (1997: 198) stand which distinguishes between lexical and anaphoric reduction. Lexical reduction provides denominative variants because the variant remains on the same conceptual level as the term. What is removed is one part that seems not essential to the term. Anaphoric reduction refers to a more generic form that is not at the same conceptual level as the term. We classify anaphoric reduction as an operation leading to a conceptual variant.

Compression
We distinguish three main types of compression: substitution, composition and initialism. Substitution applies to stems or lexical constituents of the complex terms that are replaced by morphemes. Composition lexically condenses syntagmatic compounds and generates morphological compounds or more "compound-like" patterns. Initialism scales down syntagmatic compounds to one lexical unit.

Lexeme/morpheme substitution
In the case of a semantically significant preposition, it will become a suffix if the language has a semantically equivalent affix:

$N_1\ P_2\ N_3 \rightarrow N_1\ N/Prefix_2{+}N_3$
(Computer science) Fr: *espace entre fichiers* 'space between files' → *espace inter-fichiers* 'inter-file space'
(AGR) Fr: *pourrissement après récolte* 'decay after harvest' $N_1\ P_2\ N_3 \rightarrow$ *pourrissement post-récolte* 'post-harvest decay' $N_1\ N/Prefix_2{+}N_3$

Also, a cardinal adjective (A:c) occurring inside a prepositional adverbial group of P A:c N pattern will be transformed into an affix or a stem:

> (EOL) It: *turbina eolica a tre pale* 'wind turbine with three blades' N_1 A_2 P $A{:}c_3$ N_4 → *turbina eolica tripale* 'three-bladed wind turbine' N_1 A_2 N/Prefix_3+N_4

Composition

Composition applies to syntagmatic compounds and leads to morphological compounds. One of the lexical constituent of the syntagmatic compound is reduced to a form (E) that is, or is similar to, a neoclassical stem and therefore, allows the production of the neoclassical compound. In the first example, the substitution by a neoclassical root is accompanied by a shift of the elements, the deletion of the preposition and with the insertion of a neoclassical linking vowel:

> (DIA) Fr: *résistance à l'insuline* 'insulin resistance' N_1 P_2 N_3 → *insulino-résistance* 'insulin resistance' N/E_3-N_1 where N_3 and E_3 share the same root.
> (AGR) Fr: *emballage écologique* 'sustainable packaging' N_1 A_2 → *éco-emballage* 'eco-packaging' N/E_2-N_1 where A_2 and E_2 share the same root.

Composition also applies to syntagmatic compounds to produce more concise compounds. When a term is of N P N or N P D N pattern, in Romance languages, a more concise form is made from N A pattern, with the adjective being derived from the noun. The head of the compound stays unchanged. The expansion which is a prepositional phrase is substituted by the relational adjective:

> N_1 P N_2 → N_1 A_2 where A_2 is derived from N_2
> (EOL) Fr: *fréquence de rotor* 'frequency of rotor' → *fréquence rotorique* 'rotor frequency'
> (EOL) Es: *energía del mar* 'energy of the ocean' → *energía marina* 'ocean energy'

Any preposition can be deleted: typical functional preposition Fr: *de*, Es: *de*, En: *of*, but locative prepositions too:

> (Medical-hospital) Fr: *expérimentations* ***sur*** *les animaux* 'experiments on animals' → *expérimentations animales* 'animal experiments'
> (EOL) Es: *aerogenerador* ***en*** *la costa* 'wind turbine on the coast' → *aerogenerador costero* 'coastal wind turbine'

For terms of N P N or N P D N patterns, deletion of the functional words (articles and prepositions), produces a more concise syntagmatic compound of N P N or N N patterns:

(AGR) Fr : *fixation de l'azote* 'fixation of the nitrogen' N_1 P_2 D N_3 → *fixation d'azote* 'fixation of nitrogen' N_1 P_2 N_3
(AGR) Fr: *fixation de l'azote* 'fixation of the nitrogen' N_1 P D N_3 → *fixation azote* 'nitrogen fixation' N_1 N_3

Acronym/initialism
Initialism is not generally a spontaneous mechanism replying to textual demands but rather a mechanism coming from specialists of a specific domain in order to rename long terms or organisms. An acronym is defined from the monolingual viewpoint: the variant formed from the initial letters of the elements of the complex term respects their order.

(COM) Fr: *réseaux numériques avec intégration des services (RNIS)* 'integrated services digital networks (ISDN)'
(COM) En: *integrated services digital networks (ISDN)*
(COM) Fr: *équipement terminal de traitements de données (ETTD)* 'data terminal equipment (DTE)'
(COM) En: *data terminal equipment (DTE)*
(COM) Fr: *service fixe par satellite (SFS)* 'fixed-satellite service (FSS)'
(COM) En: *fixed-satellite service (FSS)*

Some specialised domains, e.g. communication, make intensive use of this, and some languages such as English further intensify it.

Reduction
Reduction applies to syntagmatic compounds. We distinguish two types of reduction: morphological reduction and lexical reduction.

Morphological reduction
Morphological reduction applies to syntagmatic compounds, one of whose constituents is a morphological compound. Both neoclassical or native compounds are concerned. Reduction applies to neoclassical stems or lexical elements.

(EOL) En: *windmill farm* N/N_1+N_2 N_3 → *windfarm* N/N_1+N_3
(EOL) Fr: *hydrolectric power* $N/E+N_2$ N_3 → *hydropower* $N/E+N_3$

Lexical reduction
Lexical reduction is a discursive mechanism which transforms the complex term overall, by keeping its referential and notional heads and by removing one part that seems not essential to the term. Nevertheless, Haralambous and Lavagnino (2011) say that lexical reduction is not related to the immediate contextual environment. It is durable and creates variants that can in turn become terms.

Lexical reduction applies to:

1. the head noun:
   $N_1 A_2 \rightarrow N_2$
   (EOL) Fr: *énergie éolienne* 'wind power' → *éolien* 'wind'
   The relational adjective A_2 *éolienne* in feminine form is converted into a noun at the masculine form that does not allow the plural inflection.
   $N_1 P N_2 A_3 \rightarrow N_2 A_3$
   (AGR) Fr: *fromage à pâte molle* 'soft-textured cheese' → *pâte molle* 'soft texture'
2. one of the internal lexemes:
   $N_1 P N_2 A_3 \rightarrow N_1 P A_3$
   (AGR) Es: *queso de pasta blanda* 'soft-textured cheese' → *queso blando* lit. 'soft cheese'
   (AGR) Fr: *procédé de fabrication alimentaire* 'food manufacturing process' → *procédé alimentaire* 'food process'
   $N_1 P_2 N_3 P_4 N_5 \rightarrow N_1 P_2 N_5$
   (decision-making process) Fr: *processus de prise de décision* 'decision-making process' → *processus de décision* 'decision process'.

Lexical reduction does not apply to expansions of syntagmatic compounds. Expansion deletion characterises anaphorical reduction (cf. Section 3.3.2).

3.2.3 Exemplification

Exemplification is the reverse of simplification. It creates variants to fit criteria of term transparency. It is often paired with specialisation, which creates conceptual variations. We distinguish two main mechanisms that free the term structure: decompression and lexical insertion. Decompression uses substitution and partial back-compounding operations, and lexical insertion adds lexical elements to exemplify the term while still referring to the same concept. Such exemplified variants are helpful to make the meaning of the term explicit (Pecman 2014: 16). While simplification and exemplification are reverse mechanisms, they do not operate on the same lexical elements. Exemplification is close to paraphrase, whose aim is to make term designation clearer and to add aspectual elements, whereas simplification removes notional elements.

Decompression

We distinguish two main operations describing decompression: substitution and partial back-compounding. Substitution applies to affixes or neoclassical stems of complex terms replaced by lexical elements. Partial back-compounding applied to morphological compounds leads to syntagmatic compounds.

Morpheme/lexeme substitution
Back-prefixation applies to the simple term and leads to the formation of:

1. morphological compounds:
   (EOL) De: *un|unterbrochen* A/Prefix$_1$ +A$_2$ 'uninterrupted' → *unterbrechung|s|-frei* 'without interruption' A/N$_2$+*s*+A$_1$
2. syntagmatic compounds:
   (AGR) Fr: *palmer|aie* 'palm grove' N/N$_1$+Suffix$_2$ → *plantation de palmier* N$_2$ P N$_1$ 'palm plantation'
   with the syntagm *plantation de palmier* 'palm plantation' closer to the English term *palm stand*
   (EOL) Es: *aerogenerador <u>bi</u>|pala* 'bladed wind turbine ' ↔ *aerogenerador <u>de dos</u> palas* 'two-bladed wind turbine'

Partial back-compounding
When partial back-compounding is used to produce denominative variants, morphological compounds are turned into syntagmatic compounds, syntagmatic compounds from one pattern to another. We leave morphological compounds aside but the variant keeps a compound pattern. Partial back-compounding has to be distinguished from full back-compounding that creates free syntagms that are linguistic variants.

The main rules of partial back-compounding that we include in the set of denominative variants apply to the term of N/A+N or A+N and N/N+N or N P N patterns:

N/N$_1$+N$_2$ or N$_1$ N$_2$ → N$_2$ P N$_1$, seldom to N$_2$ P D N$_1$
N/A$_1$+N$_2$ → N$_2$ A$_1$
(EOL) En: *air density* N$_1$ N$_2$ → *density of air* N$_2$ P N$_1$

The preposition of the syntagmatic pattern depends on the head noun. With semantic prepositions, such as *for, in, at, on, from, with, about,* the variant generated is close to a paraphrase.

(CAN) En: *armpit lymph node* → *lymph node in the armpit*
(CAN) En: *breast cancer treatment* → *treatment for breast cancer*

Rather than partial back-compounding, we face lexical insertion that is presented below.

When partial back-compounding is accompanied with a new determination, we face a conceptual variant:

(EOL) En: *air density* N1 N2 → → *density of dry air* N$_2$ P A N$_1$
(CAN) De: *Krebs-Früherkennung* N/N$_1$-N$_2$ 'early|discovered-cancer' → *Früherkennung von Brust|krebs,* N$_2$ P N/N+N$_1$ 'early|discovered breast | cancer'.

Lexical insertion
When the term is considerably simplified, typically by using a relational adjective, the reintroduction of specifier can remove ambiguities of designation. The inserted element is able of clarify or detail the designation introduced by the relational adjective. Typical nominal specifiers belong to a closed list of nouns, such as *type, origin, colour.* The semantics of some specifiers such as Fr: *type,* Es: *tipo* can make a property clear.

(AGR) Fr: *protéine végétale* 'vegetable protein' N_1 A_2 → *protéine d'origine végétale* 'protein of vegetable origin' N_1 P N A_2.
(EOL) Es: *batería estacionaria* 'stationary battery' N_1 A_2 → *batería de tipo estacionario* 'stationary type of battery' N_1 P N A_2.

In English, verbal compounds are preferred to nominal specifiers:

(Medecine) En: *dark urine* A_1 N_2 → *dark-colored urine* A/A_1-V:mp N_2

More generally, a paraphrase can be inserted in order to explain a particularly ambiguous notion, such as the concept to which the relational adjective Fr: *biologique* organic' refers to:

(AGR) Fr: *produit biologique* 'organic product' N_1 A_2 → *produit issu de l'agriculture biologique* 'product of organic farming' N_1 A P D N A_2
(EOL) Es: *aerogenerador casero* 'homemade wind turbine' N_1 A_2 ↔ *aerogenerador de fabricación casera* 'home made wind turbine' N_1 P N A_2

3.2.4 Competing patterns

Syntagmatic compounds of length 3 and more accept competing patterns acknowledged by language grammar, or borrowed from another language.

N_1 P_2 A_3 N_4 ↔ N_1 P_2 N_4 A_3 where A_3 modifies N_4
(EOL) Es: *zona de vientos fuertes* ↔ *zona de fuertes vientos* 'area of strong winds'
N_1 A_2 P_3 N_4 ↔ N_1 P_3 N_4 A_2 where A_2 modifies N_1
(SAT) Fr: *antenne parabolique de réception* ↔ *antenne de réception parabolique* 'receiving dish'
(EOL) Es: *nivel excesivo de ruido* ↔ *nivel de ruido excesivo* 'excessive level of noise' A_1 N_2 P_3 N_4 ↔ N_2 A_1 P_3 N_4 where A_1 modifies N_2
(EOL) Es: *máxima potencia de salida* ↔ *potencia máxima de salida* 'maximum output power'
N_1 P_2 N_3 P_4 A_5 N_6 ↔ N_1 P_2 A_5 N_6 P_4 N_3
(EOL) Es: *aerogenerador para vientos de baja velocidad* ↔ *aerogenerador para bajas velocidades de viento* 'wind turbine for low wind speeds'

3.3 Conceptual variants

The term belongs to a conceptual system describing the knowledge domain. But inside a document, only a part of the domain is invoked. The term needs to be adapted to this sub-system. Expansion applies when the term denomination needs to be enlarged or detailed. Inversely, reduction is achieved when the specificity level is not judged necessary in the context. Expansion is the privileged mechanism for neonyms. Expansion is also used to describe scientific procedures involving the term or detailing its properties. The term is then inserted in a multi-word expression that is part of the phraseology of the scientific domain (Tutin 2007). On the contrary, reduction that produces generic forms "is not able to participate to the evolution of the specialised domain" (Haralambous and Lavagnino 2011:47).

A conceptual variant is constructed from a denominative variant drawn from the set of denominative variants available for the term. Identification of the denominative variants is required to access the whole set of expansions.

3.3.1 Expansion

To diversify the term use, expansion manifests itself at the level of morphology and syntax. The main linguistic operations are derivations for morphology, and predication and modification for syntax. Derivation and modification specify the term while predication shows its multiple facets, its properties and usages.

When the complex term is at the heart of the expansion process, the morphologically constructed compound is the preferred denominative variant for the predication operation, while a syntagmatic compound is preferred for a modification operation.

Derivation
Derivational variants gather variants obtained by prefixation or suffixation . The term variants make use of the common prefixes used in the native language. Here are some examples:

(EOL) Fr: *éolien* /A 'eolian' → *<u>pro</u>éolien* /A 'pro-eolian'
(EOL) De: *unterbrochen*/A 'interrupted' → *<u>un</u>unterbrochen*/A 'uninterrupted'
(EOL) Es: *síncrono*/A 'synchronous' → *<u>a</u>síncrono* /A 'asynchronous'

For some prefixes, a hyphen can mark the border between the prefix and the term.

The simple term is stated according to the possible choice of derivations: nominalisation, adjectivation, verbalisation, adverbialisation, and their combinations.

The derivational paradigm of a simple term is one of its definitional features and expresses different aspects of the term. Derivation produces a conceptual variant, when there is a terminological difference between the variant and the term, by introducing its properties or typical functions. The prototypical terminological derivation is nominalisation: (CAN) En: *embolus* → *embolism.*

Jousse and Bouveret (2003) distinguish derivations expressing semantic arguments of a predicative lexical unit, as the typical noun of the first argument, (Computer science) Fr: *programmeur* 'programmer', derived from *programmer* 'to program, the typical adjective of the second argument Fr: *imprimable* 'printable', derived from *imprimer* 'to print', the resultant adjective form *imprimé* 'printed', derived from *imprimer* 'to print', derivations expressing circumstantial changes. Derivations of simple terms are used for complex terms in order to create their derivational variants, for example:

(DIA) Fr: *insulino-sécréteur* 'insulinotropic' with *sécréteur* 'secretory', derived from the verb *sécréter* 'to secrete'.
(MOB) En: *peer-to-peer network* → *peer-to-peer networking*

Here is an example of de-adjectival variation:

N_1 A_2 → N_2 P D N_1 where N_2 is derived from A_2
(Geology) Fr: *eau profonde* 'deepwater' → *profond|eur de l'eau* 'water depth'
A_1 N_2 → N_1 N_2 where N_1 is derived from A_1
(MOB) En: *fair bandwith* → *bandwith fair|ness*
A /N_1+V_2 → N_1 N_2 where N_2 is derived from V_2
(EOL) En: *grid-connected* → *grid connec|tion*

Predication
Predication consists in inserting the term into the nominal argument structure corresponding to the left expansion. The term becomes an argument of the predicative noun or a modifier. Predication can include two terms for a two-place predicate. The predicative nouns belong to the semantic classes of process such as *study,* scientific activity such as *conversion* or *production,* or artifact (Flaux and Van de Velde 2000). Some predicative nouns express the aspects or the properties of terms such as *scale* or *length.* These predicative nouns have been studied by (Tutin 2007), and are part of the scientific transdisciplinary lexicon.

(EOL) En: *solar energy* ↔ *solar energy conversion*
(DIA) En: *sentinel node* → *sentinel node biopsy*
(EOL) Fr: *énergie éolienne* 'wind energy' ↔ *production d'énergie éolienne* 'wind energy production'
(EOL) Es: *pala* 'blade' ↔ *envergadura de la pala* 'blade length'

The nominal specifiers expressing a quantity such as *set* or a quality such as *type* could be added to the set of predicative nouns.

Modification
Modifiers can be placed before, in the middle of, or after the term. Modifiers appearing before or after the term do not break the structure of the complex term, as opposed to those that appear in the middle. Thus, two operations are distinguished, juxtaposition or insertion of the modifier. Modifiers are those used in the common language: adjective or prepositional group for noun, adjective or adverb for adjective, or adverb for adverb. In specialised languages, more specific modifiers are commonly used: groups of adverbial preposition with P A N or P N A patterns for Romance languages and verbal compounds for English:

(EOL) Fr: *à pas fixe* 'fixed-pitch'

If juxtaposition is universal, insertion is only possible for Romance languages and is not possible for En and De. Furthermore, insertion is shared with exemplification to create denominative variants. Modification applies to morphological and syntagmatic compounds.

i. *Juxtaposition*
With juxtaposition, neither the order of constituents nor the structure of the term is altered. For example, the syntagmatic sequence of N A A pattern such as Fr: *champ électrique <u>statique</u>* 'static electric field' consists in the term *champ électrique* 'electric field' of N A pattern, modified by the juxtaposition of the adjective *statique* 'static'. Juxtaposition can be carried out before of after the term.

Initial position
Modification can be carried out at the left of the term for morphological compounds and syntagmatic compounds of A N or N N patterns, adopting a right-headed order. Modification patterns of initial position are presented below, according to the nature of the compound:

Morphological compound
$N/N_2+N_1 \rightarrow N/ N+N_2+N_1$
(EOL) De: *Windpark* 'wind farm' → *<u>Meer</u>|windpark* 'marine wind farm'
$N/N_2+N_1 \rightarrow N/A+N_2+N_1$
(EOL) De: *Windgenerator* 'wind generator'→ *<u>Vertikal</u>-Windgenerator* 'vertical wind generator'
Syntagmatic compound
$N_2\ N_1 \rightarrow N\ N_2\ N_1$
(EOL) En: *wind turbine* → *<u>first-generation</u> wind turbine* $N_2\ N_1 \rightarrow A\ N_2\ N_1$
(SAT) En: *telecommunication satellite* → *<u>geostationary</u> telecommunication satellite.*

The modification of the initial position in English is often marked by a symbolic relation, i.e. a hyphen, which combines two modifiers of the term head:

geostationary-telecommunication satellite.
$A_3 N_2 N_1 \rightarrow R A_3 N_2 N_1$
(SAT) En: *geostationary satellite orbit* → *nearly geostationary satellite orbit*

Post-position
Post-position modification consists in adding a modifier to the right of the term. It applies mainly to syntagmatic compounds adopting a left-headed order. Prepositional phrase and adjective are the privileged modifiers.

The main patterns of post-positional modification are:

$N_1 A_2 \rightarrow N_1 A_2 A$
(SAT) Fr: *station terrienne* 'earth station' → *station terrienne brouilleuse* 'interfering earth station'
$N_1 P N_2 \rightarrow N_1 P N_2 A$
(EOL) Fr: *système d'énergie* 'energy system' → *systéme d'énergie hybride* 'hybrid energy system'. The adjective *hybride* 'hybrid' modifies the term *système d'énergie* 'energy system' and not the head of expansion *énergie* 'energy'.

Past and present participles are admitted post-modifiers:

(decision-making process) Fr: *processus décisionnel* 'decision-making process → *processus décisionnel unifié* 'unified decision-making process'.
$N_1 N_2 \rightarrow N_1 N_2 A$
(SAT) Fr: *modulation delta* 'delta modulation' → *modulation delta adaptable* 'adaptable delta modulation'
$N_1 P_2 N_3 \rightarrow N_1 P_2 N_3 P N$
(EOL) Fr: *vitesse du vent* 'wind speed' → *vitesse du vent de surface* 'surface wind speed'
$N_1 A_2 \rightarrow N_1 A_2$ PAN
(Transportation) Fr: *transport terrestre* 'ground transportation' → *transport terrestre à grande vitesse* 'high-speed ground transportation'
(Computer science) Es: *memoria intermedia* 'buffer' → *memoria intermedia de alta velocidad* 'high-speed buffer'

ii. *Insertion*
With insertion, the linear order and the structure of the term are modified. For instance, the sequence of N A P N pattern (SAT) Fr: *réseaux mondiaux de télécommunications* 'global network of telecommunication' is the term *réseau de télécommunications* 'network of telecommunication' of N P N pattern, modified by the insertion of the adjective *mondial* global.

The main patterns of internal modification for morphological compounds are as follow:

$N_1\ A_2 \rightarrow N_1\ A/E{+}A_2$
(EOL) Es: *acoplamiento dinámico* → *acoplamiento aerodinámico*
$N/E_1{+}N_2 \rightarrow A/E_1{+}N\ N_2$
(Energy) Ru: био|топливо 'biofuel' → био|дизельное топливо 'biodiesel fuel'

Some neoclassical and native compounds accept internal modification:

$N_1\ A/E_2{+}A_2 \rightarrow N_1\ A/E_2{+}R{+}A_2$
(DIA) Fr: *diabète insulino-dépendant* 'insulino-dependent diabetes' → *diabète insulino-non-dépendant* 'insulino-not-dependent diabetes'

The main patterns of internal modification for syntagmatic compounds are as follow:

$N_1\ A_2 \rightarrow N_1\ R\ A_2$
(EOL) Fr: *son audible* 'audible sound' → *son non audible* 'not audible sound'
$N_1\ A_1 \rightarrow N_1\ A\ A_1$
(EOL) Fr: *parc marin* 'marine park' → *parc naturel marin* 'natural marine park'
(EOL) Es: *cimentación monopilote* 'foundation of monopile' → *cimentación marina monopilote* 'foundation of marine monopile'

The insertion of an adjective into a syntagmatic compound with prepositional expansion is carried out for the closest head, before the prepositional expansion:

$N_1\ A_2\ P_3\ N_4 \rightarrow N_1\ A_2\ A\ P_3\ N_4$
(SAT) Fr: *service fixe par satellite* 'fixed-satellite service' → *services fixes nationaux par satellite* 'domestic fixed-satellite service'
$N_1\ P_2\ N_3\ P_4\ N_5 \rightarrow N_1\ A\ P_2\ N_3\ P_4\ N_5$
(SAT) Fr: *service de radiodiffusion par satellite* 'broadcasting-satellite' → *services communautaires de radiodiffusion par satellite* 'community broadcasting-satellite'
$N_1\ P_2\ N_3 \rightarrow N_1\ P\ N\ P_2\ N_3$
(EOL) Fr: *vitesse du vent* 'wind speed' → *vitesse de pointe du vent* 'high-speed wind'

Several insertions of modifiers are possible:

$N_1\ P_2\ N_3 \rightarrow N_1\ A\ A\ P_2\ N_3$
(EOL) Fr: *vitesse du vent* 'wind speed' → *vitesse annuelle moyenne du vent* 'annual average wind speed'

Insertion is often associated with partial back-compounding first transforming the morphological compound into a syntagmatic compound so as to make the insertion more natural:

$N/N_2+N_1 \rightarrow N_1\ A\ N_2$
(EOL) Ru: энерго|источник 'energy source' → источник тепловой энергии 'source of thermic energy'

3.3.2 *Anaphorical reduction*

Anaphorical reduction is obtained by ellipsis of the complex term expansion. Elliptical anaphora retain the head noun of the term referring to a more generic notion. Thus, the noun (Medicine) *process* could refer to the complex term *enzymatic process* if the latter has been previously used (Kister 2000). The possibility of using the head noun as referee depends on the degree of term lexicalisation. For example, it is impossible to retain (Computer science) Fr: *mise* for *mise à jour* 'update' and (Mobile) Fr: *modulation* for *modulation de fréquence* 'modulation of frequency'. Term anaphora is studied in some detail in the literature and as Jacques (2005) recalled, establishing the relation between the complex term and its reduced form is carried out with a definite or a demonstrative determinant. Here are some examples of anaphorical reduction where a simple noun refers to a complex term evoked before within the same paragraph:

1. (SAT) Fr: *ces réseaux* 'these networks' referred to *réseaux de télécommunications par satellite* 'satellite telecommunications networks'
2. (SAT) Fr: *cette zone* 'this area' referred to *zone des équipements de télécommunication* 'area of telecommunication equipments'

Ellipsis of a part of the expansion of the complex term is also possible when the reduced form is a term of the specialised domain:

$N_1\ P\ N_2\ A_3 \rightarrow N_1\ P\ N_2$
(EOL) Es: *fuente de energía eólica* 'source of wind power' → *fuente de energía* 'source of energy'.

Anaphorical reduction should be distinguished from lexical reduction (cf. Section 3.3.2) which does not need an earlier reference to a complex term and deletes the head or internal constituents of the term. Anaphorical reduction invokes a more generic notion to increase discourse cohesion without being acted upon by the specialised domain. Nevertheless, invocation of a generic term is a revealing clue to the domain centrality of the term (Jacques 2005).

3.4 Linguistic variants

Linguistic variants solely concern the level of language. They follow formal linguistic restrictions, the structural regularities of the vocabulary, and the functional rules of syntax. The specialised domain neither intervenes in the variant form nor in the naming function.

When the term is invoked at the discourse level, a denominative variant is chosen in the set of denominative variants. This denominative variant is then used as a lexical unit and is submitted to the orthographic and grammatical rules of the language.

We will now detail orthographic and spelling variants, inflectional variants, full back-compounding and coordination variants. For morphological and syntactic variants shared with the denominative variants, we will only observe those that will remain mainly linguistic when they are applied to a specific part of speech or semantic class. Those operations are then considered as neutral from the terminological point of view.

3.4.1 Graphics and spelling

Graphic and spelling variants consists of the following phenomena:

1. misspelling;
2. normative spelling;
3. segmentation;
4. writing convention: small letter, capital, first letter in uppercase;
5. spelling of complex terms.

Misspelling
Incorrect orthography means misspelling of writers, and all kinds of misspelling that might happen in digital document processing.

Segmentation
Complex terms accept graphical segmentation of variants. Diacritical signs such as hyphens labelling morphological compounds or spaces labelling syntagmatic compounds are deleted or substituted. A morphological compound becomes a syntagmatic compound, and conversely as its syntactical function inside the nominal phrase requires.

Space
A morphological compound is either a graphic entity, or is composed of several elements separated by diacritical signs such as hyphens or apostrophes. The morphological compound may also be written with its elements separated by a space.

(Computer science) Fr: *microordinateur* 'microcomputer' ↔ *micro ordinateur* 'micro computer'

Inversely, a syntagmatic compound of N N pattern may occur as a graphical entity.

(EOL) En: *airflow* → *airflow*

Hyphenation
A hyphen is normally used to combine elements of morphological compounds. However, this is far from being systematic. Neoclassical compounds are written nearly as often without hyphens as with hyphens. The same remark stands for morphological compounds built by affixation. The majority of morphological compounds are indifferently combined with or without hyphens.

(Computer science) Fr: *microordinateur* ↔ *micro-ordinateur* 'microcomputer'
(EOL) De: *Energieagentur* → *Energie-Agentur* 'energy agency'
(EOL) Es: *electromagnético* → *electro-magnético* 'electromagnetic'

A hyphen replaces the space appearing inside the syntagmatic compound leading to a pseudo-morphological compound.

(EOL) En: *power supply* → *power-supply*
(EOL) Es: *amperio hora* → *amperio-hora* 'ampere-hour'

Normative spelling
National languages regularly introduce spelling normalisations with the aim of simplifying spelling.

French spelling
In 1990, French spelling was reformed by the Superior Council of the French Language and French Academy. Today, the reformed spelling is systematically used. French is taught in French-speaking Belgium and the usage is also recommended in Quebec since 2005. This reform has introduced competing orthographies. Here are French examples by Fontenelle (2005):

ph ↔ **f** *nénuphar* ↔ *nénufar* 'water lily'
ie ↔ **y** *whiskies* ↔ *whiskys* 'whiskies'
é ↔ **è** the latter is in fact more faithful to the true pronunciation of verbs such as *gérera* ↔ *gérera* 'to manage (in future tense)'
î ↔ **i** *disparaît* ↔ *disparait* 'disappear'

German spelling
The reform of German spelling was introduced in 2006. As in the case of French, this reform has introduced competing orthographies. Here are German examples:

ph → **f** *Graphit* → *Grafit* 'graphite'
ti → **zi** *Potential* → *Potenzial* 'potential'
B → **ss** *Flußdichte* → *Flussdichte* 'flux density'

Americain/British spelling
British spelling differs only in some letters from American spelling. Here are American/British examples:

z ↔ **s** *polarization* (Am.) ↔ *polarisation* (Br.)
o ↔ **ou** *color* (Am.) ↔ *colour* (Br.)

Writting conventions
Writing conventions introduce capitalisation of the first letter of the term in order to mark its terminological character graphically. This is the rule in German, but several languages also use it. Capitalisation can produce spelling variants when the accent is removed from the first letter: (EOL) Fr: *éolien* ↔ *Eolien.* This transformation generates variants, without making an incorrect spelling.

Spelling of complex terms
Patterns of syntagmatic compounds introduce a large number of inflectional ambiguities on the expansion. Such phenomenon mainly concerns the following patterns:

1. (Medicine) Fr: V-N *garde-malade* 'nurse (litt. guard of patient)' ↔ *garde-malades* 'nurse (litt. guard of patients)'
2. (EOL) Fr: N P N *conservation de produit* 'retention of product' ↔ *conservation de produits* 'retention of products'

A large number of inflectional variants of the nominal expansion with the above patterns are often generated when the compound is translated from English that does not mark the plural form of the syntagmatic compound. More generally, as emphasised by Zanettin (1998), translated texts cannot represent all linguistic possibilities of the target language, and they tend to reflect idiosyncrasies of the source language as well as those of the translator. We will discuss the phenomena of translation in Chapter 7.

3.4.2 Inflection

Inflectional variants are all inflected forms. They depends on the grammatical category of the term of the language. Therefore, inflection is allowed in:

1. **number** for the nominal simple term;
2. **number, gender** for the adjectival simple term;
3. **case** in addtion for the nominal or adjectival simple term (De, Ru).

The attribution of plural form to complex terms depends on term patterns. The following rules are adopted for French, the gender and the number of N A pattern being identical to those of the noun and the adjective that compose it; the gender and the number of the N P N pattern being identical to those of the first N. For the syntagmatic compounds of N N pattern, all combination rules are possible: plural applies to the first noun, the second noun, both of them, or none of them. The plural of morphological compound follows the same rules as those used for syntagmatic compounds. Therefore, the plural form of term of A-N patterns such as (Electricity) Fr: *court-circuit* 'short' is ↔ *courts-circuits.* The plural formation of syntagmatic compounds is detailed in (Savary 2008) for English, French and Polish.

The rules for the attribution of a plural form to compounds of N P N pattern are undermined because there are many expansion variants. Therefore, with the following variants: (AGRO) Fr: *conservation de produit* 'retention of product' /*conservation de produits* 'retention of products' produce two plural forms: *conservations de produit* 'retention of product' /*conservations de produits* 'retentions of products'.

Allomorphic variants of the plural form exist in German, for instance, in some nouns in genitive:

> (Computer science) De: *Programm* 'program' → *Programms/Programmes* 'programs'

3.4.3 Derivation

Derivations that are neutral from the terminological process give more flexibility with regards to use in texts. They are verbalisation and adverbialisation, and a subset of adjectivation. These derivations hardly intervene as a naming function, as opposed to adjectivation that generates relational adjectives. They also do not lead to conceptual variants.

Derivations are carried out for simple and complex terms. Here are some examples of simple terms:

1. adjectivation (DIA) Fr: *résistance* → *résistant, résistante,* 'resistant'
2. adverbialisation (Mobile) Fr: *numérique* 'digital' → *numériquement* 'digitally'
3. verbalisation: (Computer science) Fr: *programmation* 'programming' → *programmer* 'to program'

For complex terms, the derivation paradigm is smaller:

1. adjectivation (DIA) Fr: *insulino-résistance* → *insulino-résistant, insulino-résistante,* 'insulin-resistant'
2. verbalisation (Chemistry) En: *germination stimulant* → *stimulates germination*

3.4.4 Fullback-compounding

Full back-compounding applies to the morphological or the syntagmatic compound to create a free syntagm or a verbal expression. It comes along with the inflection or permutation of its elements, and the insertion of functional words or a verb when the adjective, expansion of the syntagmatic compound, is used to predicate an attribute of the head noun compound. The following examples illustrate full back-compounding:

1. permutation and optional insertion of a preposition
   (EOL) Ru: генератор|тепловой N/N_1+A_2 → тепловой генератор A_2 N_1 'heat generator'
   (CAN) De: *Brust|drüsenentfernung* $N/N_1+A_2+N_3$ 'gland mammary ablation' → *Entfernung der Brust|drüse* N_3 P N/ N_2+A_1 'ablation of gland mammary'
2. insertion of a determiner
   (EOL) Fr: *stockage d'énergie* 'storage of energy' N_1 P_2 N_3 → *stockage de l'énergie* 'storage of the energy' N_1 P_2 D N_3
3. inflection
   (Metallurgy) De: *Edel|metall* 'precious metal' N/A+N_1 → *edles Metall* A N_1 'noble metal'

4. permutation and insertion of a determiner
   (EOL) De: *Rotor|drehzahl* $N/N_1+N_2 \rightarrow$ *Drehzahl des Rotors* N_2 T:---g N_1 'speed of the rotor'

This type of variation is not realised for all the terms. For instance, (EOL) De: *Regelenergie* 'control|energy' cannot be expressed as **Energie der Regel* 'energy of control'. The predicative variant of the complex term is allowed for the terms of N A or A N pattern. The adjective goes from the epithetic to the predicative:

$N_1\ A_2 \rightarrow N_1\ V\ A_2$
(DIA) Fr: *pectine méthylée* 'methylated pectine' → *ces pectines sont méthylées* 'These pectines are methylated'
A2 N1 → N1 V A2
(CAN) En: *digital angiography* → *angiography is digital*

3.4.5 Modification

Modification is the main operation of the expansion mechanism that leads to conceptual variants. It is also part of the exemplification mechanism that generates denominative variants. Modification variants remain generally neutral when the modifier appears at the initial position in a left-headed compound. When the modifier is postponed, the variant category depends on the conceptual addition of the modifier.

i. *Juxtaposition*
The neutral juxtaposition for a left-headed compound involves an adjective at the initial position or a preposition phrase of P N pattern:

$N_1 \rightarrow A\ N_1$
(EOL) Fr: *pale* → *vieille pale* 'old blade'
$N_1\ A_1 \rightarrow A\ N_1\ A_1$
(EOL) Es: *problema medioambiental* 'environmental problem' → *grande problema medioambiental* 'critical environmental problem'
$N_1\ A_2 \rightarrow N_1\ A_2\ P\ N$
(EOL) Fr: *générateur éolien* 'wind turbine' → *générateur éolien de référence* 'reference wind turbine'

The neutral juxtaposition at the initial position for right-headed compounds and at the final position for left-headed compounds involves the same modifiers as for conceptual variants. We provide below only one example because the same schemata of modifications are used for conceptual variants:

$N_1 N_2 \rightarrow A N_1 N_2$
(EOL) En: *wind turbine* → *typical wind turbine*

ii. *Insertion*
As for the denominative variants, the same schemata of insertions are used. For example:

$N_1 A_2 \rightarrow N_1 \underline{R} A_2$
(SAT) Fr: *réseaux numériques* 'numerical network' → *réseaux entièrement numériques* 'fully numerical network'
$N_1 P_2 N_3 \rightarrow N_1 \underline{A} P_2 N_3$
(EOL) Fr: *vitesse du vent* 'wind speed' → *vitesse relative du vent* 'relative wind speed'

3.4.6 Coordination, disjunction and enumeration

Coordination and disjunction connect terms by means of a conjunction of common coordination. In the case of the coordination, Fr: *et*, De: *und*, En: *and*, Es: *y* and for the disjunction, Fr: *ou*, En: *or*. The coordination conjunction can be omitted and replaced by a punctuation sign such as the hyphen (–) or the slash (/). Enumeration involves at least three terms coordinated with comma and a conjunction of coordination for the last coordination. Coordination is a linguistic operation that generates many ambiguities when analysed by a syntactic parser. These ambiguities are described in Chapter 7.

Coordination, disjunction and enumeration of complex terms involve morphological or syntagmatic compounds. Coordination of two compounds sharing the same pattern is the most common case. Coordination then factorises the common element. In the case of prefixed simple terms, prefixes are coordinated. In the case of neoclassical compounds, neoclassical stems are coordinated. For both cases, one of the prefixes or one of the stems is detached from its lexical element. In the case of syntagmatic compounds, the coordination factorises either the head or the expansion. The resultant coordinated form introduces common modifications to the citation form of the term, involving inflection (number, gender, case) and the determination. The coordinations of prefixed terms or morphological compounds are expansion coordinations as prefixed and morphological compounds adopt generally a right-headed order. The coordinated variant shows some surface changes when compared with the citation form of the terms that is introduced by inflection and determination. The factorisation of an adjectival expansion introduces a plural inflection.

i. *Head coordination*

With head coordination, the whole expansion is factorised as well as the determinant preceding the head. Head coordination is often difficult to distinguish from coordination between a simple term and a syntagmatic compound.

The main rules of coordination are:

1. Two terms of N P N pattern where:
   a. the article introducing the head noun and the expansional preposition phrase are identical.
   $(D_0)\ N_1\ P_2\ N_3,\ (D_0)\ N_4\ P_2\ N_3 \rightarrow D_0\ N_1\ C\ D_0\ N_4\ P_2\ N_3$
   (EOL) Fr: *(la) production d'électricité,* 'generation of electricity' *(la) distribution d'électricité* 'distribution of electricity' → *la production et la distribution d'électricité* 'generation and distribution of electricity'
   b. the prepositional phrase is shared: same preposition, same nominal expansion head.
   $N_1\ P_2\ N_3,\ N_4\ P_2\ N_3 \rightarrow N_1\ C\ N_4\ P_2\ N_3$
   (SAT) Fr: *élévateur de fréquence* 'upconverter (litt. raiser of frequency)', *abaisseur de fréquence* 'downconverter (litt. reducer of frequency)' → *élévateurs et abaisseurs de fréquence* 'upconverter and downconverter (litt. raiser and reducer of frequency)'
   c. only the head of expansion is shared.
   $N_1\ P_2\ N_3,\ N_4\ P_5\ N_3 \rightarrow N_1\ C\ N_4\ P_2\ N_3$
2. Two terms of N A pattern where:
   a. an adjective or an adjectival expansion sequence is shared.
   $N_1\ A_2,\ N_3\ A_2 \rightarrow N_1\ C\ N_3\ A_2$
   b. the article introducing the head noun and the adjectival expansion are shared.
   $N_1\ A_2,\ N_3\ A_2 \rightarrow D_0\ N_1\ C\ D_0\ N_3\ A_2$

The rules of head coordination can be complicated in the case, for instance, of a coordination between two terms of different patterns:

$N_1\ P_2\ N_3,\ N_4\ P_5\ N_6\ Sp_2\ N_3 \rightarrow N_1\ C\ N_4\ P_5\ N_6\ P_2\ N_3$
Es: *instalación de aerogeneradores* 'installation of wind turbines', *puesta en marcha de aerogeneradores* 'start up of wind turbines' → *instalación y puesta en marcha de aerogeneradores* 'installation and start up of wind turbines'.

ii. *Coordination of expansion*

With expansion coordination, the head of the complex term is factorised. Elements of coordinated expansions often are of the same pattern. The factorisation of the head may introduce a plural inflection. The main patterns of coordination and enumeration on the expansion of prefixed term and morphological compounds are:

1. coordination:
   A/E_1+A_3, $A/E_2+A_3 \rightarrow E_1$ C A/E_2+A_3
   (Maths) Fr: *bidimensionnel* 'bidimensional', *tridimensionnel* 'tridimensional' → *bi et tridimensionnel* 'bi- and tridimensional'
   (EOL) Fr: *hypersynchrone* 'hypersynchronous', *hyposynchrone* 'hyposynchronous' → *hyper et hyposynchrone* 'hyper- and hyposynchronous'
2. disjunctive enumeration:
   A/E_1+A_4, A/E_2+A_4 $A/E_3+A_4 \rightarrow E_1$, E_2 A/E_3+A_4
   (Maths) Fr: *monodimensionnel* 'one-dimensional', *bidimensionnel* 'two-dimensional', *tridimensionnel* 'three-dimensional' → *mono-, bi-, ou tridimensionnel* 'one-, two-, three-dimensional'

The main patterns of coordination and enumeration for the expansion of the syntagmatic compounds are:

1. Two terms of N_1 P N_2 or N_2 N_1 pattern where N_1 is the head and P N_2 or N_2 is the expansion:
   a. Two heads and the preposition introducing the expansion are identical: The rule of coordination is the following:
      N_1 P_1 N_2, N_1 P_1 $N_3 \rightarrow N_1$ P_1 N_2 C P_1 N_3(SAT) Fr: *équipement d'émission* 'equipment of broadcasting', *équipement de transmission* 'equipment of transmission'→ *équipement d'émission et de transmission* 'equipment of broadcasting and transmission'

      Here is the rule of enumeration:
      (SAT) Fr: *système de surveillance* 'system of monitoring', *système d'alarme* 'system of alarm', *système de commande* 'system of control' → *systèmes de surveillance, d alarme et de commande* 'system of monitoring, alarm and control'
   b. Only the two heads are identical:
      N_1 N_2, N_3 $N_2 \rightarrow N_1$ C N_3 N_2
      (SAT) En: *transmit equipment, receive equipment* → *transmit and receive equipment*
      N_1 P_1 N_2, N_1 P_2 $N_3 \rightarrow N_1$ P_1 N_2 C P_2 N_3
      (SAT) Fr: *systèmes en câble* 'system of cable, *systèmes à satellites* 'systems of satellite'→ *systèmes en câble et à satellites* 'systems of cable and satellite'
2. Two terms of N A or A N pattern where N is the head and A is expansion:
   The coordination rule is:
   N_1 A_1, N_1 $A_2 \rightarrow N_1$ A_2 C A_1
   (EOL) Fr: *axe horizontal* 'horizontal axis', *axe vertical* 'vertical axis' → *axe vertical ou horizontal* 'horizontal or vertical axis'

(AGR) Fr: *alimentation animale* 'animal food', *alimentation humaine* 'human food' → *alimentation animale et humaine* 'animal and human food'
$A_1 N_1 \rightarrow A_1 C A_2 N_1$
(EOL) De: *elektrischen komponenten* 'electrical component', *elektronischen komponenten* 'electronical component' → *elektrischen und elektronischen komponenten* 'electrical and electonical component'

The enumeration rule is:
$A_1 N_1 \rightarrow A_1 C A_2 C A_3 N_1$
(EOL) Ru: механическая энергия mechanical energy, электрическая энергия 'electrical energy', тепловая энергия 'thermal energy' → механическая, электрическая и тепловая энергия 'mechanical, electrical, or thermal energy'

3. Two terms of N P N A pattern where the syntagmatic compound of N P N pattern is shared:
$N_1 P N_2 A_1, N_1 P N_2 A_2 \rightarrow N_1 P N_2 A_1 C A_2$
(EOL) Es: *fuente de energía eólica* 'wind energy source', *fuente de energía solar* 'solar energy source' → *fuente de energía eólica y solar* 'wind and solar energy source'
4. Two terms made from different patterns, for example, one of N A pattern and the other of N P N pattern. The first element of the coordinated structure is the term of N A pattern, and more generally the shorter term. This property is rather remarkable in the case of the relational adjective:
$N_1 P N_2, N_1 A \rightarrow N_1 A C P N_2$
(SAT) Fr: *service spatial* 'space service', *service de Terre* 'service of the Earth' → *services spatiaux et de Terre* 'space and terrestrial services'

When the head and the expansion head are identical and only differ from the preposition that is employed, an expansion coordination is preferred to the head coordination:

(SAT) Fr: *couplage avant amplification* 'coupling before amplification', *couplage après amplification* 'coupling after amplification' → *couplage avant amplification ou après amplification* 'coupling before or after amplification'

In order to keep the parallelism of patterns in the coordination between two terms, the denominative variant may be preferred. In the example below, the syntagmatic compound of N P N pattern is preferred to the denominative variant of N A pattern in order to form a coordination of homogeneous expansion of P D N pattern:

$N_1 A_2, N_1 P N_3 \rightarrow N_1 P D N_3 C P D N_2$ with A_2: derived from N_2
(EOL) Fr: *circuit rotorique* 'rotor circuit', *circuit du stator* 'stator circuit' → *circuit du stator et du rotor* 'stator and rotor circuit'

3.5 Variants of register

In the preceding section, we illustrated the linguistic variants generated from a denominative variant selected from among a set of denominative variants. The choice of a denominative variant is either arbitrary, or is subject to syntactical constraints. It can also respond to a communicative situation and personal interaction. We call this a "register variant".

Otmam (1996) remarks that usages relating to the metaphorisation or the vulgarisation of the topic are in competition. Cabré (1998: 188) indicates possible differences of register such as *penitentiary/prison/clink.*

Register variants allow to distinguish between communication levels, such as scientific and popular scientific discourses, or for and against points of view. "Communication level", which is a corpus feature, is introduced in Section 5.1.1. Shift of register will normally select a term but, when the concept cannot be avoided, a denominative variant judged more or less scientific, or more or less favourable according to the scientific viewpoint will be selected.

3.5.1 Variation of scientification/popularisation

The variation of scientification is used in specialised domains where the expert needs to communicate with non-specialists, such as in medicine. Two linguistic operations are favoured to go from one register to the other: synonymic substitution capable of generating either a specialised or a common variant of the term, and anaphorical reduction that generalise the term notion.

Synonymic substitution
The scientification variant is created by substituting one of the element of the complex term by another element that is of greater scientific form than the other. Scientification can be applied to any element of the morphological or syntagmatic compound. The symbol $>_s$ means, in the following examples, that the left variant is terminologically stronger than the right variant.

For some denominal derivations, many suffixes compete with each other and one of them is judged to be more scientific than the other. In French, the suffixes of denominalisation make it possible to oppose the scientific and the popular register:

Scientific	Popular
-aire	*-ier*
-al or *-il*	*-el*
-ain	*-in*

In the case of compounding, the competition between two neoclassical compounds generates a variant of scientification when for a lexeme there are two lexical forms, i.e. neoclassical and common:

(Energy) Fr: *hydrocarbure/hydrocarbone* 'hydrocarbon' where *carbure* 'carbide' is the neoclassical noun of *carbone* 'carbon'.
(Energy) Es: *hydrocarburo/hydrocarbono* 'hydrocarbon' where *carburo* 'carbide' is the neoclassical noun of *carbono* 'carbon'.

The derived form of a neoclassical root is often judged as more scientific than the native word:

(Energy) En: *carbon* $>_s$ *coal*
(MED) Fr: *ophélète* $>_s$ *aidant* 'carer'

Anaphorical reduction
Anaphorical reduction is commonly used to go from a scientific register to a common one. Lexical reduction eliminates elements of the complex term judged too scientific.

(DIA) En : *diabetes melitus* $>_s$ *diabetes*

3.5.2 Variants of position

Terms are linked to concepts whose existence and usage in discourse are connoted, either negatively or positively. Terminology becomes subjective, at the origin of favourable or unfavourable sentiment. Some terms and term variants have to be banished in order to neutralise scientific discourse. For example, in tourism when agencies advertise for an area, the industrial infrastructure is hidden, or disguised in such way that the industrial connotation is neutralised. The term of (Energy) Fr: *lac artificiel* 'artificial lake' is preferred to *centrale hydroélectrique* 'hydroelectric plant' and (EOL) Fr: *nouveau moulin à vent* 'new wind mill' to *éolienne* 'aerogenerator'.

3.6 Borders between categories of variants

We have described so far the mechanisms and the linguistic operations that generate a category of variants. Some linguistic operations such as modification are used as much to produce conceptual variants as stand-alone linguistic variants. Other operations are specific to one category of variants. It is a matter of choice to assign an operation to a category of variant. Other choices will be discussed presently.

3.6.1 Denominative and linguistic variants

Denominative variants realised by initialism can be introduced for the purpose of economy. Its existence is only valid at the document level and such a local acronym is not retained as a denominative variant.

(AGR) Fr: *synthèse organique* 'organic synthesis' → *SO*
(Chemistry) Fr: *hydrocarbure* 'hidrocarbon' → *HC*
(Chemistry) En: *hydrocarbon* → *HC*

3.6.2 Denominative and conceptual variants

The boundaries between denominative and conceptual variants are blurred because of the collusion between the naming and neonymy processes. Derivation that generates an inherent derivative paradigm to a term calls for their inclusion in the conceptual category, indeed, (Pastry) Fr: *fraise* 'strawberry' and *fraisier* 'strawberry cake' are two terms.

Another choice might have been made that includes all aspectual variants obtained by derivation in the set of denominative variants. Such aspectual variants gather typically the argument of the predicative noun, and the modifiers which semantics describes as a property, a cause or a result. Whatever the retained category of derivational variants, either conceptual variants or denominative variants that include aspectual differences, these variants, and more generally the derivational paradigm of a term, are terminologically crucial. The same remark applies to the prefixation variants: a prefix introduces either an aspectual difference, such as (Sciences of education) Fr: *citation/co-citation*, or leads to two distinct terms such as (Computer science) Fr: *apprentissage* 'machine learning' / *surapprentissage* 'overlearning'.

3.6.3 Conceptual and linguistic variants

The expansion of the term, thanks to modification, is at the heart of the expansion process that leads to the generation of conceptual variants. This modification may remain of a qualitative nature without leading to a new term. Thus, (SAT) Fr: *fixed antenna* is a conceptual variant of *antenna* on the contrary of *old antenna* which is a linguistic variant only: the adjective *old* only brings a qualitative aspect to *antenna*. The decision to categorise a variant as conceptual or solely linguistic requires terminological criteria and the study of the semantics of the modifier. A well-known clue to opt for a conceptual variant for Romance languages during an adjectival modification is the use of a relational adjective. We will use this criterion to label the relation between the term and the variant in Chapter 4. Modification by epithetic adjectives is more difficult to classify. Thus, the epithetic adjective *old* that currently occurs in linguistic variants may lead to a conceptual variant in another specialised domain such as: (Linguistic) Fr: *langue ancienne* 'historic language' is a clear distinct concept of *langue* 'language'.

In this chapter, we have described the variants of terms with regards to the mechanisms and the linguistic operations that are employed for their creation. Denominative and linguistic variants keep term monosemy, contrary to conceptual variants that lose it, introducing a conceptual difference. The following chapter will examine a few semantic and conceptual relationships that link the term and the conceptual variant.

CHAPTER 4

Semantics of conceptual variants

In this chapter, we will pursue the conceptualisation of variants. In Chapter 3, we only observed variants from the point of view of their creation. We identified the main mechanisms and the linguistic operations of orthography and grammar involved to generate a category of variants. We will now examine the nature of the link between term and variant.

As the label of a concept within a domain, a term does not stand alone. It is part of the terminology that reflects the conceptual system of the specialised domain. A term is in close relationship with other terms. The notion of relation is crucial for the building of terminological resources. Recent specialised dictionaries, termbanks, or thesauri, aim not only to register terms, but also to model the structure of specialised domains, with the help of internally labelled relations between terms. This work of structuring uses relations that have been defined in terminology or in lexicography. A conceptual relation exists between two terms of a specialised domain whereas a semantic relation exists between two words of the language or between the constituent elements of complex terms.

Although a variant is only a potential term, the relation between term and variant is similar to the relation between two terms. Denominative variants are mainly synonymic variants. Conceptual variants show various relations with the term, among which hierarchical relations and collocations are preponderant. First, we will recall the main terminological and semantic models employed to label the relation between two terms. Then, we will provide the main relations characterising the link between the term and the variant: fundamental relations, complex relations, and two additional relations, predication and instance.

4.1 Structuring terms

In this section, we summarise the relations currently employed to qualify the link between two terms. There are many works dedicated to this topic, see for example (Otman 1996) for a review of the semantic relations and (Nastase 2003) for a review of the intra-nominal relations.

4.1.1 Conceptual and semantic relations

Inside a specialised domain, terms are members of a terminology and in relation with other terms. These relations are labelled with conceptual or semantic tags.

Conceptual relations
Conceptual relations aim to structure the domain by using hierarchical relations. The basic conceptual relations following Cabré (1998: 176) are:

1. Generic relations: Generic – Kind: *building – house, edifice, garage.* Generic relations adopt a heritage principle where the designation of a given notion relies on a larger notion that needs to be specified (Lethuillier 1989).
2. Partial relations: All – Part : *body – head, torso, member.*

With these two relations alone, terminologists managed to build sizeable representations of the terminology of specialised domains. But there are other types of conceptual relations called "complex contextual relations" by Sager (1990: 34–35). They depend on the terminology domain and, at the same time, on the application. Let us show two examples:

> Cause – Effect: *nuclear fallout* are caused by *nuclear weapons test*
> Activity – Place: *coal mine* is the place of the *coal mining*

Other conceptual relations have been proposed by Otman (1996) in order to elaborate the Terminological Semantic Network model, such as:

1. associative relations (that the terms share):
   a. kind-of: Fr: *caméra* 'camera' – *appareil de prise de vue* 'image pick-up apparatus'
   b. part-of: *compressor – turbine*
   c. function-of: the function of *loam* is to make a *tissue*
   d. proximity-of: *printer – toner*
2. The distinctive relations (properties that the terms don't share):
   a. contrast-with: *propeller – jet aircraft*
   b. equivalent-of: (with the factor of distinction): Fr: *transparent* (transparent) (France) – *acétate* 'acetate' (Québec).

4.1.2 Classic semantic relations

The classic semantic relations reflect the relations between the words of a language. Cruse (1995) studied in detail four lexical semantic relations: synonymy, antonymy, hypernymy and meronymy, and proposed paradigmatic tests to identify them.

Polguère (2003) defined such relations as "fundamental semantic relations". They shape the organisation of the lexicon of a language.

Synonymy

Two words are synonyms if their meanings are identical. Thus, they can substitute themselves, whatever the context. Such synonyms are "absolute synonyms" (or perfect synonyms). Absolute synonyms have to be distinguished from "near-synomyms". Near-synonyms share meaning and are similar only in given contexts. Murphy (2003) distinguished quasi-synomys with six main differences of meanings. Degree of specialisation is one of them, and thus a hypernym is a possible near-synonym in context.

Antonymy

Two words are antonyms if their meanings are opposite. As for synonymy, there are two kinds of antonyms: "absolute antonyms" and "near-antonyms". Absolute antonyms (Cruse 2004) are gradable opposites, mainly adjectives, which stand at the opposite extreme of a dimension scale such as *warm/cold.* Near-antonyms are similar in every dimension of meaning, except in a specific one. Among classic types of opposites, reversible antonyms are two verbs or predicative nouns that describe two reverse actions such as *install/uninstall.*

Hypernymy

Two words are hyponyms if the meaning of one, the hyponym, is entailed in the meaning of the other, the hypernym. Hypernymy is an oriented and transitive relation. It has been formalised for the building of semantic hierarchies and ontologies.

Meronymy

Two words are meronyms if one, the meronym, is part of the second, the holonym. Meronymy is an oriented and transitive relation and is a base-relation for the building of semantic hierarchies and ontologies. As for synonymy and antonymy, "absolute meronyms" have the properties of functionality, homeomerity and separability (Winston et al. 1987). They have to be distinguished from the "near-meronyms" which involve other types of inclusion than meronyms. Hypernyms are included in the near-meronym set. Hypernymy and meronymy are hierarchical relations.

The basic terminological relations and the classical semantic ones are comparable. The conceptual relation "Generic – Kind" matches hypernymy. The conceptual relation "All – Part" matches meronymy. A conceptual relation involves two terms referring to two concepts, whereas a semantic relation links two words with different meaning.

From the point of view of the General Theory of Terminology (Wüster 1968), synonymy is not a conceptual relation because the univocity and the monoreferenciality of the term are definitional properties. In the daily practice of terminology, and even inside a specialised domain, equivalent terms exist in order to facilitate a discourse (Malrieu and Rastier 2002).

4.1.3 Collocation

A collocation is a number of words that co-occur frequently and stem principally from the linguistic competence of native speakers (Firth 1968). It is "an arbitrary and recurrent word combination" (Benson 1990).

Collocations are semi-idiomatic expressions with at least one of the constituents, the base, keeping its original meaning while the meaning of the collocate is neutralised. For example, in *to take a walk,* the word *walk* maintains its meaning, but the verb that goes along with it is devoid of its original meaning. In this case, this is a support verb, free of meaning. Furthermore, in many cases this type of expressions cannot be translated literally, the arbitrary element of the collocate requires that we know the correct form for each language. For example, in French we can say *forte pluie* 'lit. strong rain', to express intensity, whereas in English if we wanted to express the equivalent meaning, we would use *heavy rain.* The collocate substitutability is limited. This means that when substituted only a few other words keep their meaning, even if they fit syntactically and semantically. The majority of the substituted words yield understandable but slightly odd expressions: *amour fou* 'deep love' / **amour dément* 'crazy love'.

The study of collocation is above all aimed at assisting language learners and translators in their tasks. The lexicographical school seeks to formalise collocations so as to include them in dictionaries (Haussmann 1985, Benson 1990). The phenomenon of collocation is fully in place and in force in specialised domains. Martin (1992) introduced "conceptual collocation" and gave some examples in the metallurgy domain of adjectives: *centrifugal, electric, selenoid* occurring with *switch.* The terms *electric switch, centrifugal switch, selenoid switch* are all hyponyms of *switch.* A collocation is a combination of lexical units whose intra-relation between the base and the collocate has to be specified. Lexical functions have been designed for this aim.

4.1.4 Lexical functions

Lexical functions (LF) are used to model semantic and conceptual relations and a subset of collocations, the restricted lexical co-occurrences (CRL). Mel'čuk et al. (1984: 4) defined the CRL as "the capacity of lexemes to combine within syntagms to express a given meaning. A lexical co-occurrence is restricted if a lexeme *A* with the meaning 'A' and a lexeme *B* with the meaning 'B' cannot be combined to express the compound meaning 'A + B', even if it is syntactically allowed."[1] The definition of a CRL is similar to the criterion of non-compositionality in lexical semantics.

LF are mathematical functions f(x) = y that involve a keyword (x) whose values (y) are associated with a given meaning. The notation f(x) = y means that a lexical relation f holds from x to y. We choose as an example the standard LF of the highest intensification, called CULM, which applies to the noun Fr: *joie* 'joy' generates the value:

CULM(joie) = *comble* [*de la joie*] 'overjoyed'.

There are 60 simple standard lexical functions that gather miscellaneous relations. LF are able to express:

1. Paradigmatic relations such as syntactic derivations associated with their FL: adjectivation (A_0), nominalisation N_0, verbalisation (V_0). The complete list of derivations is provided by Jousse and Bouveret (2003);
2. Syntagmatic relations such as CRL. Another example of CRL is *beurre rance* 'butter', where the noun *beurre* cannot be substituted by other nouns belonging to the class of dairy products: **fromage rance* 'rancid cheese'; conversely within the CRL *désir ardent* 'burning desire', the adjective cannot be substituted by other synonyms: **désir embrasé* 'engulfed desire', **désir enflammé* 'inflamed desire', **désir incandescent* 'incandescent desire'.

Some paradigmatic semantic relations accept syntagmatic expressions. FL provides a unified framework capable of expressing both paradigmatic and syntagmatic expressions. The FL MULT, a regular set of *X*, is an example of paradigmatic semantic relation with both paradigmatic and syntagmatic expressions:

MULT(*dog*)= *litter*,MULT(*bee*) = *sworn* [*of bees*].

Within the paradigmatic LFs, we have the classic semantic relations:

synonymy SYN(*car*)= *automobile*
antonymy ANTI(*respect*) = *disrespect* and conversive antonymy CONV_{31} (*buy*)= *sell*
hypernymy GENER(*gaz*) = *substance* and hyponymy SPEC.

1. Our translation of "Par co-occurrence lexicale, on entend la capacité des lexèmes de se combiner en syntagmes pour exprimer un sens donné. On parle de co-occurrence lexicale restreinte si un lexème *A* signifiant 'A' et un lexème *B* signifiant 'B' ne peuvent pas se combiner pour exprimer le sens composé 'A + B', cela n'étant pas interdit par la syntaxe."

Some of the FL describe the intra-nominal relations. We illustrate some FL which involve two nouns and a noun and an adjective:

1. F(N) = N for a syntagmatic compound of N P N pattern
   SING a regular < portion > of
   SING(*snow*) = *flake* [*of snow*]
   MULT a regular set of
   MULT(*bee*) = *sworn* [*of bees*]
   MAGN intensification
   Fr: MAGN(*mémoire*) = [*mémoire d'*] *éléphant* 'like an elephant memory'
2. F(N) = A for a syntagmatic compound of N A pattern
   MAGN intensification
   MAGN(*memory*) = *prodigious*
   VER as it should be, correct
   VER(*expectation*) = *legitimate*
   BON good – as it should be expressed in the language
   BON(*advice*) = *valuable*
   POS positive evaluation
   POS(*opinion*) = *favourable*

The values obtained for a keyword with the FL SING and MULT are similar to the part-of and set-of conceptual relations.

Lexical relations were studied by L'Homme and Dancette (2004) to build terminological databases that encode the conceptual relation that holds between two terms. The retained FL are those capable of expressing classic semantic relations such as:

1. synonymy SYN (*mél* 'email' – *courriel),*
2. antonymy ANTI (*acquitter* 'acquit' – *condamner* 'condemn'),
3. taxonymy GENER et SPEC (*fruit* 'fruit' – *pomme* 'apple'),
4. meronymy PART (*moteur* 'motor' – *piston* 'piston'),

but also several other relations such as:

1. singulative or unit SING,
2. collective or set MULT,
3. adjectival passivisation A_2,
4. verbalisation V_0.

L'Homme et Dancette's (2004) model gathers 28 lexico-semantic relations. FL fits well to express classic lexical relations and numerous complex conceptual relations. Furthermore, standard lexical functions are shared by all languages.

4.2 Fundamental relations between term and variant

A term and a variant are linked by a semantic relation. We adopt the notions of lexical semantics as the terminological character of the variant is only potential. The two fundamental relations that hold between term and variant are synonymy and hierarchy. We apply the notion of lexical function proposed by L'Homme and Dancette (2004) in order to describe the basic terminological relations.

4.2.1 Synonymy

Given that terminologies are concerned exclusively with one specialised domain, absolute synonyms are rare, but near-synonyms are usually employed in context. Denominative variants attest a near-synonymy relation. The main linguistic operation to generate a synonym variant is the synonymic substitution. Full substitution applies to simple terms; full or partial substitution to complex terms (cf. Section 3.2.1). The relation of synonymy is established between a term and its variant if compositionality (Partee 1984) is verified. Therefore, a term and its variants are considered as synonyms if at least one of their components in the same syntactic position are synonyms and the other component is the same (Hamon and Nazarenko 2001). For example, from the fact that we face synonymy between two words, (EOL) Fr: *rotor* and *turbine*, the terms (EOL) *Darrieus rotor* and *Darrieus turbine* also are synonyms. We extend these properties from syntagmatic to morphological compounds.

Definition

Complex term, synonymic variant
A complex term and its variants, both of them being of morphological or syntagmatic compounds type, are synonyms if at least one of their components in a syntactic position is synonym and the other components remain identical.

Morphological compound
synonymic substitution on the modifier for a right-headed compound

> (EOL) SYN(*aéro*) = *éolien*, term: *aérogénérateur* 'aerogenerator', variant: *générateur éolien* → SYN(*aérogénérateur*) = *générateur éolien*

Syntagmatic compound
synonymic substitution on the head for a left-headed compound

(EOL) Fr: SYN(*éolienne*) = *aérogénérateur,* term: *éolienne à axe horizontal,* variant: *turbine à axe horizontal* → SYN(*éolienne à axe horizontal*), = *aérogénérateur à axe horizontal*

The situation can be extended to a complex component of the term as in the following example:

(EOL) It: SYN(*turbina eolica*) = *areogeneratore,* term: *turbina eolica ad asse vericale* → SYN(*turbina eolica ad asse vericale*) = *areogeneratore ad asse vericale)*

We will exploit this definition to automatically discover synonymic variants of complex terms in Chapter 8.

4.2.2 Hierarchical relations

Hierarchical relations apply to conceptual variants. The specification of a term is carried out by using the expansion process and the modification operation presented in Section 3.3. According to the lexical hypothesis of Kleiber and Tamba (1990), there is a hierarchic subsumption between two terms when one of them is lexically included, in a syntactic position given, in another term. We will extend this property from two terms to a term and a variant, and from a syntagmatic compound to a morphological compound.

Definition

Complex term, hierarchical variant
A complex term and its variants are linked by a hierarchical relation if the term is lexically included in a morphological or syntactic position in the variant.

Morphological compound
(EOL) Fr: term: *pale,* variant: *monopale* → SPEC(*pale*) = *monopale* and GENER(*monopale*) = *pale.*

Syntagmatic compound
(EOL) Fr: term: *éolienne* 'rotor', variant: *éolienne tripale* 'three-blade rotor' → SPEC(*éolienne*) = *éolienne tripale* et GENER(*éolienne tripale*) = *éolienne.*

This phenomenon of specialisation is recurrent and can be applied to complex terms:

(EOL) Fr: term: *éolienne tripale* 'three-blade rotor', variant: *éolienne tripale à tour tubulaire* 'tubular-tower three-blade rotor' → SPEC(*éolienne tripale*) = *éolienne tripale à tour tubulaire* and GENER(*éolienne tripale à tour tubulaire*) = *éolienne tripale.*

If a hierarchical relation naturally refers to hypernymy, it can also denote a relation of meronymy between the term and the expansion of the variant:

(EOL) Fr: term: *éolienne tripale* 'three-blade rotor', variant: *éolienne tripale à tour tubulaire* 'tubular-tower three-blade rotor' → PART(*éolienne tripale*) = *tour tubulaire* 'tubular tower'

Condamines (2009) indicates that the preposition *avec* 'with' is a typical marker of meronymy, while the preposition *de* is used in a very marginal way. Let us see some examples:

(EOL) En: term: *wind plant,* variant: *wind plant with two-blade rotor* → PART(*wind plant*) = *two-blade rotor*

The preposition *with* remains semantically ambiguous when the meronymical meaning is in competition with the more common accompaniment meaning such as:

(EOL) En: *annoyance with wind turbine*

Nevertheless, if the including property is necessary to qualify a hierarchical variant, it is not sufficient. Other relations can be characterised by the inclusion criterion: complex relations.

4.3 Complex relations between term and variant

The term and its variants may be linked by other relations than the fundamental ones. Some of these relations are similar to complex conceptual relations with the difference that the variant has only an intermediate terminological status. Derivation and modification engender a variety of semantic relations which distinguish the term and the variant. They can both be used to generate a relation.

Antonymy
Near-antonymy between a term and its variant is qualified by the inclusion property extended to the morphological element. We include, in the set of near-antonyms, contrasting term-variant pairs which have a conceptual, semantic or cultural opposition (Chaffin and Hermann 1984).

Morphological antonymy is expressed by the prefixes Fr: *in (im), ir, dé, non(-)*. Prefixing can be carried out upon:

1. the modifier:
   (AGR) Fr: term: *solubilisation micellaire* 'micellar solubilisation' variant: *insolubilisation micellaire* 'micellar insolubilisation' → ANTI(*solubilisation micellaire*) = *insolubilisation micellaire*
2. the head:
   (AGR) Fr: term: *phénol polymérisé* 'polymerized phenol' variant: *phénol non-polymérisé* 'unpolymerized phenol' → ANTI(*phénol polymérisé*) = *phénol non-polymérisé*
   (CAN) En: term: *cyclical breast pain* variant: *non-cyclical breast pain* → ANTI(-*cyclical breast pain*) = *non-cyclical breast pain*

Syntagmatic antonymy is expressed by modification with a adverb of negation such as Fr: *non*. This adverb is juxtaposed:

1. at initial position:
   (CAN) En: term: *cell-cycle specific* variant: *non cell-cycle specific* → ANTI(*cell-cycle specific*) = *non cell-cycle specific*
2. inserted in N A pattern:
   (AGR) Fr: term: *levure floculante* 'flocculating yeast' variant: *levure non floculante* 'non-flocculating yeast' → ANTI(*levure floculante*) = *levure non floculante*

The unique status of *non* as both a prefix and a negation adverb generates competing antonymic patterns such as:

> (DIA) Fr: *diabète non insulino-dépendant/diabète insulino-non-dépendant* 'diabetes'

4.3.1 Result

FL S_{RES} refers to the state which is a result of an action or a process: S_{RES}(to *print*) = *printout*.

S_{RES} is expressed by:

1. the suffixes Fr: *age, ade, erie* on the head of the compound:
   S_{RES}(*filetage du saumon*) 'salmon filleting' = *filet de saumon* 'salmon fillet';
2. the suffixes Fr: *age, ade, erie, ment, tion, ure* on the modifier of the compound:
   S_{RES}(*congélation des aliments*) 'food freezing' = *aliment congelé* 'frozen food'

4.3.2 Plurality

FL MULT(L) refers to a set *of* L.

Full substitution may be used to generate a plurality variant of the simple term. When L is not present in the value, the operator =// is used:

(Trade) term: *customer,* variant: *clientele* → MULT(*customer*) =// *clientele*

But the plurality of a term is usually carried out by using the expansion process.

The morphological plurality is expressed by the suffixes Fr: *ade, aille, aie.*

(AGR) Fr: term: *rose,* variant: *roseraie* → MULT(*rose*) = *roseraie*

This example illustrates a complex conceptual relation Element–Collection where all the parts belong to the same species.

(AGR) Fr: term: *citron* 'lemon', variant: *citronnade* 'lemon juice' → MULT(*citron*) = *citronnade*

This example illustrates a complex conceptual relation Substance–Whole which expresses 'a preparation made of'.

The syntagmatic plurality is expressed by predication with quantifiers such as Fr: *ensemble* 'set'.

(AGR) En: term: *bee,* variant: *swarm of bees* → MULT(*bee*) = *swarm of bees.*

4.3.3 Spatiality

FL S_{RES} refers to spatiality. The spatiality of a term is usually carried out by using the expansion process.

The morphological spatiality is expressed by the suffixes Fr: *ie, -oir.*

(AGR) Fr: term: *sucre de betterave* 'beet sugar', variant: *sucrerie de betterave* 'beet sugar factory' → S_{loc} *(sucre de betterave)* = *sucrerie de betterave*

The syntagmatic spatiality is expressed by modification. It is quite current in the medical domain.

(CAN) Fr: term: *curage axiliaire* 'axillary node dissection', variant: *curage axiliaire droit* 'right axillary node dissection' → S_{loc} *(curage axiliaire)* = *curage axiliaire droit*

(CAN) En: term: *lymph node,* variant: *cervical lymph node* → S_{loc} *(lymph node)* = *cervical lymph node*

4.3.4 Temporality

FL S_{temps} refers to the temporality. The temporality of a term is usually carried out by using the expansion process.

(CAN) Fr: term: *effet secondaire* 'side effect' variant: *effet secondaire immédiat* 'immediate side effect' → S_{temps} *(effet secondaire)* = *effet secondaire immédiat*
(EOL) En: term: *power production,* variant: *annual power production* → S_{temps} *(power production)* = *annual power production*

4.3.5 Quality

Relations of quality were introduced by Nastase and Szpakowicz (2003) to explain intra-nominal semantics. They gather miscellaneous sub-relations such as content, container, manner, measure, and so on. These sub-relations also apply to the term and its variants.

Measure the variant indicates either a value associated with a unit of measure, or an intensification of the term (FL MAGN). Intensification is gradable with the possibility to express the maximum intensity (FL CULM).

(EOL) En: term: *rotor diameter,* variant: *100-metre rotor diameter*
(MOB) En: term: *global operator,* variant: *large global operator*
→MAGN(*global operator*) = *large global operator*
(MOB) En: term: *global operator,* variant: *giant global operator*
→MAGN(*global operator*) = *giant global operator* with *giant* > *large*
(EOL) En: term: *low temperature,* variant: *extremely low temperature*
→ CULM(*low temperature*) = *extremely low temperature*

Manner the variant explains how to use or characterise the term. This sub-relation may advocate a favourable sentiment (FL BON). Manner is expressed thanks to the adding of an adverb or an adjective modifier.

(MOB) En: term: *grid connection,* variant: *smooth grid connection*
(CAN) En: term: *significant peak,* variant: *statistically significant peaks*
(MOD) En: term: *bandwidth,* variant: *fair bandwidth*
→ BON(*bandwidth*) = *fair bandwidth*

4.4 Other relations between term and variant

For many conceptual variants, it is difficult to label the link between the term and its variants using a semantic or conceptual relation. We retain, as other relations, predication and instance.

4.4.1 Predication

Variants obtained by predication refer to aspects or properties of the term, to its typical action on a domain object (Heid 1993). The term becomes a typical argument or modifier of a predicative noun.

(EOL) En: term: *wind turbine,* variant: *health effects of wind turbines*
(CAN) En: term: *anastrozole,* variant: *benefit of anastrozole*
(CAN) En: term: *lymph node,* variant: *involvement of lymph node*

Such predicative noun expressions are similar to the collocations verb + term where the term is the argument of the verb, either subject or object.

(MOB) En: term: *grid connexion,* variant: *to connect grid.*

4.4.2 Instance

Conceptual variant may also refer to a unique reference of the invoked concept that we call an "instance". A unique reference designs a particular entity which is a singular object. This singular object describes a place entity, a product, a name entity, a mathematical or scientific symbol. The instance of a term is a variant without any semantic or conceptual relation. An instance takes different values along time. It has more singular properties than the term it relates to.

Each term may, under certain conditions, accept an instance. The instance is obtained by the expansion of a name entity or a symbol:

1. at initial position:
   (EOL) En: term: *standard deviation,* variant: *Cn standard deviation*
   (EOL) En: term: *wind farm,* variant: *Jepirachi wind farm*
   (MOB) En: term: *mobile operator,* variant: *Citycell mobile operator*
2. at final position:
   (EOL) En: term: *tip-speed ratio,* variant: *tip-speed ratio* λr

The instance may be substituted for the term in discourse as (MOB)*Citycell* for *Citycell mobile operator.*

This review of the semantic relations between the term and the variant shows a huge diversity. The objective of this chapter was not to enumerate exhaustively all the relations but rather to illustrate the richness of semantics between term and variant. For most relations obtained by derivation, the semantic label can be directly assigned from the pair term/variant sharing a typical pattern and the semantics of the suffix. For example, given a term of N_1 P_2 N_2 pattern, given a variant of N_3 P_2 N_2 pattern, with the expansion P_2 N_2 shared, N_1 and N_3 having the same stem, N_3 built with a suffix belonging to the list Fr: *aie, erie, oir,* then locativity relation is inferable between the term and its variant, such as (AGR) Fr: S_{LOC}(*huile de palme* 'palm oil') = *huilerie de palme* 'oil palm mill'. The semantic qualification of the semantic relation could be added to the variant grammar rules as the one described in Chapter 7. The variants obtained by derivation and their particular feature are a small subset of the variants when compared to the set of conceptual and denominative variants. In the second part of our study, we will look at the automatic detection of variants and its categorisation depending on the main categories of variants: denominative, conceptual or only linguistic. A more fine-grained categorisation is beyond the scope of our study. However, we will suggest some measures which automatically assigned hierarchical relations in Chapter 7, and synonymy and antonymy in Chapter 8.

PART II

Automatic discovery

CHAPTER 5

Primitive exploration of variants using comparable corpora

If we want to study term variants across languages and domains, we need several comparable corpora of specialised domains. First, we recall the definition of corpus and its main properties. When several properties of monolingual corpora are shared across languages, we assume that they are comparable. Our study is based on several comparable corpora of different domains, languages and communication levels of which we present the main features. Then, we carry out a primitive exploration using these comparable corpora. N-gram calculation is a simple method that can be used to observe variants in the same way that collocations of multi-word expressions in comparable specialised corpora were observed by Forchini and Murphy (2008). Applying n-grams will allow us to validate our specification on the data and to observe variants when diversifying corpus features such as domain, language and communication level. Our primitive corpus-based exploration uses computational tools. We focus on variants of some central terms in the domains of our corpora.

5.1 Comparable corpora

5.1.1 Corpus

According to Sinclair (2003: 4), a corpus is: "a collection of pieces of language that are selected and ordered according to explicit linguistics in order to be used as a sample of the language." In our study, the "pieces of language" means a text by adopting Rastier's (2002) position about this subject: "If the word [...] is the elementary unit, the text is the minimal unit for an advanced linguistics, and the corpus is a collection where this unit can find its meaning". The collected texts enhance specialised domains and build a "sample" of these domains. The representativeness of the corpus for the study of variants is arguable like any study on corpus linguistics. The features of the texts, their availability, authors, language, genre, productive condition, influence the selection of a term, and also variants to be observed. In addition to these properties, there are conditions under which texts are gathered.

They can be collected manually, semi-automatically or fully automatically. In the case of a contrastive study of a specialised domain covering several languages, collected corpora of a specialised domain must be comparable.

5.1.2 Properties

Our investigation on variants is carried out on comparable corpus of specialised domains. All texts in a corpus enhance the same "language" and the same "communication level". The genre of document intervenes to decide on a specialised domain and to judge of the communication level at the same time. The size of the corpus is determined by its exploitability and the time needed for text gathering. The aimed minimal size of a corpus should be 200,000 words, which must be balanced in length and width. In other words, not only the number of words, but also the number of texts must be taken into account (Williams 1999).

Genre

Genres, according to Biber (1989), are text categories distinguished spontaneously by the speakers of a language. For example, genres in English include novels, articles of newspapers, editorials, research papers. This categorisation loses its spontaneity in front of the proliferation of document genres found on the web. The notion of genre becomes more diffuse because of the interconnection and combination of documents. The list of genres on the web changes constantly and some genres are underrepresented. There are several typologies of web genres, from the most concise (8 genres) to the most exhaustive (2,000 genres) as shown by Crowston et al. (2010). As for specialised languages, Montesi and Navarette (2008) count 28 genres and 10 subgenres for the available documentation on the Web consulted by a computer engineer. In general, texts of the same genre share the same communicative function as well as a number of linguistic and structural features. For example, scientific papers adopt the same structure concerning title, keywords, summary, introduction, state of art and bibliography. A classification by genre guarantees the homogeneity of the corpus, and the volume of texts ensures the usability of the corpus (Bommier-Pincemin 1999).

Domain

The notion of domain is as difficult to define as the notion of genre. The domain can be generic like the large domains of science and technology, or it can be more precise by detailing subdomains of a generic domain such as, for science and technology, computer science, physics, then these subdomains can be divided themselves into themes such as computer science of software technology, artificial intelligence, data science, and so on. As an example, *Trésor de la langue française* (TLF) considers 758 domains classified by hierarchical order on 3 levels, and *Cambridge International Dictionary of English* (CIDE) has 900 hierarchical domains on 4 levels. Depending on the nomenclatures, a domain can appear as a subdomain of another domain. For example, medicine is a subdomain of science and technology in TLF, although it is an entire domain in CIDE. Domain is assimilable to a theme, a subject, an activity or a problematic concerning a specific research. Sager (1990) talked about "Language for Special Purposes (LSP)". In Termium, the system of classification of domains includes 3 levels: classes or large domains, divisions and sections. For example, medicine is composed of one class containing divisions such as digestive device, respiratory device, diagnostic methods, surgery, pharmacology, and so on. The surgical division is distributed into sections such as anesthesia and resuscitation, heart surgery, dental surgery, and so on. In general, it is the section (more precisely the subdomain) which appears on the terminological record. Therefore, Termium is composed of 24 large domains of terminological sets, and each domain is divided into 10–12 subdomains on average. These subdomains are then subdivided into more subdomains with an approximate total of 1,600 nodes of classification (Pavel and Nolet 2001).

A term is defined according to a domain, and the notion of domain is essential. The more the domain becomes general, the more the terminology becomes important and less detailed. On the contrary, a detailed domain generates a narrowly-specialised terminology of small size. Proximity and interconnection of domains make it difficult to delimit a domain strictly. Barrière (2010) points out that in *Grand Dictionnaire Terminologique* (GDT), domain borders are ambiguous: for example, metallurgy and mining industry, or energy and electricity.

Communication level

The textual unit guarantees the necessary discourse dimension for the observation and the analysis of terms and variants. For Malrieu and Rastier (2002), a text of a specialised domain belongs to the scientific or popular scientific discourse. The former collects works written by experts or initiated persons to experts or initiated persons. The latter integrates different degrees of popularisation: writing made by experts or initiated persons to uninitiated persons, as well as writing made by uninitiated persons to uninitiated persons. Bowker and Pearson (2002) prefer the term "communication level" to the term "discourse". A communication level distinguishes communications between experts, from an expert to an initiated person, from an expert to an uninitiated person, and from a professor to a student. A specialised text is written by an expert of the domain to other experts. It belongs to the scientific discourse.

The categories of variants that will be observed are conditional upon the corpus. A corpus of a given specialised domain, gathering texts of one single genre and one communication level, will probably yield a preponderant category of variants. Thus, a corpus made from scientific articles, written by experts to experts, gathered over a short duration of time, shall provide us with an inventory of the conceptual variants of the term studied. A corpus with several genres of documents, of one single communication level, shall provide us with more denominative variants and fewer conceptual variants than a corpus only made of scientific articles.

5.1.3 Collecting comparable corpora

Texts may be manually collected from scientific portals with open archives. Portals and archives adopt a classification of domains or subjects, and guarantee an indexation of documents with key-words belonging to a controlled vocabulary. Texts are selected by using a search engine, a thematic search engine, or an internal search engine of the portal. Key-Words for this search are manually provided or are calculated by using other texts. The compilation of the list of key-words of a domain is an essential step to collect a homogeneous corpus of a pre-specified domain. The list is made by introspection, by consultation of encyclopedias, of existing terminological databases, and by the examination of typical relevant texts of the domain. Generally, the list is a compromise between specificity and productivity. Document genres marked on the portals are restricted, with a predominance of papers and scientific reports for scientific domains.

Automatically building specialised corpora from the web is also possible with a topic specific monolingual crawler (Bergmark et al. 2002). A web crawler is a program which downloads, when one or more boots of a lexical type or URL are given, the web pages associated with these boots. It extracts the hyperlinks in which the boots are included and continues to download in a recursive way the web pages identified by these hyperlinks (Olston and Najork 2010). Topic crawlers use search engines and guide the acquisition of texts with seed words extracted from texts in specialised domains. New seed words are extracted from the retained texts to complete the original list of seed words. The performance of a topic crawler depends mainly on two aspects: first, the list of seed words, or of seed URL that are provided as the main terms of the specialised domain. These lists are constructed either manually, semi-automatically or fully-automatically; second, the ranking and the filtering of the URL and the texts. Topic crawlers harvest monolingual domain-specific corpora to initiate the acquisition of comparable corpora in several languages. Well-known topic crawlers for the building of comparable corpora are BootCaT (Baroni and Bernadini 2004), Ardo[1] or Babouk (De Groc 2011).

1. combine.it.1th.se

5.1.4 Comparability

Comparable corpora are composed of texts written in different languages which are not mutual translations. The term *comparable* is used in order to indicate that these collected texts share a number of features, such as the domain, period or communication level (Bowker and Pearson 2002: 93). Other criteria can be taken into account in the construction of comparable corpora such as the comparability of size (number of texts, of words, or of sentences) (Maia 2003), the method for collecting texts, the distribution into different genres, and so on. The exploitation of comparable corpora as well as the methods used for this procedure also are parameters of comparability (Saralegi et al. 2008).

5.2 Comparable corpora used in this study

The comparable specialised corpora used in this study gather technical and scientific texts with a high degree of specialisation: we can thus expect a significant density of terms. We have three comparable corpora, namely two semi-manually extracted corpora of breast cancer [CAN] and diabetes [DIA], and an automatically collected corpus of wind energy [EOL]. Breast cancer and diabetes are subdomains of the medical domain, and wind energy is a subdomain of the energy domain. All documents comprising our comparable specialised corpora have been normalised through the following linguistic pre-processing steps: tokenisation, part-of-speech tagging, and lemmatisation.

Comparable corpora used for this primitive exploration of variants will also be used for automatic variant recognition (cf. Chapters 7 and 8, and for automatic term extraction with variant recognition (cf. Chapter 9).

Breast cancer

Our comparable corpora of breast cancer are available in two types of discourse, i.e. scientific discourse and popular scientific discourse, and three languages, i.e. French, English and German. Scientific discourse texts were selected among scientific articles on the *Elsevier*[2] website and on *Google Scholar*.[3] As for texts of popular scientific discourse, they are popular scientific papers written for patients and their relatives. Documents have been collected in order to comply with the following comparability criteria:

2. www.elsevier.com

3. scholar.google.com

Table 5.1 Features of multilingual corpora of breast cancer [CAN].

	Fr	En	De
Science			
Number of words	267,180	198,244	197,187
Number of documents	78	70	103
Popular science			
Number of words	184,504	218,336	201,760
Number of documents	217	272	162

Table 5.2 Features of French corpora of diabetes and food [DIA].

	Fr	
	Science	Popular science
Number of characters	2,668,783	2,845,114
Number of words	425,800	267,900
Number of papers	65	183

a. contain the seed term *cancer du sein* for French (or its equivalent terms in other languages: *breast cancer* for English and *Brustkrebs* for German);
b. published in the period 2001–2008;
c. comparable size as regard to other sets of papers in other languages.

Diabetes

Our comparable corpora of diabetes are available only in French. The aim of the corpus is to compare discourses in the medical domain. The central topic is diabetes and food. This topic assures a diversity of document genres having a scientific or a popular scientific scope. A general search engine was used to pick up the documents with the help of search elements, made from various combinations of seed terms such as *alimentation* 'food', *diabète* 'diabetes', and *obésité* 'obesity'. Only the documents in html and pdf formats were kept, then they were manually classified into the scientific or the popular scientific category. Documents are differentiated by genre, sociolinguistic environment of production and mode of transmission. Scientific documents are presented in medical portals like CISMeF. The collection process was carried out in 2006.

Renewable energy

Our comparable corpora of renewable energy domain are available in seven languages, i.e. French, English, German, Spanish, Russian, Latvian and Chinese. Corpora were collected from web pages by using the topic crawler Babouk (de

Groc 2011). Some of the monolingual corpora have been extended with manually collected documents on the Web in order to satisfy the minimal size, set to 300,000 words. The collection of documents was carried out in 2010.

Corpora of the renewable energy domain are downloadable.[4]

Table 5.3 summarises the sizes of French, English, German, Spanish and Russian corpora by number of words and number of papers that will be used for this study.

Table 5.3 Features of multilingual corpora of renewable energy [EOL].

	Fr	En	De	Es	Ru
Number of words	313,943	314,549	358,602	453,953	323,929
Number of papers	11	28	34	46	48

5.3 Looking for variants

When a term is given, it is easy to extract from a corpus the n-grams containing the term in question. A unigram contains the search string, a bigram contains the search string as well as another string that might be a previous one or a following one. As for an n-gram, it contains the search string and *n* additional strings. These n-grams display all the occurrences of the term, including the majority of variants where the form of the term is not modified. The goal is to observe all the occurrences of a term in the corpus and to compare the variants detected by our typology of variants proposed in Chapter 3. This method is easy to perform but is only exploitable for some n-grams or some languages.

5.3.1 Implementation

The study of variants by examining n-grams is carried out on [EOL] comparable corpora for the five languages. We calculate the n-grams of the term *blade* for these languages. *Blade* is a simple term, central to the wind energy domain. It is a non-predicative noun.

N-grams have been computed by software AntConc,[5] version 3.2. Collecting the n-grams including a term can be carried out in two ways: by the search string which is a word surrounded by two delimiters of words, or by the search string which is a string able to appear within a longer string surrounded by two delimiters

4. www.lina.univ-nantes.fr/?Ressources-linguistiques-du-projet.html

5. antlab.sci.waseda.ac.jp

of words. The first type of collection of n-grams was obtained with a "search by word", and the second type was obtained with a "search by subword". In order to extract the morphological variants of the term, a search by subword was carried out. The set of word separators includes the hyphen. The punctuation appearing between two words of a n-gram with $n > 1$ is not taken into account. However, the method is case-sensitive.

5.3.2 N-gram massive data

The number of n-grams increases exponentially, so if the number of a simple term's unigrams is n, the maximum number of bigrams becomes n^2, the maximum number of trigrams becomes n^3, and so on (Manning and Schütze 1999: 192). In practice, the number of n-grams > 1 is greatly lower to these bounds, but it still represents a considerable mass of data. Such mass of data is too noisy to be used as it is, since a majority of n-grams are not variants and its size is crippling to study manually, except for German. To illustrate this statement, Table 5.4 supplies the numbers of n-grams with n from 1 to 5, for the simple term *blade* from [EOL] for French, English, German, Russian and Spanish. The instantiation of the search is detailed in Appendix C. The number of n-grams can be reduced by disregarding the case and by adding constraints such as:

Table 5.4 N-grams of the term *blade* for [EOL] in De, En, Es, Fr and Ru – Search by subword.

Languages	**En**	**De**	**Es**	**Fr**	**Ru**
Simple term	blade	Blatt blätt	pala	pale pâle	лопасть
1-gram					
Number	30	47	16	20	38
Occurrences	1,428	178	917	680	788
2-grams					
Number	798	251	594	473	890
Occurrences	2,776	330	1,778	1,235	1,477
3-grams					
Number	2,615	435	1,597	1,117	1,747
Occurrences	4,073	461	2,600	1,729	2,090
4-grams					
Number	4,466	565	2,773	1,698	2,286
Occurrences	5,349	576	3,392	2,181	2,606
5-grams					
Number	5,923	669	3,725	2,118	2,727
Occurrences	6,571	674	4,161	2,572	3,063

1. the preliminary segmentation of the corpus into sentences in order to limit the collection of n-grams to the context of the sentence;
2. the filtering of the grammatical words in order to compute n-grams of lexical words only.

The context of the sentence is an acceptable constraint which increases the precision without deleting variants. The filtering of grammatical words eliminates a number of denominative variants and loses information of surface forms of the variant.

5.3.3 Unigrams

The number of unigrams given in Table 5.4 is close to completeness for their study. The chosen term *blade* is a simple term, and is central to the wind energy domain. The search of unigrams is carried out by indicating a common root to the inflection forms such as: Ru: Лопасть and by making the graphic variants of these roots clear: Fr: *pale/pâle;* De: *Blatt/Blätt.* Appendix C supplies the unigrams extracted for De, En, Es, Fr and Ru. The simple term *blade* is shown in all languages, except for De because *Blatt* is associated with *Rotor* for almost all occurrences.

Derivations and compounds

Unigrams calculated from the string *pale* illustrates how languages behave for linguistic and inflectional variants as well as conceptual variants obtained by derivation or morphological compounding.

German morphological compounds behave differently: they are native compounds and bigrams and trigrams of the other languages. For example, De: *Rotorblatt* is instantiated in French by *pale de rotor* but more generally by *pale,* En: *rotor blade,* Es: *pala del rotor,* Ru: лопасть ветроколеса 'wind wheel blade'.

Table 5.5 N-gram of the term *pale* for [EOL] in De, En, Es, Fr and Ru – Search by subword. Comparative unigrams with or without a hyphen.

Languages	En	De	Es	Fr	Ru
Simple term	blade	Blatt blätt	pala	pale pâle	
1-gram without -					
Number	8	45	13	16	38
Occurrences	1,428	172	917	680	788
Correct number	8	26	11	12	38
Correct occurrences	1,428	142	903	538	788

(*continued*)

Table 5.5 (*continued*)

Languages	En	De	Es	Fr	Ru
1-gram with -					
Number	30	47	15	20	38
Occurrences	1,428	172	917	680	788
Correct number	26	26	13	16	38
Correct occurrences	1,424	142	903	538	788

Conversely, prefixations such as *bipale* or *tripale* are common in En, Es, Fr, Ru, but they do not appear in De. Other remarks can be made:

1. Native compounds in Ru include lit. 'quadriblade' and lit. '6-blades' which do not appear in the other languages;
2. Only in Fr, the morphological variant of the diminutive *palette* appears. It is used as a competing element of the syntagmatic compound *petite pale* 'small blade'.

Word splitting characters

The hyphen was considered as a separator of the term for the computation of unigrams shown in Table 5.4. We perform a new computation of unigrams with the hyphen as a character of the term. Table 5.5 shows that the number of unigrams is still stable as a whole for De, Es, Fr and Ru, with or without the hyphen as a word delimiter. Unigrams which include a hyphen are mainly graphic variants of compounds: Fr: *mono-pale/monopale*, En: *two-bladed/twobladed.*

For English, the number of unigrams with a hyphen grows considerably: the number of different unigrams goes from 8 to 30. This observation acts as a proof of the use of the hyphen as a marker of morphological relation for native compoundings such as *rotor-blade.* Some unigrams, which can be qualified as correct without the inclusion of the hyphen, proved to be incorrect, such as the occurrence *blade-radius.*

Reliability of unigrams

Table 5.5 summarises the unigrams that have been collected. Clearly, search by subword permits to easily identify many morphological variants as well as graphical variants. In spite of that, even at the unigram level, the search is noisy, especially for English and German. Russian unigrams are all valid.

Unigrams allow us to identify and characterise variants that comply with our specifications of different categories of variants. We analyse unigrams by presenting a table summary by language. In each table, we show linguistic, denominative, and conceptual variants. Some of the conceptual variants have denominative variants.

Table 5.6 Summary of variants identified from unigrams in [EOL] Fr: *pale.*

	Term	**Linguistic variants**	
		Graphic	**Inflection**
	pale	*pale*	*pale* (175)
			pales (287)
		pâle	*pâles* (3)
	Conceptual variants	**Linguistic variants**	
		Graphic	**Inflection**
Derivation	*palette*	*palette*	*palettes* (4)
Compounding	*monopale*	*monopale*	*monopale* (1)
		mono-pale	*mono-pale* (4)
			mono-pales (2)
Prefixation	*bipale*	*bipale*	*bipale* (14)
			bipales (4)
Prefixation	*tripale*	*tripale*	*tripale* (29)
			tripales (7)
Compounding	*multipale*	*multipale*	*multipale* (1)
			Multipales (2)
		multipale	*multipale* (1)
		Multi-pale	*multi-pale* (2)
			multi-pales (2)

Linguistic variants gather the various forms of the term occurring in the corpus. Each form is associated to its number of occurrences in brackets. The form of conceptual and denominative variants appearing in the tables are generic. They group together many linguistic variants, of which some may not occur in the corpus, such inflectional or graphical variants. For clarity reason, we remove inflectional and derivational variants for a graphic variant. This is an arbitrary choice of data presentation. When a conceptual variant admitted its variants, we systematically assigned to it term status in order to present its denominative and linguistic variants.

Analysis of Fr unigrams

Table 5.6 summarises variants of Fr *pale.* Many conceptual variants are identified. All of these variants are built by prefixation. There is no denominative variant for the term nor for its conceptual variants. As for linguistic variants of graphic type, they are numerous since the hyphen is optionally employed for compounding. A recurrent spelling mistake appears by emphasising the vowel *a* of *pale.* All inflections of variants do occur. Derivational variants are rather rare. Variants obtained by prefixation with the prefix *bi-*, or compounding, with the root *mono-*, allow us to clarify the number or the quality of *pales.*

Analysis of En unigrams

Table 5.7 summarises the variants of En *blade.* As for linguistic variants of graphic type, there are numerous since the hyphen is optionally employed for compounding. Unigrams applied to English allow us to identify several conceptual variants obtained by morphological compounding. Denominative variants appear when con-ceptual variants are created by compounding. For example, the conceptual variant *rotor-blade* gets one denominative variant, *turbine-blade,* and the conceptual variant *two-blade* also gets one denominative variant, *2-blade.* There are a large number of linguistic variants of graphic type, because of, again, the optionality of the hyphen when compounding. As for linguistic variants of derivational type, only one kind was detected, i.e. the adjectival form *bladed* which is used as much as the nominal term.

Table 5.7 Summary of variants identified from unigrams in [EOL] En: *blade.*

Term	**Denominative variants**	**Linguistic variants**	
		Graphic	**Inflection or derivation**
blade	*blade*	*blade*	*blade* (910)
			blades (372)
			bladed (5)
Conceptual variants	**Denominative variants**	**Linguistic variants**	
Compounding		**Graphic**	**Inflection/derivation**
one-blade	*one-blade*	*one-blade*	*one-bladed* (1)
	single-blade	*single-blade*	*single-bladed* (1)
two-blade	*two-blade*	*two-blade*	*two-blade* (7)
			two-bladed (11)
		Two-blade	*Two-bladed* (1)
		twoblade	*twobladed* (1)
	2-blade	*2-blade*	*2-blade* (19)
			2-blades (1)
		2blade	*2blade* (1)
three-blade	*three-blade*	*three-blade*	*three-blade* (3)
			three-bladed (28)
		threeblade	*threebladed* (1)
	3-blade	*3-blade*	*3-blade* (25)
			3-bladed (22)
		3blade	*3blade* (2)
four-blade	*four-blade*	*four-blade*	*four-bladed* (1)
multi-blade	*multi-blade*	*multi-blade*	*multi-bladed* (1)
		Multiblade	*Multibladed* (1)
rotor-blade	*rotor-blade*	*rotor-blade*	*rotor-blades* (1)
		rotorblade	*rotorblade* (1)
	turbine-blade	*turbine-blade*	*turbine-blades* (1)
blade-element	*blade-element*	*blade-element*	*blade-element* (5)

Analysis of Es unigrams

Table 5.8 summarises the variants of Es *pala.* Unigrams applied to Spanish allow us to identify many conceptual variants obtained from prefixation or compounding. No denominative variant was detected for the term nor for its conceptual variants. Linguistic variants of graphic type are rare compared to Fr or En. Many inflectional variants are found. No derivational variant was detected. Variants obtained by prefixation with the prefix bi-, or by compounding with the root *mono-*, allowing, like Fr and En, to make clear the number or the quantity of blades.

Table 5.8 Summary of variants identified from unigrams in [EOL] Es: *pala*

	Term	Linguistic variants	
		Graphic	Inflection
	pala	*pala*	*pala* (277) *palas* (533)
	Conceptual variants	Linguistic variants	
		Graphic	Inflection
Compounding	*monopala*	*monopala*	*monopala* (13) *monopalas* (3)
Prefixation	*bipala*	*bipala*	*bipala* (21) *bipalas* (8)
		bípala	*bípala* (1)
Prefixation	*tripala*	*tripala*	*tripala* (20) *tripales* (6)
Compounding	*multipala*	*multipala*	*Multipala* (11) *multi-pale* (7)
		multipala	*multipala* (2)
		multipala	*multipala* (2) *multi-pales* (2)
Compounding	*pala-buje*	*pala-buje*	*pala-buje* (1)
Compounding	*pala-rodamiento*	*pala-rodamiento*	*pala-rodamiento* (1)

Analysis of De unigrams

Table 5.9 summarises the variants of De *Blatt-* Unigrams applied to German allow us to identify numerous conceptual variants built by compounding. Many inflectional variants of the simple term are present. It is possible to distinguish three groups of conceptual variants. The first group corresponds to variants which are already identified for Fr, En and Es, featuring the number of blades. Nevertheless for De, the paradigm is more restricted: only three and more blades are specified. The second group corresponds to constitutive elements of the blade: the nose, the head, a section, the front edge, or to its physical features such as the shape. The third group treats more typical actions carried out on the blade, such as the adjustment that the blade should undergo such as the heating system or the icing. The predominance of morphological compounds allow us to identify with the sole unigrams, conceptual variants of conceptual variants, that we call conceptual variants of level 2. These conceptual variants of level 2 presented in Table 5.10 advocate the status of conceptual variants of the variants of level 1 from which they are built.

Table 5.9 Summary of variants identified from unigrams in [EOL] De: *Blatt.*

Term	**Linguistic variants** **Inflection**
Rotorblatt 'rotor blade'	*Rotorblatt* (32) *Rotorblätter* (51) *Rotorblättes* (7) *Rotorblättern* (19)
Conceptual variants **Compounding**	**Linguistic variants** **Inflection/derivation**
Dreiblattrotor 'three-blade rotor'	*Dreiblattrotor* (1)
Vielblattrotor 'multi-blade rotor'	*Vielblattrotor* (2)
Rotorblattnase 'nose of the rotor blade'	*Rotorblattnase* (1)
Rotorblattprofil 'shape of the rotor blade'	*Rotorblattprofil* (2) *Rotorblattprofile* (1) *Rotorblattprofilen* (1)
Rotorblattschnitt 'section of the rotor blade'	*Rotorblattschnitt* (1)
Rotorblattspitze 'head of the rotor blade'	*Rotorblattspitze* (1)
Rotorblattvorderkante 'front edge of the rotor blade'	*Rotorblattvorderkante* (1)
blattgeregelte 'adjusting of the rotor blade'	*blattgeregelten* (1)
Rotorblattaerodynamik 'aerodynamics of the rotor blade'	*Rotorblattaerodynamik* (1)
Rotorblattfertigung 'production of the rotor blade'	*Rotorblattfertigung* (1)
Rotorblattheizung 'heating of the rotor blade'	*Rotorblattheizung* (5)
Rotorblattlast 'load on the rotor blade'	*Rotorblattlasten* (1)
Rotorblattvereisung 'icing of the rotor blade'	*Rotorblattvereisung* (4)
Rotorblattverstellung 'change of position of the rotor blade'	*Rotorblattverstellung* (5)
Standortblatt 'location of the rotor blade'	*Standortblätter* (1)

Analysis of Ru unigrams

Table 5.11 summarises derivational and inflectional variants of Ru лопасть. Table 5.12 shows conceptual variants. We find the variants we have already collected in other languages, as for the number of blades, with a new distinction which permits to indicate a small number of blades. The conceptual variant малолопастные 'with few blades' looks less stable as two denominative forms exist: малолопастные and двухтрехлопастней '2 or 3 blades'. The other compounds describe the physical properties of the blade, which is narrow or flat. We also have encountered these properties in Spanish.

Table 5.10 Summary of conceptual variants of level 2 identified from unigrams in [EOL] De: *Blatt.*

Term	**Linguistic variants** **Inflection**
Rotorblattheizung 'heating of the rotor blade'	*Rotorblattheizung* (5)
Conceptual variants **Insertion**	**Linguistic variants**
Rotorblattnasenbeheizung 'heating of the nose of the rotor blade'	*Rotorblattnasenbeheizung* (1)
Term	**Linguistic variants** **Inflection**
Rotorblattvereisung 'icing of the rotor blade'	*Rotorblattvereisung* (4)
Conceptual variants **Insertion**	**Linguistic variants** **Inflection/derivation**
Rotorblattnasenvereisung 'icing of the nose the rotor blade'	*Rotorblattnasenvereisung* (1)
Rotorblattvereisungsform 'type of icing of the rotor blade'	*Rotorblattvereisungsformen* (1)

Table 5.11 Summary of linguistic variants identified by unigrams in [EOL] Ru: лопасть 'blade'.

Term	**Linguistic variants**	
	Derivation	**Inflection**
лопасть	лопасть N	лопасти (291)
		лопастей (276)
		лопастями (84)
		лопасть (58)
		лопастях (22)
		лопастью (4)
		лопастям (4)
	лопастной A	лопастного (5)
		лопастные (4)
		лопастной (3)
		лопастным (1)
		лопастных (1)

Table 5.12 Summary of conceptual variants identified by unigrams in [EOL] Ru: лопасть 'blade'.

Conceptual variants Compounding	Denominative variants	Linguistic variants Inflection
однолопастное A 'single-blade'	однолопастное	однолопастные (2) однолопастное (1) однолопастных (1)
двухлопастное A 'two-blade'	двухлопастное	двухлопастного (2) двухлопастное (2) двухлопастные (2) двухлопастный (1)
трехлопастное A 'three-blade'	трехлопастное	трехлопастная (1) трехлопастное (1) Трехлопастной (1)
малолопастные A 'with few blades'	малолопастные 'with a few blades'	малолопастные (2)
	двухтрехлопастной '2 or 3 blades'	двухтрехлопастной (1)
четырехлопастное A 'four-blade'	четырехлопастное	четырехлопастное (1) четырехлопастный (1) четырёхлопастные (1)
шестилопастного A '6-blades'	шестилопастного	шестилопастного (1)
многолопастное A 'multi-blade'	многолопастное	многолопастные (11) многолопастное (2) многолопастный (2) многолопастных (2) многолопастные (1) многолопастным (1)
узколопастные N 'narrow blade'	узколопастные	узколопастные (1)
прямолопастных N 'flat blade'	прямолопастных	прямолопастных (1)

5.3.4 Skip-grams

Skip-grams are discontinuous n-grams. They are adapted for detecting complex terms' variants because they allow us to identify variants of insertion applying to compounds. Insertion leads to the creation of denominative, conceptual and linguistic variants. To extract skip-grams, it is necessary to check the identity at the borders of the lexical forms of the term and to request the insertion of one or more lexical forms of any grammatical category at specified positions inside the term. Such queries have been used to detect skip-grams of terms of length 2 in [EOL].

These variants do not exist in De and En, whose modification is only performed by juxtaposition. As for Ru, only the linguistic variants of coordination are detected by skip-grams. For Fr and Es, the number of variants depends on the morphosyntactic pattern: terms adopting the N P N pattern accept more linguistic modifications by insertion than those of the N A pattern. Tables 5.13, 5.14 and 5.15 illustrate insertions we obtained for two terms: (EOL)*wind farm* and (EOL)*wind speed* in [EOL], for Fr, Es and Ru. Insertions in the N A pattern are rare but reliable, contrary to the insertions we found in the N P N pattern. In particular, the corpus does not include variants of the N A pattern with more than one inserted modifier. For the variants of the N P N pattern, the insertion of several modifiers are attested in Fr and Es. Variants with only one modifier inserted in the N P N pattern are generally reliable. When the number of insertions grows, these skip-grams are not variants of the term any more. Linguistic variants of coordination are well captured by skip-grams but accompanied by many occurrences that are not coordinative variants of the term. As a result, skip-grams are a reliable and effective method for detecting variants when the insertion is limited to only one element.

Table 5.13 Identified variants related to bigrams Fr: *parc éolien,* Es: *parque eólico* of N A pattern and Ru: скорость ветра of N N pattern.

Term	Conceptual variants Modification
parc éolien (267)	*parc national éolien* (1) *parcs industriels éoliens* (1)
parque eólico (470)	*parque híbrido eólico-solar* (1) 'wind solar hybrid park'
	Coordination
скорость ветра (208)	скорость и направление ветра (4) 'wind speed and direction'

Table 5.14 Variants identified by insertion concerning bigrams Fr of N P N pattern.

Term	**Linguistic variants** **Modification**
vitesse du vent (813)	*vitesses élevées de vent* (1) *vitesse faible du vent* (1) *vitesse relative du vent* (2) *vitesse non perturbée du vent* (2)
	Coordination
	(la) vitesse et la direction du vent (1) *(la) vitesse et la fréquence des vents* (1)
	Conceptual variants **Modification**
	vitesse moyenne du vent (6) *vitesse maximale du vent*(2) *vitesse nominale du vent* (4) *vitesse instantanée du vent* (3)
	Linguistic variants
vitesse moyenne du vent (6)	*vitesse moyenne v m du vent* (1)

Table 5.15 Identified variants by insertion related to a bigram Es of N P N pattern.

Term	**Linguistic variants** **Modification**
velocidad del viento (518)	*velocidad incidente del viento* (1) *velocidad normal del viento* (2) *velocidad relativa del viento* (1) *velocidad no perturbada del viento* (5)
	Coordination
	(la) velocidad y dirección del viento (18) *(la) velocidad y la dirección del viento* (1) *velocidad y perfil del viento* (1)
	Conceptual variants **Modification**
	Velocidad instantánea del viento (1) *velocidad media del viento* (63) *velocidad nominal del viento* (1) *velocidad real del viento* (3) *velocidad superficial del viento* (2)
	Linguistic variants
velocidad media del viento (63)	*velocidad media anual del viento* (4) *velocidad media máxima de viento* (1)
	Denominative variants
	velocidad promedio del viento (3)

5.3.5 Categories of variants facing data

Variants are classified depending on three major groups: conceptual, denominative and linguistic variants. We carried out two simple methods, unigrams and skip-grams, for the gathering of variants that supply exhaustive results. The analysis of the variants detected by these methods strengthens our conceptualisation of variants and our variant categories. Linguistic and conceptual variants are numerous. Denominative variants are also present for some languages, but the method of uni-grams is only capable of detecting a few subsets of them. The appropriate precedence suggested by the relationship between variant categories is indeed: conceptual variant >> denominative variant >> linguistic variant. This first exploration allows us to strengthen properties or difficulties related to the study of variants:

1. The systematic instability, property of neologisms (Cabré 1998), features the derivational paradigms updated by unigrams. We outline:
   a. Derivational holes that affect the derivative forms. These holes characterise the parasynthetic derivation where the prefixed derivation form exists while the derivative form does not, such as *hyperglycémiant* without the occurrence of *glycémiant;*
   b. Syntagmatic holes that affect syntagmatic compounds. These holes characterise variants obtained by modification where a double modified form exits with no trace of a simply modified form, such as *vitesse non perturbée du vent* 'not disturbed wind speed' without the occurrence of *vitesse perturbée du vent* 'disturbed wind speed';
2. The precedence of variants types is sometimes difficult to rule because of systematic instability;
3. The recursive character of the conceptual variation;
4. The paradigms of variants by languages show that variants are shared between languages. This remark indicates the artificial character of the separation of mechanisms of prefixation and compounding on the one hand, and compounding and modification as well as syntagmatic expansion on the other hand.
5. Different automatic methods depending on languages will be required in order to carry out a valid terminological comparative analysis of variants. In particular, it will be necessary to segment the morphological compounds in De and Ru, which was predictable, but also in En and Es because of the emerging phenomenon of compounds built with borrowing elements.
6. The ambiguity between categories of linguistic and conceptual variants when the modification operation is applied. Modified complex terms found by ship-grams are either conceptual or linguistic variants.

Table 5.16 Summary of identified variants using unigrams of Fr: *glycémie* in [DIA].

	Term Fr	PS	SC
Base	***glycémie***	1,013	536
	glycémique	808	419
	Conceptual variants		
Prefixation	***hyperglycémie***	235	218
	hyperglycémiant	97	45
	antihyperglycémiant	0	3
	hyperglycémique	6	35
	hypoglycémie	213	289
	hypoglycémiant	17	151
	hypoglycémique	36	34
Compounding	***englycémie***	0	4
	insulino-glycémie	0	2
	normoglycémie	0	2
	normoglycémique	2	1
	perglycémie	0	2

Table 5.17 Summary of Fr identified variants using unigrams of *insulin* in [DIA].

	Term Fr	PS	SC
Derivation	***insuline***	1,150	769
	insulinique	10	34
	insulinés	0	2
	Conceptual variants		
Prefixation	***anti-insuline***	0	10
	hyper-insulinique	1	2
	hyper-insulinisme	1	24
	hypo-insulinique	0	1
	hypo-insulinisme	0	2
	pro-insuline	0	1
	pro-insulinisme	0	2
Compounding	***insulinémie***	2	30
	insulinémique	0	1
	hyperinsulinémie	0	20
	hyperinsulinémique	0	5
	hypoinsulinémique	0	1
	hypo-insulinémie	0	2
	insulino-déficience	0	1
	insulino-dépendance	0	7
	insulino-dépendant	101	185
	non-insulino-dépendant	6	11
	insulinoglycémie	0	2
	insulino-nécessitance	0	1
	insulino-nécessitant	3	3

Table 5.17 (*continued*)

	Term Fr	PS	SC
	insulinoObésité		2
	insulinopéniques		2
	insulino-requiérance	0	1
	insulino-requérant	9	2
	insulino-résistance	121	209
	insulino-résistant	0	6
	insulino-sécréteur	0	8
	insulino-sécrétion	4	71
	insulino-sécrétoire	0	4
	insulino-sécrétrice	0	2
	insulinosécrétagogues	0	3
	insulino-sensibilité	3	6
	insulino-sensible	0	5
	insulino-thérapie	34	156
	insulino-traité	3	16
	insulinome	0	13
	insulinopénie		11
	insulinopénique	0	5
	insulinotrope	0	1

Table 5.18 Summary of identified variants by unigrams Fr: *ménopause* and En: *menopause* in [CAN].

	Term Fr	PS	SC
	ménopause		
Derivation	*ménopausée*	53	122
	ménopausique	0	5
	Conceptual variants		
Prefixation	***pré-ménopause***	1	3
	pré-ménopausée	2	18
	préménopausique	0	3
	post-ménopause	0	9
	post-ménopausées	0	6
	post-ménopausique	0	4
Compounding	***périménopause***	0	3
	Term En		
	menopause		
Derivation	*menopausal*	42	61
	Conceptual variants		
Prefixation	***pre-menopausal***	12	70
	post-menopausal	10	128
	postmenopausally	0	1
Compounding	***perimenopausal***	0	1

5.4 Comparison according to communication levels

If on the level of communication two comparable corpora are available, it is possible to observe the variants generated by each level. For this study, our two basic methods, unigrams and skip-grams are used. The aim is to check if variants characterise generally more a communication level than another, or if a type of variants might be more prone to appear only in one communication level.

5.4.1 Unigrams

Corpus Diabetes in Fr

With the corpus [DIA], we examine variants of two central terms of the diabetes domain, namely *glycemia* and *insulin.* The results of unigrams are shown in Tables 5.16 and 5.17. For the aim of simplification, we do not include linguistic, graphic and inflectional variants. We can point out two things: firstly, variants are presented at the two communication levels, and secondly, variants are considerably more numerous at the scientific communication level. Derivation and compounding are quite frequently used, confirming their status of privileged mechanisms of neonymy in medicine. Derivational paradigms are systematically produced from derivations, such as the neoclassical compound *insulinemia* and its derived elements: *hyperin-sulinésie, hyperinsulinésique.* The presence of derivation and compounding paradigms from a derived term gives a clear clue to the importance of the denomination of the concept in the subdomain.

Table 5.19 Summary of identified variants by unigrams in [CAN] Fr: *mammaire* and En: *mammary.*

	Term Fr	PS	SC
Base	***mammaire***	232	408
	Conceptual variants		
Prefixation	***extramammaire***	0	1
	intermammaire	0	1
	intramammaire	1	2
	sous-mammaires	0	1
Compounding	***échomammographie***	0	1
	mammectomie	48	22
	post-mammectomie	0	1
	mammo-échographique	0	1
	mammoglobine	1	2
	mammographie	394	154
	mammographe	5	4

Table 5.19 (*continued*)

	Term Fr	PS	SC
	mammographique	9	48
	mammographiquement	0	1
	mammopexie	0	1
	mammoplastie	0	12
	mammotome	1	1
	mammoscintigraphie	0	1
	Term En		
	mammary	3	30
	Conceptual variants		
Compounding	***mammogram***	86	31
	mammography	19	133
	mammographic	6	23
	mammographically	0	11
	mammoplasty	0	6
	mammotome	2	

Corpus Breast cancer in Fr and En
Concerning the corpus [CAN], we examine variants for two central terms of the domain (CAN) Fr: *menopause* and Fr: *mammaire,* En: *mammary.* The results of unigrams are shown in Tables 5.18 and 5.19. The results are similar to those of the domain of diabetes. Conceptual variants are considerably more numerous in the scientific corpus than in the popular science corpus. In addition, all variants appearing in the popular scientific corpus also appear in the scientific corpus.

5.4.2 Skip-grams

Corpus Diabetes in Fr
For the corpus [DIA], we examine variants of two complex terms Fr: *masse corporelle* 'body mass' and Fr: *traitement du diabète* 'treatment of diabetes'. The results of skip-grams are shown in Table 5.20 where we did not include graphic and inflectional variants. These results confirm those obtained by unigrams. Variants of modification appear mainly at the scientific communication level. They are linguistic variants such as *traitement idéal du diabète* 'ideal treatment of diabetes', or conceptual variants such as *traitement médicamenteux du diabète* 'medical treatment of diabetes'. The low frequency of the term *masse corporelle* 'body mass' in the popular scientific corpus explains the absence of variants. However, the frequency of the term *masse corporelle* 'body mass' is comparable to the frequency of the term *traitement du diabète* 'treatment of diabetes' which has many variants. The presence

of a paradigm of modification from a complex term supplies, as in the case of the morphological compound, a clue to the importance of the concept denomination that needs to be specified or qualified.

Table 5.20 Summary of identified variants by insertion concerning bigrams Fr: *masse corporelle* and *traitement du diabète* in [DIA].

Term Fr	PS	SC
masse corporelle	7	35
Variants		
masse grasse corporelle	0	1
Term Fr		
traitement du diabète	92	99
Variants		
traitement idéal du diabète	0	1
traitement initial du diabète	0	1
traitement médicamenteux du diabète	1	1
traitement préventifdu diabète	0	1
traitement principal du diabète	0	1

Corpus Breast cancer in Fr and En

For the corpus [CAN], we examine variants of two complex terms Fr: *ganglion sentinelle,* En: *sentinel node* and Fr: *cancer du sein,* En: *breast cancer.* The results of skip-grams are shown in Table 5.21 where we did not include graphic and inflectional variants. Variants of modification are numerous at the scientific communication level and they are all conceptual variants.

The popular scientific corpus for Fr has two variants obtained by modification that are conceptual variants: *cancer avancé du sein* and *cancer héréditaire du sein.* These variants do not occur in the scientific corpus. Modifiers employed in popular communication belong to general language, such as *avancé* 'advanced', *héréditaire* 'hereditary' and those at scientific communication level are neoclassical or derivative adjective, such as *hormonodépendant, infiltrant, invasif.* For En, there is no variant in the popular scientific corpus. In the scientific corpus, a conceptual variant obtained by coordination occurs: *breast/ovarian cancer* with / used as a coordination conjunction. This substitution of the coordination conjunction belongs to the mechanism of simplification of denominative variant (cf. Section 3.2.2), that, here, applies to linguistic variants.

The comparative study of variants in several languages strengthens the need of treating morphological and syntagmatic compounds in a uniformed way, as well as derived terms by prefixation and morphological compounds. The study also reveals semantic paradigms which are similar in the languages, but they are expressed in a different way from the linguistic point of view. The study of variants at two levels of communication, i.e. sciences and popular sciences, has indicated the predominance of variants in scientific communication. There is no linguistic operation at the origin of a variant that could be specific to popular science communication. Almost all the variants detected in the popular scientific corpus also occur in the scientific corpus. Popular scientific communication limits the number of conceptual variants. These observations deny a few terminological studies carried out on terminological variation from different angles (Freixa 2002; Ciapuscio 2003; Haralambous and Lavagnino 2011). These studies linked the increase of the denominative variants to the decrease of text specialisation. If linguistic variants are similar in number at each communication level, our study shows a decrease of both conceptual and denominative variants in the popular scientific courpus. Of course, this observation is limited as we perform variant detection with n-grams only. N-grams are simple and exhaustive, but they do not allow us to detect all variants and to label the linguistic operation that may be used to categorise the variant. What we need is more sophisticated methods, which will be the topic of the next chapters.

Table 5.21 Summary of identifed variants by insertion concerning bigrams Fr: *ganglion sentinelle*, En: *sentinel node* and Fr: *cancer du sein*, En: *breast cancer* in [CAN].

Term Fr	PS	SC
ganglion sentinelle	24	276
Variants		
ganglion axillaire sentinelle	0	2
ganglion lymphatique sentinelle	0	2
ganglion non sentinelle	0	20
Term En		
sentinel node	23	74
Variants		
sentinel lymph node	0	4
Term Fr		
cancer du sein	980	997
Variants		
cancers avancés du sein	2	0
cancer bilatéral du sein	0	1
cancers héréditaires du sein	1	0
cancers hormonodépendants du sein	1	0
cancer infiltrant du sein	0	1
cancer invasif du sein	0	2
cancer primitif du sein	0	14

(continued)

Table 5.21 (*continued*)

Term En	PS	SC
breast cancer	1783	1366
Variants		
breast/ovarian cancer	0	2

CHAPTER 6

Processing methods for the detection of variants from corpora

The aim of this chapter is to propose a survey of the processing methods for the detection of variants in corpora. In Chapter 5, we investigated the variants of a few key terms of the specialised domains in our corpora using the basic method of n-grams. N-grams are language-independent and implemented in numerous tools of corpus exploration. The methods we present now are more sophisticated. They are options of some tools dedicated specifically to the detection and exploitation of term variants. Some of these tools will be presented in-depth in Chapter 10. After outlining the prerequisites, we will look at very useful methods for the automatic detection of variants. The first family of methods belongs to natural language processing (NLP): they exploit the linguistic properties of the variant. NLP methods carry out two types of analyses: syntagmatic analysis and paradigmatic analysis. The second family of methods are string searching algorithms: they are used to locate the base-term as a substring of a longer string that is the variant, and to measure the distance between the term and the variant. Other methods that tackle variant detection are reviewed briefly. Closely linked to the method for seeking a variant consists in observing how the base-term and the variant occur in the corpus. We distinguished three types of occurrences. We are speaking of families of methods because the detection of all kinds of variants requires to aggregate various methods, each of them dealing with a particular variant detection. There is no unified framework for detecting variants.

But before going any further, if might be useful to recall the basis of the automatic detection of variants from corpora. In Section 5.1, we introduced corpus properties and we stressed how they influence the categories of variants to be observed. Size and language are major factors: a small corpus cannnot be used for some processing methods such as distributional analysis; some NLP corpus processing operations requiring to apply a given method are not available because the language is under-resourced or the open-source license is too restrictive, and so on. The domain, the register and the communicative settings of the corpus documents also are key properties. Some domains show a distinct preference for some kinds of variants. The domain of telecom is filled with initialisms, aeronautics with abbreviations, medicine with neoclassical compounds, and so on. With regards to the register or the genre of documents, a corpus composed of published articles incorporates very few misspellings and will not require full graphical variant detection. We observed in Section 5.4 that conceptual variants are avoided in the popular science discourse.

6.1 Linguistic-based methods

NLP methods differ according to the linguistic level and the linguistic units they apply to. Morphological analysis deals with words and computes their features. Syntactic analysis examines words in the context of a sentence. Lastly, paradigmatic analysis shapes the word according to all its contexts in corpora.

6.1.1 Morphological analysis

Morphological analysis is carried out by using appropriate tools, or by using lexical bases listing inflections and derivations of words. Inflectional dictionaries permit to connect inflected forms and lemmas such as Lefff[1] (Sagot 2010) for French, or the Multext multilingual lexicon[2] for French, English, Italian, German, Spanish. The morphological dictionaries pair to a generic form, root or lemma, its derived forms. Among morphological dictionaries, the CELEX[3] (Burnage 1990) database is available for German, English, and Dutch. Derivation rules for English appear under the record of each lemma. For example, the rule: *((celebrate [V]), (ion)([NV.])[N])* means that the noun *celebration* is built from the verb *celebrate* with the suffix *-ion*.

The problem of a lexical base is its coverage which can never be exhaustive, especially in specialised domains. There are NLP tools dedicated to morphological analysis that can be used for the morphological analysis of terms such as the following programs:

> **Stemming** of simple terms such as the Porter's stemmer, SNOWBALL,[4] for which there are adaptations in many languages. The stem is a prefix substring shared by many inflectional and derivational forms of a word. It has to be differentiated from the linguistic root of an existing word.

1. http://atoll.inria.fr/~sagot/lefff.html

2. http://catalog.elra.info

3. http://www.lands2.let.kun.nl/members/software/celex.html

4. snowball.tartarus.org

Lemmatisation or inflectional analysis of simple terms such as FLEM for French (Namer 2000). Lemmatisation is a derived product of the part-of-speech tagging: once the grammatical category of a word is known, the lemma is deduced. The lemma is an attested form in the language chosen in an arbitrary way. It refers to the inflectional paradigm of the word.
Splitting or segmentation of morphological compounds such as Morfessor (Creutz and Lagus 2005) or the method of Koehn and Knight (2003). Generally automatic splitting consists of breaking down an unknown morphological compound into some known (in-lexicon) components.
Morphological analysis, such as SMOR, developed for German (Schmid et al. 2004) or Derif for French (Namer 2003). The morphological analysis carries out an analysis of the word morphemes. Morphemes are labelled by part-of-speech, and their order of application is explicit. Morphological analysis applies to compounding and derivation.

Table 6.1 illustrates for French the generic forms obtained with different types of morphological analysis.

Table 6.1 Example of the results provided by the morphological processing tools.

Type of analysis	Inflectional form	Computed form
stemming	*génératrices*	*générat*
lemmatisation	*génératrices*	*génératrice*
splitting	*aérogénératrice*	*aéro génératrice*
morphological analysis	*décomposition/N*	[[*dé[composer* V] V] *ion* N]

6.1.2 Syntagmatic and paradigmatic analysis

Syntagmatic analysis focuses on the combination of lexical units within the framework of the sentence. A syntagm is a group of linguistic units forming a unit of the lexical network of the sentence. The syntagmatic axis reflects the combination. Paradigmatic analysis combines lexical units by semantic relations. In the distributional theory introduced by the American linguist Leonard Bloomfield (Bloomfield 1935), a lexical unit is defined by the overall contexts where it appears. A distributional class will gather lexical units that appear in the same context. The distributional axis reflects the selection as emphasised by Harris (1954: 156):

> Difference of meaning correlates with difference of distribution.

Grefenstette (1994a) formed part of the distributional framework to automate the creation of a first-draft thesaurus from raw text. He introduced the concept of "affinity" that specifies the interrelationship of words. Grefenstette (1994a: 279) defined third-order affinities that can be derived from the analysis of a corpus of text:

> **First-order affinities** describe which other words are likely to be found in the immediate vicinity of a given word (syntagmatic type of relation);
> **Second-order affinities** operate between words sharing the same contexts of occurrence. It is not necessary that words sharing second-order affinities appear together themselves (paradigmatic type of relation);
> **Third-order affinities** operate between subgroups of words that are similar in a distributional way (extraction of classes).

Syntagmatic variants of terms are collected thanks to a syntactic analysis. They are a subset of first-order affinities. Detection of paradigmatic variants of terms requires a distributional analysis that can be based on a prior syntactic analysis to isolate syntagms inside the sentence. Paradigmatic variants are a subset of second-order affinities.

Syntagmatic and paradigmatic variants are equitably distributed across our main categories of variants defined in Section 3.1.1: each category has syntagmatic and paradigmatic variants, but some are more specific to one category of variants. Syntagmatic variants are used to specialise and to provide a context to a term, they are specific to conceptual variants.

6.1.3 Syntactic analysis

Partial analysis recognises non-recursive kernels of the sentence phrases, "chunks", and recovers surface syntactic information (Abney 1996). It is efficient compared to traditional parsers on unrestricted text and can be easily implemented with regular expressions either at the character level, "basic regular expressions", or on annotations that have been added to strings, "regular expressions on annotations". Basic regular expressions are part of most programming languages such as Perl, Java, Python. Specific components were developed to deal with regular expressions on annotations, such as TokenRegex (Chang and Manning 2014) integrated in *Standford CoreNLP*[5] or RUTA (Kluegl et al. 2016) part of Apache UIMA.[6] We will introduce UIMA TokenRegexp in Section 10.3.2, the component part of TermSuite framework that expresses regular expressions on annotations within the UIMA framework.

5. nlp.stanford.edu/software/corenlp.shtml

6. uima.apache.org/ruta.html

Table 6.2 Example of the modelling of the context of the term *wind turbine geobox* in the sentence *A main supplier of wind turbine geoboxes recently inaugurated testing facilities.*

Context	Example	
window	*main, supplier, recently, inaugurated*	span of 3 words
dependence	<*turbine* dep → *wind*>, <*geoboxes* dep → *turbine*>, <*recently* dep → *geoboxes*>	binary and oriented dependencies given by MaltParser[7]

The grammar performing partial analysis is composed of rules applying to a linguistically preprocessed corpus with grammatical, even morphological, annotations added to the text tokens. These rules, called "patterns", are regular expressions defined on the alphabet constituted of part-of-speech categories and lexical items, either stem, lemma or full forms. When regular expressions only make use of part-of-speech tags, they are called "morphosyntactic patterns". When at least one element of the regular expression belongs to a closed list of words, the term "lexico-syntactic pattern" is used. Patterns explicitly specify the linear pattern of the linguistic string searched for. Patterns are expressive enough to allow us to describe the patterns of the terms and their variants. Partial analysis is the state-of-the-art method for detecting syntagmatic variants of terms.

6.1.4 Distributional analysis

Distributional analysis models the context by word, then compares contexts in order to calculate a distributional similarity.

Context is considered either as a lexical context that gathers the cooccurences of words appearing in a window of words (Sahlgren 2008), or as a syntactic context treating all syntactic relations of dependency in which the word is implied (Baroni and Lenci 2010). Lexical contexts are configured according to the size of the window, span of the left and right word. Syntactic contexts are produced by a syntactic parser and are expressed traditionally in the triplet form: < *word1*, RELATION, *word2* > with RELATION being a syntactic relation such as SUBJECT or OBJECT for the verbs, or < *word1*, LEMMA, *word2* > where LEMMA instantiates the verb predicate. Table 6.2 illustrates context modellings for the complex term *wind turbine geobox*. Lexical contexts such as syntactic ones are weighted according to the values of a measure of association (Evert 2008). Grefenstette (1994b) noticed that lexical contexts were more effective for less frequent words, and more recently Baroni and Lenci (2010) demonstrated that the two methods were globally equivalent.

7. http://www.maltparser.org/userguide.html#inout

Distributional similarity is computed by comparing word contexts. For each word *w*, context comparison is performed using a similarity measure. There are numerous similarity measures, such as the cosine similarity, the Dice coefficient, or the weighted Jaccard index (Jurafsky and Martin 2009: 666).

The application of similarity measures outputs a ranked list of distributional related words for *w*. Words at the top of the list are words closest to *w*. One difficulty lies in choosing the number of closed-words to keep. Only the first distributional word may be kept, TOP_1, or the first five words, TOP_5, the first ten words, TOP_{10}, and so on. The ranks of a word vary depending on the similarity measure. The choice of the number of the distributional related words to keep is thus critical if one for example wishes to compare several similarity measures. Similarity measures favour words sharing similar distributions in the corpus (Weeds 2003). Thus, they are inappropriate in discovering denominative variants of low frequency or showing a distribution different from the term.

Distributional analysis depends on several parameters: corpus properties, in particular its size, the context definition, which includes the size of the context, the kind of elements to consider as part of the context and their ranking thanks to association measures, and the similarity measures. If each parameter impacts the ranking, the combination of some parameters is decisive. Turney and Pantel (2010) demonstrated that the combination of an association measure and a similarity plays a major part.

6.2 Algorithms on strings

The distances between strings of characters are frequently used for detecting the orthographical variants coming most often from misspellings, either generated by the author or introduced after the application of cleaning programs or text conversion. Misspellings generated by programs are caused by various factors, for example:

1. bad segmentations of the end of sentence, caused by pagination that were not corrected,
2. conversion of a coding of characters, often caused by the loss of accent.

Measures of distance allow us to compare the strings of characters. They are applied to letters, to grams of letters or to words. They need to be adapted according to the considered elements. Distances may be used to detect morphological variants, or syntactic variants when they are applied to words. The main measures are distances calculated from common substring and distances of edition that build alignments between strings.

Before introducing distances, we recall the terms we will used for describing them:

> **String of characters** is a contiguous set of characters. The character belongs to an alphabet;
> **Length:** the length of a string s, |s|, is the number of characters that compose the string;
> s[i]: the character at the i^e position with $1 \le i \le |s|$; the string of length 0, ε, is called the empty string;
> **Subsequence:** a subsequence of *s* is a sequence of characters of *s* in the same order that they occur in *s*, obtained by keeping only some characters of *s*;
> **Substring:** a substring of *s* is a string formed by contiguous characters of *s*, obtained by deleting some characters at the beginning of at the end of *s*; the substring $s[i]s[i+1]\ldots s[j]$ with $1 \le i \le j \le |s|$, more simply $s[i..j]$, is the one in which the first character is the i^e character of *s* and the last one the j^e character of *s*;
> **Prefix:** a prefix of *s* is a substring $s[1..j]$ with $0 \le j \le |s|$; if $j = 0$, $s[1..0]$ is the empty string which is prefix of any string;
> **Suffix:** a suffix of *s* is a substring $s[i..|s|]$ with $1 \le i \le |s| + 1$; if $i = |s| + 1$, $s[|s| + 1..|s|]$ is the empty string which is the suffix of any string.

Table 6.3 Example of calculation of distance between the strings of characters *environmental* and *environmemtal* with |*environmental*|=|*environmemtal*|=13.

Distance	String	Value
prefix	*environme*	8
suffix	*tal*	20
substr	*environme*	8
subseq	*environmetan*	2

6.2.1 Distance computed from common substrings

Popular distance measures compare two strings by calculating the number of characters they have in common without looking at the characters they share. Distances are computed respectively to a key position, at the initial position or at the final position of the string. Well-known string distances are defined from the lengths of common substrings:

Given two strings *x* and *y* of respective lengths $|x|$ and $|y|$, the well-known string distances which are defined from the lengths of common substrings are:

Distance of the longest common prefix:

$d_{prefix}(x, y) = |x| + |y| - 2 * |lcpref(x, y)|$

where *lcpref* (*x*, *y*) is the longest common prefix in *x* and *y*.

Distance of the longest common suffix:

$d_{suffix}(x, y) = |x| + |y| - 2 * |lcsuf(x, y)|$

where *lcsuf* (*x*, *y*) is the longest common suffix in *x* and *y*.

Distance of the longest common substring:

$d_{substr}(x, y) = |x| + |y| - 2 * |lcstr(x, y)|$

where *lcstr* (*x*, *y*) is longest common substring in *x* and *y*.

Distance of the longest common subsequence:

$d_{subseq}(x, y) = |x| + |y| - 2 * |lcseq(x, y)|$

where *lcseq* (*x*, *y*) is the longest common subsequence in *x* and *y*

These measures computed a similarity score between two strings. The greater the value of the distance becomes important, the more the words are considered as distant. Table 6.3 illustrates these distances calculated from lengths of common substrings.

All of these distances cause specific problems. They can generate linguistic errors: false positive errors, i.e. they give values of low distances to strings of characters which do not have any linguistic relationship, or inversely, false negative errors, i.e. they assign a high distance to linguistically close strings. For example, the distance of the longest common prefix (lcpref) shows a big distance and does not allow to detect morphological variants (false positive): $d_{prefix} = 19$ for Fr: *synchrone/asynchrone;* the distance of the longest common prefix supplies a low distance to strings without any linguistic relationship (false negative): $d_{suffix} = 3$ for Fr: *aération/itération.* Distances computing common subsequences of characters are much more efficient than distances calculated against the substrings only. But, the performance of the algorithms implementing the computation of the longest subsequences are for most of them quadratic in both time and space, even if, for a range of differing conditions, speed-up solutions have been proposed. Moreover, skip-characters are at the origin of important linguistic distances. They need to be constrained in order to minimise the production of false negative.

In this way, Kraif (2002) introduced a new common subsequence distance for detecting similar words in two languages. Its d_{subseq} forbids the skip of contiguous characters. Only d_{subseq} with skips of at least one character will be retained. For example, no distance will be computed for *pragmatic* and *paradigmatic* because of the skip of *di* is of two consecutive characters.

Another way to compute proximity between two strings is to assign a fixed value to strings that are close. Similarity measures highlight the proximity between two strings. Strings are closer when values are bigger. Other modifications of the distance computing have been proposed such as Kraift's (2002) normalisation according to the longest word rather than the average length of two words:

$$d_{subseq}(x, y) = \frac{|lcseq(x, y)|}{max(|x|, |y|)}$$

6.2.2 Edit distances

Edit distances align local similarities and differences between strings and calculate string-alignment. Distance is no longer calculated from common substrings but from the number of necessary operations for transforming the first string into the second. Crochemore et al. (2001: 227) propose the following definition of the alignment:

> if *A* is the common alphabet to *x* and y, if ε is a symbol representing a "gap", an alignment of *x* and *y* is a string made for the alphabet $(A \cup \{\varepsilon\}) \text{ x } (A \cup \{\varepsilon\}) \backslash \{(\varepsilon, \varepsilon)\}$.

An alignment between *x* and *y* about *A* describes the transformation of *x* into y. The result is a basic editing operation that transforms a character of $A \cup \{\varepsilon\}$ into another. Three basic operations are generally considered, and each of them is associated with a weight (a, $b \in$ A):

1. the insertion in *x* of a character $y\,[j]$ with $1 \leq j \leq |y|$, a pair of type $(\varepsilon, y[j])$ with a weight of inserting: $ins(\varepsilon, b)$ denoted by $ins(b)$;
2. the deletion in *x* of a character $x[i]$ with $1 \leq i \leq |x|$, a pair of type $(x[i],\varepsilon)$ with a weight of deleting: $del(a, \varepsilon)$ denoted by $del(a)$;
3. the substitution in *x* of a character $x[i]$ by a character $y[j]$, either a matching (if $x[i] = y[j]$), or a replacement (if $x[i] \neq y[j]$ with a weight of replacing: $sub(a,b)$.

The edit distance *Lev*, as defined by Wagner and Fisher (1974), is the minimal cost of transforming string *x* into string y. Distance computes the best alignment with the algorithm:

$$\begin{aligned}
&dist(x_{1,i}, y_{1,j}) = \\
&\quad \min(dist\,(x_{1,i-1}, y_{1,j}) + ins(x_i), \\
&\quad dist(x_{1,i}, y_{1,j-1}) + del(y_j), \\
&\quad dist(x_{1,i-1}, y_{1,J-1}) + sub(x_i, y_j) * dist(x_{i,i}, y_{j,j}))
\end{aligned}$$

and on the borders:

$$dist(0,0) = 0$$
$$dist(0, y_{1,j}) = dist(0, y_{1,j-1}) + del(y_j)$$
$$dist(x_{1,j}, 0) = dist(x_{1,j-1}, 0) + ins(x_j)$$

Many algorithms for edit distances are selected and evaluated by Stephen (1994) and Crochemore et al. (2007).

The calculation of the edit distance produces three optimal alignments between the words `environmental` and `environmemtal` with the costs: *ins*=*del* = 1 and *ins* = 2. The distance between these strings *dist* (`environmental,environmemtal`) is equal to 2. The first alignment suppresses the character `N` and inserts the character `M`, the second inserts the character `M` and suppresses the character `N`, and the third substitutes the character `N` with `M`. All the other characters align themselves.

```
E N V I R O N M E N ε T A L    |   E N V I R O N M E ε N T A L
E N V I R O N M E ε M T A L    |   E N V I R O N M E M ε T A L
                  D I          |                     I D

             E N V I R O N M E N T A L
             E N V I R O N M E M T A L
                               S
```

The value of the edit distance for a misspelling is equal to the value of two words that differ by one letter.

Fr: *évaluation, évacuation,*
Lev(`évaluation,évacuation`) = 2.

Adapting edit distance to a language requires resetting the weights assigned to basic operations depending on particular characters. Thus, a lighter weight for substitution will be assigned to two phonetically close letters, or a null weight of substitution if the two spellings are similar (cf. Section 3.4.1). As for Fr, sets of phonetically close characters are: {e,é,è}, {a,â}, {f,v}, {s,x,z}, {c,q}. A character substituted by a character belonging to the same subset will receive a lower cost than a letter belonging to another subset. Furthermore, it is opportune to compute edit distance on strings that have a first letter in common, at the diacritic character nearby (Hauer and Kondrak 2011).

As for distances computed from common substrings, edit distance is often normalised according to the longest string. The lower the cost is, the more strings are similar. And, rather than computing the distance, similarity between to strings can be calculated by:

$$Sim_{Lev}(x,y) = \begin{cases} 1\_(Lev(x,y)/|x|) & \text{if } |x| >= |y| \\ 1\_(Lev(x,y)/|y|) & \text{otherwise} \end{cases} \quad (6.1)$$

Thresholding the value of the distance in order to make a decision on the similarity between two strings depends on language. Threshold setting needs several experiments to be performed on textual data. Different thresholds may be chosen for different lengths of strings. A rather trustful threshold for Sim_{Lev} which applies to several languages is 0.9. To make the decision upon the proximity of two strings, there are other similarity measures that are not computed from edit distances. Frunza and Inkpen (2009) made a survey of them.

Edit distances are commonly used to detect misspelling variants. They can be applied at the word level with the objective of building inflectional paradigms, or at the stem level to elaborate derivation paradigms to fill the gap in the absence or in addition to lexical resources or morphological tools (cf. Section 6.1.1). In particular, when stems are submitted to allomorphy, edit distances are useful to detect alternative stems, such as (AGR) Fr: *forêt*, *forest*, two stems of *forestier*. For our study, edit distances are used for compound splitting and graphical variant recognition, and included in TermSuite that will be presented in Chapter 10.

Edit distances were adapted for detecting syntactic variants of terms. Tartier (2003) computes the edit distance between two syntactic compounds at the term level. Basic editing operations apply to the term components, such as in the example of term alignment shown below:

diffusion	cohérente	inélastique	de_electron	
diffusion	cohérente		du_ncutron	thermique
		D	S	I

The weights of the edit operations are set according to the level of syntactic dependency of the term component with regard to its head. Alignments are not possible if components do not share the same level of dependency. Each level of dependency is denoted by an integer: the head of the nominal phrase has a level equal to 0 and each of its arguments and modifiers have a level equal to 1, modifiers of modifiers have a level equal to 2, and so on. The occurrence Fr: *diffusion inélastique de neutrons thermiques* is labelled with the following pattern and levels of dependency:

form	diffusion	inélastique	de neutrons	thermiques
lemma	diffusion	inélastique	de_neutron	thermique
pattern	N	A	P_N	A
level	0	1	1	1

Morphological weights are added to syntactic weights. A substitution of component by one of its derivative is less weighted than an insertion, and a head substitution is heavily weighted:

`diffusion`	`de_neutron`	`diffusion neutronique`	0.5
`diffusion`	`neutronique`	`diffusion élastique de_neutron`	1.5
`diffusion`	`de_neutron`	`diffraction de_neutron`	7.5

Edit distances between variants of terms were computed to observe terms and their variants across periods of times. They provided temporal fingerprints of a specialised domain and resumed its evolution.

6.3 Statistical methods

There is a battery of statistical methods for knowledge extraction from texts (Manning and Schütze 1999; Ibekwe 2007), but most of them are barely adapted for detecting variants because of the difference of the statistic distribution between the term and the variant. Most variants are much less frequent than the term. Many variants are rare events. Several methods that have proved their effectiveness and robustness for many NLP applications do not fit variant discovery, because they do not discriminate between variants and other strings.

We have shown in Chapter 5 that one of the most popular methods, n-grams, is not adapted to the discovery of variants. Variants are collected but they are flooded in the set of n-grams. To discriminate variants from other strings, n-grams need to be constrained to unigrams and skip-grams with one word wild-card unigrams computed from a stem, collect misspellings, some morphological variants and morphological compounds. Skip-grams with one word wild-card retrieve precisely syntactic variants with an inserted modifier.

Other methods such as clustering methods that compute third-order affinities can be used for gathering the term and its variants. The hierarchical agglomerative clustering (HAC) and its extensions are one of them. AHC are bottom-up algorithms in which words are merged together to form dendrograms. It considers each word as its proper class. At each iteration, it agglomerates pairs of words sharing the highest value of similarity measure until the depth of the dendrogram is reached. Each class regroups a set of lexical units. The results will be similar n-gram results: some variants will be identified but it will be difficult to isolate them inside classes with a limited number of classes.

6.4 Typology of variant occurrences

The choice of an automatic method depends on the way in which the term and the variant occur in the text. We need to distinguish two contexts: the local context that spans in a short window of words up to the sentence, and the extended context that is the whole corpus. Between the sentence and the whole corpus, there are other units of segmentation that could have been considered such as the paragraph or the document. Paragraph is the context in which conceptual variants obtained by anaphoric reduction occur, document is the one in which linguistic variants obtained by initialism occur. As a matter of simplification, the extended context is defined as trans-sentence. The proposed typology of variant occurrences relies on the hypothesis that the corpus includes both the term and its variant. This hypothesis can be released if the term, its grammatical category and its pattern are known elsewhere.

6.4.1 Isolated variant occurrences

The variant only appears in the local context. The term occurs in the extended context. The linkage between the term and the variant is an alignment problem that requires to examine all terms occurrences. The alignment is carried out either by computing the distance between two strings of characters (cf. Section 6.2), or by performing a distributional analysis (cf. Section 6.1.4). The distances between strings of characters allow us to detect:

1. the orthographic variants such as:
   (EOL) Fr: *éolien* → *Eolien*
2. the derivational variants with allomorphy:
   (MED) Fr: *hygiène*/N/*hygién|ique*/A

The alignment based upon a distributional analysis or an external lexical resource allows us to detect denominative variations obtained by synonymic substitution. Distributional analysis compares the contexts of the term and the variant by using a similarity measure. In the following example, the relationship between *energy* and *power* is either supplied by a lexical resource that registers word synonyms, or discovered by distributional analysis.

(EOL) En: *wind energy* ↔ *wind power*

6.4.2 Inter-mixed term and variant occurrences

The variant and the term are inter-mixed and occur in the same phrase. The integration is either morphological, syntactic, or both morphological and syntactic.

Morphological integration
The variant and the term share the same root. They belong to the same inflectional or derivational paradigm. It is typically the case of variants obtained by prefixation such as:

(EOL) De: *unterbrochen*/A 'interrupted' → *un̲u̲nterbrochen*/A 'uninterrupted'

or by compounding:

(EOL) De: *Windpark* 'wind farm' → *Meerwindpark* 'offshore wind farm'

Lexical integration
The variant and the term share the same content word. The variant is built from the term to which lexemes are added or omitted. These syntagmatic variants are built by the following linguistic operations:

modification
(SAT) Fr: *modulation delta* → *modulation delta adaptable* 'adaptative delta modulation'
predication
(EOL) En: *solar energy* ↔ *solar energy conversion*
coordination
(EOL) Fr: *axe horizontal, axe vertical* → *axe vertical ou horizontal* 'vertical or horizontal axis'

Morphological and lexical integration
The variant and the term share the same lexemes but those differ morphologically. The variant includes additional morphemes and lexemes, or inversely, components of the term have been removed. Variants are obtained by the exemplification process: the term is a morphological compound and the variant is a syntagmatic compound with an additional morphological or lexical element:

(CAN) De: *Krebs-Früherkennung* $N/N_1–N_2$ 'early detection of cancer' → *Früherkennung von Brustkrebs*, 'early detection of breast cancer'.

The identification of the inter-mixed term and variant is carried out by using grammar rules. A regular grammar is enough to express term and variant patterns. Grammar rules must be constrained in order to check the match between common morphemes or lexemes of the term and the variant. Further constraints may be added to check the grammatical category or the form of the inserted or deleted element. In the case of morphological or mixed integrations, a morphological segmentation is preliminarily necessary before applying grammar rules.

Table 6.4 Method of discovery of such category of variants with regards to the occurrence type.

Analyses	Occurrences	Main categories
syntactic	inter-mixed	denominative, conceptual, linguistic
syntactic	separated	denominative, conceptual
morphological	inter-mixed	conceptual, linguistic
distributional	isolated	denominative
distance	isolated	linguistic

6.4.3 Separated term and variant occurrences

The variant and the term occur in the same local context. More precisely, the variant is introduced before or after the term thanks to a textual marker. Textual markers are linguistic clues that are typical of a defining context. Typical markers are punctuation clues such as the parenthesis that are used to define acronyms:

> (DIA) Fr: *L'obésité est définie par un Indice de Masse Corporelle (IMC)* 'Obesity is defined by a Body Mass Index (BMI)'

or denominative variants:

> (DIA) Fr: *L'insulino-déficience responsable de l'hyperglycémie du diabète de type 2 est précédée par 10 ou 20 ans d'hypersécretion insulinique (hyperinsulinisme) secondaire à une insulino-résistance des tissus périphériques* 'The insulino deficiency because of the hyperglycemia of the diabetes of type 2 is preceded by 10 or 20 years of insulin hypersecretion (hyperinsulinism), secondly to an insulin resistance of peripheral tissues'

Another linguistic marker is the conjunction of coordination such as the disjunctive conjunction *or:*

> (DIA) Fr: *Le diabète non insulino-dépendant ou diabète de type 2 résulte de la conjonction de plusieurs gènes de susceptibilité* 'the non-insulin dependent diabetes or diabetes of type 2 is caused by the conjunction of many susceptibility genes'

The identification of the term and of the variant when they co-occur separately is carried out by using lexico-syntactic patterns.

6.5 Relationship between processing methods and types of occurrences

We have surveyed a large pallet of methods for the detection of term variants without claiming for completeness. Applying one method depends on whether we are looking for variants of a simple term or a complex term and of the type of occurrences of the variant with the term. A method never covers the detection of all occurrences of one category of variants because there are several linguistic operations leading to as many types of occurrences. In order to capture orthographic variants, only the measure of distance can be used. We propose in Table 6.4 a synthesis of methods allowing to detect such categories of variants depending on the type of occurrences of the variant.

In the two following chapters, we will pursue the topic of automatic detection of variants. We will investigate the behaviour of linguistic methods for variant detection for several languages and specialised domains. Chapter 7 will design a generic grammar of variants based on syntactic analysis. Chapter 8 covers a distributional analysis for the detection of denominative variants of complex terms obtained by synonymic substitution. Both syntactic and paradigmatic analysis will be associated with morphological analysis of varied complexity.

CHAPTER 7

Grammar of variants

A grammar of variants is designed for occurrences where the term and its variant are inter-mixed. Grammar is used to perform syntagmatic analysis and recognises subsets of the three main categories of variants: denominative, conceptual and linguistic variants. We demonstrated in Chapter 5 that ngrams containing co-occurrences of the complex term and additional strings are not appropriate to detect variants. Remember as well the statement of Jacquemin (2001: 216) which observed English complex terms of the medical domain occurring in a textual window of 26 words: "Only 46.1% of the co-occurrences actually correspond to a term variant."

A grammar of variants will permit the identification of term variants with a greater reliability than the simple co-occurrence of its constituents. We propose a generic grammar for the recognition of variants that will be adjusted for separate languages. As a preamble, its application requires linguistic processings that are part-of-speech tagging, splitting of compound terms, and stemming of simple terms and components of complex terms. Other more sophisticated processing than part-of-speech tagging might be employed, such as chuncking or dependency parsing. Stemming can be replaced by a morphological analysis as well. As our goal is to design a generic grammar for languages from different families, we prefer to use robust linguistic processing available for many languages. Thus, our grammar of variants will be homogeneous for any language.

7.1 Specifications and properties

A grammar of variants contains a set of rules. A rule marks the term and the expected variant by using a sequence of grammatical categories. Each rule allows us to pair a term and a variant. The pairing is executed when the lexical or morphological and the grammatical matches succeed. A rule allows us to recognise many variants for a term. One detected variant can be assigned to many terms.

7.1.1 Expressivity of the syntagmatic rules

Term and variant patterns are expressed by regular expressions. In the recognition rules, what is picked up from the context of the variant occurrence should be distinguished from the elements that are part of the variant. We illustrate different rule types for a typical case of syntactic variants: insertion in a complex term.

Structural rules

To illustrate a structural rule, the complex term is a term of length 2 and its variant is of superior length with inserted elements. The most generic method simply checks similar forms or sub-forms between the term and its variants:

(R0) Term: $X_1\ X_2 \rightarrow$ Variant: $X_1\ X\ X_2$

Similarity: of forms is expressed by similar small numbers assigned to symbols. The term may be of any pattern and inserted elements of any grammatical category. This rule matches the meta-rule defined for modifications and substitutions by Jacquemin (2001: 163). This rule is picked up too permissively and restrictions expressed for grammatical categories are necessary for the morphosyntactic description of the term and for inserted elements.

To check grammatical categories, the generic symbol X of the rule R0 is instantiated by the part-of-speech tag featuring the components of the complex term and its variant. For example, the following rule allows us to express a variant of internal modification between the term and the variant. The term of N A pattern is changed by the insertion of an adjective:

(R1) Term: $N_1\ A_2 \rightarrow$ Variant: $N_1\ A\ A_2$

Rule (R1) limits the insertion to only one element of a given grammatical category. Other rules can be more permissive by allowing insertion of many modifiers:

(R2) Term: $N_1\ A_2 \rightarrow$ Variant: N_1 ((R)*A)+ A_2

Rule R2 allows us insertion of many adjectives. Each adjective can be modified by one or many adverbs. The adverbial modification remains optional. Usually, a generic rule cannot check the presence of constituents of the term. It can accept an insertion (R3-1) or many insertions (R3-2), without checking the grammatical category of inserted elements:

(R3-1) Term:$N_1\ A_2 \rightarrow$ Variant: $N_1\ X\ A_2$
(R3-2) Term:$N_1\ A_2 \rightarrow$ Variant: N_1 (X)+ A_2

When the insertion is limited to one element, true genericity is obtained for some variants, such as coordination of expansion (Jacquemin 2001: 167) and insertion.

Morphological patterns
The constraint of the identity of forms of the term and variant constituents is based upon the inflection form, the lemma or the stem. The lemma of a lexical element is commonly calculated by part-of-speech tagging. The application of patterns to lemmas allows us to generalise the detection of variants to its inflectional paradigm.

Let us take a complex term as example of the rule (R1), (AGR) Fr: *pays tropical* N/N A 'tropical country' and its variant *pays forestier tropical* N/N A A 'tropical forest country'. Rule R1 detects the following occurrences when it is applied to:

1. The inflectional forms *pays* 'country' and *tropical:* the single pair *pays tropical* 'tropical country' /*pays forestier tropical* 'tropical forest country'
2. The lemmas *pays* and *tropical* (the two pairs are picked up from the inflectional paradigm of the N A pattern): *pays tropical/pays forestier tropical* and *pays tropicaux/pays forestiers tropicaux*
   The generalisation based upon lemmas permits the detection of occurrences of false positive variants. Therefore, the detection of the occurrence *pays forestiers tropicaux* can be a sub-sequence of the string *les palmiers de pays forestiers tropicaux* 'the palm trees of tropical forest countries' where the adjective *tropical* modifies *palmier* 'palm tree' and not *pays* 'country'; for this occurrence, the pair *pays tropicaux/pays forestier tropicaux* is incorrect.
3. The stems *pays* and *tropical* (the two pairs are picked up from inflectional and derivational paradigms): *pays tropical* 'tropical country' /pays *tempéré intertropical* 'intertropical temperated country'. The generalisation based upon stems when computed by stemming leads to the extraction of false positive variants without relation with the term such as: *pays tropical/paysage agricole tropical* 'tropical agricultural landscape' where *pays* 'country' and *paysage* 'landscape' are paired, though actually, they should not.

Structural rules augmented with lexical filtering
Checking grammatical categories can be accompanied by positive or negative lexical constraints.

Positive constraint: only some of the forms are accepted:

(R4) Term: $N_1\ A_2 \rightarrow$ Variant: N_1 P N*type, base, …* A_2

Rule R4 suits the detection of denominative variants obtained by exemplification when it is useful to constraint the inserted lexical forms to a closed list of nouns, such as *type:*

(Chemistry) Fr: *agrégation hydrophobe* 'hydrophobic aggregation'/*agrégation de type hydrophobe* 'hydrophobic-typed aggregation'.

Negative constraint: lexical forms are rejected:

(R5) Term: N_1 A_2 → Variant: N_1 Adv!*puis* 'then', *alors* 'thus', … A_2

Rule R5 describes the insertion of an adverbial modifier inside a syntagmatic compound of N A pattern. Some phrasal adverb modifiers, such as *puis* 'thus', are prohibited to avoid wrong pairs, such as:

(Chemistry) Fr: *calcium ioniser* 'lit. calcium to ionise' / *calcium puis ioniser* 'calcium then ionised' where the sequence of lemma *calcium ioniser* 'lit. calcium to ionise' matches inflectional forms such as *calcium ionisé* 'ionised calcium'. The detected variant is a substring of the sequence: *trempé dans du chlorure de calcium puis ionisé* 'soaked in calcium chloride then ionised'.

Structural rules augmented with contextual filtering
Parts of speech used in rules R1, R2, and R3 describe the term and its variant patterns. In order to reduce the rule scope, it is sometimes useful to look into the adjacent contexts of the variant pattern. Therefore, the preposition expressed in italics in rule R6 is a contextual filter to avoid false positive insertion variants of the term of N P N pattern:

(R6) Term: N_1 P_2 N_3 → Variant: N_1 (X)+ P_2 N_3 *P*

Rule R6 allows us insertion in the syntagmatic compound of N P N pattern only if the variant is followed by a preposition. This contextual restriction discards the pair:

(MED) Fr: *facteur de forme* 'form factor' / **facteurs de risque de forme diverse* 'risk factors of miscellaneous forms'

where in the false positive, the expansion of the term, *de forme,* is actually the head of the prepositional modifier *de forme diverse* of the syntagmatic compound *facteurs de risque* 'risk factor'.

Constitutive and contextual elements of the pattern need to be distinguished so that contextual elements do not appear as part of the variant. Ville-Ometz et al. (2007) established twenty rules for contextual filtering for English that increase the precision of the insertion and coordination rules by 0.9 at least.

7.1.2 Core operations

Core operations are permutation, insertion, juxtaposition, susbtitution and deletion. Permutation, substitution and deletion are editing operations. Insertion and juxtaposition are two processes of the editing operation of addition. These operations are applied to autonomous constituents of the syntagmatic compound, or to morphological components of the morphological compound. A single operation involves one linguistic element and generates a simple variant. We now detail these operations:

1. **Insertion (I):** this transformation inserts elements between the constituents of the term without changing their order.
   Term: X_0 X_1/ Variant: X_0 X^* X_1
   The nature of inserted elements depends on the term pattern, of the compound type and of the language. The inserted elements are either of grammatical or lexical nature. Typical insertions are:
   a. variants obtained by internal modification, such as the insertion of an adjective in a syntagmatic compound:
      Fr: Term: N_0 A_1/ Variant: N_0 A A_1
   b. coordination variants: Fr:
      Term: N_0 A_1/ Variant: N_0 A C A_1
   Other elements can be inserted, such as grammatical words:
   Term: N_0 N_1/ Variant: N_0 P D N_1
   Segmentation (Sg) is a distinguished type of insertion when diacritical sign or space are inserted.
2. **Permutation (P):** this transformation changes the order of the elements of the complex term. Permutation comes along generally with an insertion.
   Term: X_0 X_1 / Variant: $X_1X^*X_0$
   For English, the basic permutation rule is applied to syntagmatic compound and uses a preposition as pivot: N_0 N_1 = N_1 P N_0
3. **Juxtaposition:** this transformation adds elements to borders of the term. Juxtaposition of elements can be carried out to the left **(El)** or to the right **(Er)** of the term.
   Term: X_0 X_1 / Variant: $X_1X_0X^+$ or $X^+X_1X_0$
   The typical juxtaposition concerns the expansion variants obtained by modification from a syntagmatic compound:
   Fr: Term: N_0 A_1 / Variant: N_0 A_1 A
4. **Deletion (R):** this transformation deletes constitutive elements of the term without changing the order of its components:
   Term: X_0 X_1 / Variant: X_0 or X_1

A typical deletion is anaphoric reduction when only the head of the compound is kept:
Fr: Term: N_0 A_1 / Variant: N_0
5. **Substitution (Sb):** this transformation substitutes constitutive elements of the term without changing the order of its components. The substitued elements are lemmas or identical stems but different grammatical categories:
Term: X_0 X_1 / Variant: X X_1 or X_0 X
Derivation (D) is a distinguished type of substitution when a lexical element is substituted by one of its derivatives.

The variants of permutation, insertion and deletion are considered by Jacquemin (2001: 160) as characteristic operations of basic variations of syntagmatic compounds. We describe coordination variants with insertion or juxtaposition operations while Jacquemin, (2001) considered coordination as a separate operation. Juxtaposition was not included by Jacquemin (2001) in the set of core operations. Nevertheless, in Romance languages juxtaposition or insertion are in competition for expressing the same conceptual variant:

> (TEL) Fr: Term: *antenne de réception* 'receiving antenna' / Variant: *antenne parabolique de réception* 'lit. parabolic antenna of receiving'/*antenne de réception parabolique* 'parabolic receiving antenna'.

7.1.3 Ambiguity of the syntactic analysis

When the term and the variant are inter-mixed, syntagmatic analysis produces ambiguities depending on the number of constituents and the length of the complex term.

One term
With a complex term, there are many ambiguities arising from the choice of the term and the operation. Three analyses are possible for a complex term pattern: a complex term of length *n*, a modified complex term of length ≤*n*−1, a reduced complex term of length >*n*. For example, for a pattern N A and the French term: *énergie renouvelable,* or for a pattern A N and the term En: *renewable energy,* the interpretations are:

1. a complex term: Fr: *énergie renouvelable;* En: *renewable energy*
2. a conceptual variant obtained by modification of a simple term: Fr: *énergie;* En: *energy* modified by the adjective Fr: *renouvelable;* En: *renewable;*
3. a conceptual variant obtained by anaphoric reduction: Fr: *énergie renouvelable éolienne;* En: *renewable wind energy* where the adjective Fr: *éolienne;* the noun En: *wind* have been deleted.

When dealing with corpora, variants of length 3 built by expansion from a term of length 2, and the term of length 2 occur as isolated or separated occurrences. With the occurrences of several variants of length 3, the term of length 2 becomes ambiguous. For example, the French occurrence: *énergie éolienne* 'wind energy' can be analysed as a denominative variant obtained by lexical reduction of one of the following terms of length 3: *énergie d'origine éolienne, énergie renouvelable éolienne* or *énergie du système éolien,* a conceptual variant obtained by anaphoric reduction of one of the following terms of length 3: *énergie éolienne du système, énergie éolienne offshore,* a linguistic variant obtained by coordination: *énergie éolienne et solaire,* or by modification: *énergie éolienne compétitive,* and we do not mention the complex terms of length $\geq n + 1$. The same phenomenon is reported for En: *renewable energy* can be a denominative variant obtained by lexical reduction: *renewable energy resources,* a conceptual variant obtained by anaphoric reduction: *hybrid renewable energy, marine renewable energy,* a linguistic variant obtained by coordination: *renewable and spare energy,* or by modification: *alternative renewable energy, clean renewable energy.*

With terms of length 3, the number of variants obtained by exemplification or expansion will decrease, while the number of variants obtained by reduction will increase. Let us take for example the patterns: Fr: N A P N and En: A N N, and the occurrences: (EOL) Fr: *machine synchrone à excitation* and En: *excited synchronous machine.* The interpretations are:

1. a complex term of N A P N pattern: Fr: *machine synchrone à excitation;* A N N En: *excited synchronous machine;*
2. a conceptual variant of the complex term of N P N pattern: Fr: *machine à excitation;* A N En: *excited machine* modified by the adjective Fr: *synchone;* En: *synchronous;*
3. a conceptual variant of the complex term of N A pattern: Fr: *machine synchrone*; En: *synchronous machine* modified by a prepositional group Fr: *à excitation;* by an adjective En: *exited;*
4. a conceptual variant obtained by anaphoric reduction of the complex term of N A P N A pattern: Fr: *machine synchrone à excitation alternative;* N A N N En: *AC excited synchronous machine* where the adjective *alternative* and the acronym *AC* of the term *aternative current* have been deleted.

Of course, depending on the languages and on complex term patterns, some interpretations are more or less legitimate. For example, for English, interpretation 2 has not to be formulated even if the term *excited machine* exists.

Several terms

Linguistic variants obtained by coordination implies two complex terms sharing constituent part. One pattern Fr: D N_1 C D N_2 A_3 produces three possible analyses depending on the occurrence they met:

1. a complex term of D N_1 C D N_2 A_3 pattern, such as (Energy) Fr: *coût d'installation et de raccordement* 'installation and connexion cost';
2. a linguistic variant involving two complex terms such as in (EOL) Fr: *la consommation et la production éolienne* 'wind energy consuption and production' with the complex terms *consommation éolienne* 'wind energy consuption' and *production éolienne* 'wind energy production';
3. a coordination of a simple term and a complex term: (Energy) Fr: *le chauffage et l'eau chaude* 'heating and hot water': the simple term *chauffage* 'heating' and the complex term *eau chaude* 'hot water'.

The coordinated structure, proposed by analysis (1), is not a term pattern and examples of such terms are rare. Ambiguities (2) and (3) are frequent and difficult to resolve. A contextual constraint and a lexical constraint can be added that check, for a head coordination, that a determinant occurs before the coordination pattern and that this determinant is of the same category than the determinant of the coordination pattern. For example, the head coordination in French requires the occurrence of definite articles dependent on the coordinated head nouns. The same constraint applies for an expansion coordination above the preposition that should be shared by two expansions. For example, for French the expansion coordination variants of the complex term (Energy) Fr: *pertes par conduction* 'losses by conduction' will only be those using the preposition *par* 'by' twice such as: *pertes par conduction et par commutation* 'losses by conduction and by switching'.

Another clue for eliminating the ambiguity between analyses (2) and (3) is the occurrence of two coordinated structures whose order of elements is permuted around the conjunction of coordination, such as for: (Energy) Fr: *réserve primaire 'primary reserve'/réserve primaire et secondaire primary and secondary reserve/ réserves secondaires et primaires* 'secondary and primary reserves'.

7.2 Generic grammar of recognition of variants

We write a generic grammar of recognition of variants (GGRV) valid for several languages. The GGRV applies to morphosyntactically analysed terms. Constitutive elements of terms can be autonomous components, i.e. lexical units of the syntag-matic compound, or non-autonomous elements of the morphological compound, i.e. neoclassical elements or prefixes.

The GGRV consists of three kinds of set of rules:

1. competing structures that generate denominative variants such as simplification and exemplification variants, and linguistic variants of segmentation;
2. augmented or reduced structures that generate conceptual and linguistic variants such as expansion or reduction variants;
3. contextual structures that generate linguistic variants such as coordination or full back-compounding.

Each set of rules is composed of rules that either apply to syntagmatic or morphological compounds. Depending on the language, the subsets of rules for syntagmatic compounds and for morphological compounds have a greater or a lesser number of rules. Each rule of the GGRV will have morphosyntactic productions that differ depending on the language.

Given *A*, *B* and *C*, the components of a complex term, and X any lexical element. The notation found between square brackets [AB] means that A and B are constituent elements of a lexical unit. These constituent elements may be concatenated or separated by a hyphen.

7.2.1 Competing structures

Competing structures requiring morphological processing are the linguistic variants of segmentation (cf. Section 3.4.1) and the denominative variants obtained by compression (cf. Section 3.2.2).

Length 2
For a complex term composed of two lexical elements A B, the competing structures are:

Segmentation (Sg) identical lemmas: [AB] = A B
Derivation (D) identical stems: A B (or [AB]) → C B with morpho(A, C) or A D with morpho(B, D)
Permutation (P) AB (or [AB]) → B A

Length 3
For a complex term composed of three lexical elements A B C, the competing structures are:

Segmentation (Sg) identical lemmas: [ABC] = [AB] C = A [BC] = A B C
Derivation (D) A B C (or [ABC]) → D B C with morpho(A, D) or A E C with morpho(B, E) or morpho(B, D) or A B F with morpho(C, F)
Permutation (P) A B C = C A B = A C B

7.2.2 Augmented/reduced structures

The augmented or reduced structures apply to syntagmatic or morphological compounds. The element to be added to or to be removed from the term is either a lexical unit or a morphological element.

Length 2

For a complex term composed of two elements A and B, the augmented/reduced structures are:

Insertion (I) A B → A X_{1-2} B
Permutation and insertion (PI) AB → BX_{1-2} A
Right juxtaposition (Jr) A B → A B X_{1-2}
Left juxtaposition (Jl) A B → X_{1-2} A B
Right deletion (Rr) A B → A
Left deletion (Rl) A B → B

Length 3

For a complex term composed of three elements A, B and C, the augmented/reduced structures are:

Insertion I1 A B C → A X_{1-2} B C
or **I2** A B C → A B X_{1-2} B C
Permutation and insertion (PI) A B C → BCX_{1-2} A or A B C → B X_{1-2} C A
Right juxtaposition (Jr) A B C → A B C X_{1-2}
Left juxtaposition (Jl) A B C → X_{1-2} A B C
Permutation and right juxtaposition (PJr) ABC → X_{1-2} C A B
Permutation and left juxtaposition (PJl) A B C → C A B X_{1-2}
Right deletion (Rr) A B C → A B or A B C → A
Left deletion (Rl) A B C → B C or A B C → C
Center deletion (Rc) A B C → A C

For terms of length ≥ 3, core operations are used in combination. The variants generated involved several basic operations. Here is an example of such combination of operations: [AB] C D → [AE] B D, the element E is inserted and the element C is deleted, such as (EOL) En: *fixed-speed wind turbine* → *fixed-rotational speed turbine.* These rules, including many basic operations, are complex. They may generate variants whose meaning is far from the term concept. Furthermore, complex rules are not generic rules: they apply to very few terms. Even, many complex rules only apply to one term and generate only one variant.

7.2.3 Contextual structures

Contextual structures are described with the same operations as for the competing and the augmented or reduced structures. Coordination variants involving at least two terms are described with the help of insertions and left and right juxtapositions. The non-modified form of the term such as in (EOL) En: *sustainable energy* in *renewable and sustainable energy* matches a left juxtaposition (J1). The modified form of the term such as (EOL) En: *renewable energy* in *renewable and sustainable energy* matches one insertion (I1). The insertion is operated at position 1 and of C N pattern. These rules describing insertions of coordination, enumeration or argument structures are useful in order not to lose occurrences of terms. Futhermore, the fact of having met the term in a coordination, an enumeration or as an argument, and not as an isolated occurrence, may be interesting within the scope of the exploitation of variants for terminology structuring or control indexing.

7.2.4 Function words

It might be interesting to keep the grammatical words of the term patterns and to observe their insertion, deletion or substitution. These rules will be identical to those that have already been written for lexical and morphological elements. The substitution of preposition picks up a denominative variant. Prepositions forming a closed class of words, substitution identifies a variant as soon as another preposition occurs inside the term. For other synonymic substitutions involving content words or morphological elements, substitution rules can be used, by they need to be associated with lexical filtering. Synonyms of the complex term component to be substituted must be listed. Using substitution rules to model synonymic substitutions implies creating nearly as many rules augmented with lexical filtering as complex terms. To discover denominative variants obtained by synonymic substitution, paradigmatic analysis is more appropriate than syntagmatic analysis and will be described in Chapter 8.

7.2.5 Ad-hoc rules

The GGRV applies to terms of predefined patterns, but the linguistic processing assigns wrong grammatical tags to words. In order to correct some tagging errors, correction rules can be written. These rules apply, for example, when a term gets two tags such as Fr: *physique* A 'physical' or N 'physics'; or Fr: *congelé:* A 'frozen' or V.

Substitution (Sb) same lemmas or stems but with different tags:

A B (or [AB] or [A-B]) → C B or A B → A D

The number of ad hoc rules must be limited. If not, the genericity of the GGRV is lost.

Table 7.1 Features of the GGRV: number of rules by language, by structure type, and by morphological or syntagmatic nature with CP: competing structures, AR: augmented/reduced structures, CT: contextual structures, M: morphological rule, S: syntagmatic rule.

		De	**En**	**Es**	**Fr**	**Ru**
CP	M	3	3	2	2	4
	S	2	5	4	5	1
AR	M	6	5	2	4	2
	S	8	17	17	13	5
CT	M	0	2	0	2	0
	S	11	9	15	11	4
Total	M	9	10	4	8	6
	S	21	31	36	29	10
Nb rules		30	41	40	37	16

7.3 Variant grammars for specific languages

The GGRV is instantiated for five languages: French, English, Spanish, German and Russian. Instantiations for other languages have been written for Japanese (Takeuchi et al. 2004), Italian (Haralambous and Lavagnino 2011) or Malagasy (Daille et al. 2000), but they are not included in this study. For each language, three set of rules are paired with the three types of structure alterations detailed: competing, augmented/reduced and contextual structures and apply to the main term patterns listed in Section 2.5. For each rule set, morphological rules are distinguished from syntagmatic rules. Variant rules focus on complex terms. A rule is classified as morphological when a morphological splitting is required. Each rule supports a basic operation with some exceptions. Rules of GGRV are listed in Appendix D.

Describing the combination of operations will imply an explosion in the number of rules for a poor coverage of terms and variants. Our choice is to ensure the genericity of the GGRV. We should avoid including in-depth analyses to handle variants of a specific language wherever possible. Jacquemin (2001) wrote a wide coverage grammar of variants for English. Our English GGRV includes one subset of Jacquemin's rules designed for terms of A N, N N and N P N patterns, but it enlarges the grammar by including rules that apply to more complex term patterns, such as A N N and N N N. Some morphological rules such as the permutation of morphological components of a morphological compound, have been added; these cases were extremely rare, but judged important by Bowker and Hawkins (2006).

Table 7.1 summarises the number of rules by language of the GGRV. The Russian grammar contains the smallest number f rules (16 rules) and the English grammar contains the most (41 rules). Of course, the GGRV is not exhaustive and many rules can be added. Inversely, some of the rules can be deleted or con-strainted in order to improve their precision. The category of variant searched for is strongly related to the study or the application. It is difficult to disable a rule a priori, especially if it belongs to the augmented/reduced structures that may identify terminologically interesting variants.

Table 7.2 Statistics concerning the variants detected by the GGRV in [EOL] with T number of triplets <Term, Variant, Rule>, and |T| number of occurrences of triplets <Term, Variant, Rule>.

	CP		A/R		CT		Total	
	T(%)	|T|(%)	T(%)	|T|(%)	T(%)	|T|(%)	T(%)	|T|(%)
Fr	182	898	7,874	13,310	621	2,325	8,677	16,533
	(2.1)	(5.43)	(90.74)	(80.51)	(7.16)	(14.06)		
En	610	10,763	10,152	16,221	933	1,596	11,695	28,580
	(5.22)	(37.66)	(86.8)	(56.76)	(7.98)	(5.58)		
Es	104	401	22,489	30,987	3,190	14,617	25,783	46,005
	(0.4)	(0.87)	(87.22)	(67.36)	(12.37)	(31.77)		
De	125	291	7,679	10,489	1,431	5,417	9,235	16,197
	(1.35)	(1.8)	(83.15)	(64.76)	(15.5)	(33.44)		
Ru	21	33	4,106	6,055	320	3,010	4,447	9,098
	(0.47)	(0.36)	(92.33)	(65.55)	(7.2)	(33.08)		

Table 7.3 The most detected rule by the GGRV in [EOL].

	Cat	M/S	SCat	Patterns	T	|T|	Example
Fr	AR	S	J1	$N_1\ A_1/N\ P\ N_1\ A_1$	1,808	3,109	*parc éolien / installation de parcs éoliens*
En	AR	S	Jl	$A_1\ N_1/R\ A_1\ N_1$	210	1,241	*turbulent wind / unusually turbulent wind*
Es	AR	S	Jl	$N_1\ A_1/N\ P\ N_1\ A_1$	5,010	7,047	*energía eólica / potencia de energía eólica*
De	AR	S	Jl	$A_1\ N_1/A\ A_1\ N_1$	2,648	3,076	*zeitlich auflösung / hohe zeitliche auflösung*
Ru	AR	S	Jl	$N_1\ N_2/A\ N_1\ N_2$	2,626	3,407	порыв ветра/ когерентный порыв ветра

7.4 Cross-lingual observations

The GGRV is applied to the comparable specialised corpora [EOL] and [CAN] (see Section 5.2 for corpora description). The implementation of the GGRV is executed in TermSuite (cf. Section 10.3). We have observed two steps, the first one studies the coverage of rules without assuming their reliability in [EOL], and the second examines the syntactic correction on a subset of variants of central terms of the domains reflected in [EOL] and [CAN]. Evaluation of the syntactic correction is followed by the evaluation of the classification of the variants according to their categories (cf. Section 3.1.1) provided by the three types of structures of the GGRV.

Table 7.4 The triplet <Term, Variant, Rule> with the biggest number of occurrences in [EOL].

	Cat	M/S	SCat	Patterns	Term/variant	|T|
Fr	CT	S	I	$N_1\ A_1/N_1\ A, A\ C\ A_1$	*énergie électrique / énergie utilisable, mécanique ou électrique*	1,232
En	CP	M	Sg	N/NN	*windturbine / wind turbine*	1,583
Es	CT	S	I	$N_1\ P_1\ N_2/N_1\ C\ N\ P_1\ N_2$	*velocidad del viento / velocidad y directión del viento*	400
	CT	S	El	$N_1\ P_1\ N_2/N\ C\ N_1\ P_1\ N_2$	*directión del viento / velocidad y dirección del viento*	400
De	CT	S	El	$A_1\ N_1/A\ C\ A_1\ N_1$	*erneuerbaren energie / energie-effizienz und erneuerbaren energie*	215
	CT	S	Er	$A_1\ N_1/A_1\ N_1\ C\ N$	*erneuerbaren energie / erneuerbaren energie und energieeinsparung*	215
Ru	CT	S	I	$A_1\ N_1/A_1\ C\ A\ N_1$	окружающая среда / окружающая и социальная среда	212

7.4.1 Coverage

The coverage of the GGRV rules applied to five languages is estimated by examining the detected variants by the three types of structures: competing structures (CP), augmented/reduced structures (A/R) and contextual structures (CT). The detection of a variant is featured by a triplet <Term, Variant, Rule> whose meaning is 'Variant result of the application of Rule to Term'. The number of occurrences of triplets are counted. Table 7.2 gives the number of triplets (T) and their numbers of occurrences (|T|) for each type of structure and each language in [EOL]. The average number of variants by term ranges from 1.75 for German to 2.44 for English. The averages of French (1.9), Spanish (1.78) and Russian (2.05) are included between these two bounds. We notice that the size of the grammar in number of rules has little influence on the number of detected variants: the Russian GGRV is the smallest grammar but the average number of variants is close to the upper bound.

There is a very large number of variants detected by augmented/reduced structures, between 80% and 90% of the detected triplets. The contextual structures have a coverage between 7% and 15%. Finally, the competing structures are the rarest between 0.4% and 6%. The observation of the number of occurrences of triplets rebalanced these figures: competing and contextual structures cover between 30% and 40% of the total number of the detected variants.

Table 7.3 provides for each language the rule that applied the most to different terms. All of them involve juxtaposition rules of augmented/reduced structures. These frequent rules apply once or twice for each term, with the exception of the rule for English. The English rule stipulates the adverbial modification of the term of A N pattern and supplies mainly linguistic variants. This rule can be deleted in the English GGRV or can be lexically constrainted in order to accept only deadjectival adverbs as modifiers. Such adverb are more likely to be used in the scope of conceptual variants such as *rotationally augmented flow* that common adverbs such as *nearly augmented flow.* Table 7.4 gives for each language the triplet with the most occurrences. All of them involve coordination or segmentation rules included in contextual and competing structures respectively.

Table 7.5 Extract of the list of variants to be evaluated. Example of variants of the term En: *blade element* in [EOL].

T	blade element
V	combined blade element (1) [ann: combined blade element] {is_ variant:_1_} and analysis environment, the blade element and momentum theory (BEM). To aid the understanding of combined blade element and 2.3 Turbine generator momentum theory it is useful initially to consider the rotor as an actuat
V	ith blade element (6) [ann: ith blade element] {is_variant:_1_} ratio of rotor: design tip-speed ratio: local tip-speed ratio: local tip-speed ratio for the ith blade element: local tip-speed ratio at the hub: corresponding axial induction factor at of an airfoil: design lift coefficient of an airfoil: tip-loss factor: tip-loss factor for the ith blade element: number of blade elements: number of blades of a rotor: axial induction factor at rotor plane:
V	elements of an airscrew blade (1) [npnn: element of airscrew blade] {is_variant: _1_} Engineering, Vol.14 No.2, 1990 12- Lock, C. N. H., "Experiments to Verify the Independence of the Elements of an Airscrew Blade", Br. A.R.C.R and M.953, 1924 13-Wilson, R. E., Lissaman, P. B. S., Walker, S. N., "Aerodynamic Pe
V	annular blade element (2) [ann: annular blade element] {is_ variant: _1_} wake: rotor thrust: rotor torque: drag force on an annular blade element: lift force on an annular blade element: force on an annular element tangential to the circle swept by the rotor: drag coefficient of an Bernoulli's constant between outflow and far wake: rotor thrust: rotor torque: drag force on an annular blade element: lift force on an annular blade element: force on an annular element tangential to the circle swe

7.4.2 Precision

Our goal is to evaluate the quality of the variants detected by the GGRV. Evaluation is carried out by native speakers for each language. They must judge whether the identified variant is linguistically correct, given a valid term. For each variant, its number of occurrences and its pattern are detailed. The sentences in which the variants occur are provided. At least one sentence is supplied as an example for one variant, up to five. This evaluation is carried out for all variants and is interested in the first hundred variants of candidate terms provided by the term extraction tool, TermSuite, that ranks candidate terms according to a specificity score (cf. Section 9.3). When the hundred variants are based upon a candidate term that accepts further variants, all variants of the candidate from the hundred are taken. Table 7.5 shows an extract of detected variants for (EOL) En: *blade element.* Three different variants are identified. The number between brackets indicates the number of occurrences of the variant, therefore *combined blade element* occurs once. The pattern of the variant and its lemma appears between square brackets. The field {is_variant:_0_1_} should be set by the evaluator to 0, if incorrect, or 1 if correct. Looking at the example of Table 7.5, all identified variants are judged as linguistically correct.

Table 7.6 Statistics and precision of the variants of top candidate terms in [EOL].

	De	En	Es	Fr	Ru
Nb candidate terms	816	341	36	93	23
Nb valid/invalid candidate terms with variants	34/41	16/17	1/1	3/3	3
Nb distinct variants of valid/invalid terms	72/101	102/103	164/164	104/104	127/127
Nb valid/invalid variants	57/72	96/102	123/164	78/104	118/127
Precision	79	94	75	75	93

Table 7.7 Statistics and precision of the variants of top candidate terms in [CAN].

	En	Fr
Nb candidate terms	231	132
Nb valid/invalid candidate terms with variants	12/13	3/3
Nb distinct variants of valid/invalid terms	105/107	137/137
Nb valid/invalid variants	94/105	105/137
Precision	90	77

Tables 7.6 and 7.7 summarise by language the number of candidate terms retained in order to reach the minimum number of a hundred variants. Table 7.6 shows variants that have been identified in [EOL]. For Spanish, they are linked to a sole term: *parque eólico,* for Russian, to two terms: скорость ветра 'wind farm', электростанции 'farm', and for French, to three terms: *vitesse de rotation* 'rotational speed', *turbine éolienne* 'wind turbine', and *système de stockage* 'storage system', whereas for English, to 17 terms, such as *angle of attack, tip-speed ratio,* or *wind generator,* and for German, to 41 terms. Table 7.7 shows the variants that have been identified in the corpus [CAN]. For French, they are linked to 3 terms: *effet secondaire* 'side effect', *cellule cancéreuse* 'cancer cell', *curage axillaire* 'axillary dissection', and for English, to 13 terms, such as *chemotherapy, cancer cell,* or *lymph node.*

Some of these candidate terms are not syntactically valid. In this case, variants are not judged. Accordingly, the number of terms with variants is reduced for [EOL], to 16 for English, and 34 for German, and for [CAN], to 12 for English. As for other languages, all candidate terms are syntactically correct. The number of a hundred variants to be judged will therefore be reduced for German in [EOL] to 72 evaluated variants. Concerning other languages in [EOL] and in [CAN], the minimum number of a hundred variants is reached. A variant matches a unique triplet <Term, Variant, Rule>. A triplet judged as correct on one occurrence is assumed to be valid for all its occurrences. No further checking is carried out. The variant precision is only calculated for the syntactically correct candidate terms. It always exceeds a precision of 75%. The most precise variants are variants in Russian and English and the noisiest are those observed in Spanish and French. The size of the grammar again has no influence on precision because the Russian grammar has the smallest number of rules and the English grammar has the highest number of rules. The explanation comes from the more important number of concurrent structures in Russian and English than in any other languages. Rules of concurrent structures are generally far more reliable that rules of augmented/reduced or contextual structures. The number of examined terms is also an important factor. For Spanish, French and Russian, candidate terms are central terms of the domain. They accept many variants obtained by juxtaposition featuring conceptual variants. These are distributed almost equally between left and right juxtapositions. Juxtapositions are less precise than insertions. Tables 7.8 and 7.9 detail the precision of variants according to the nature of the rule, morphological (M) or syntagmatic (S), the type of structures, competing (CP), contextual (CT) or augmented (AR), and specify the operations for the augmented structures: left juxtaposition (Jl) or right juxtaposition (Jr), insertion (I) and permutation (P). Comparing the results with the naive approach of Chapter 5, insertions are still precise but rare. Constrained expansions by the help of syntagmatic rules are much more precise than the n-grams and supply quite interesting results. However, their high number compared to other categories of variants argues in favour of a further refining of the category of conceptual variants in sub-categories more semantically circumscribed. Frequent conceptual variants are more likely to be terms than variants. Another solution would have been to remove them from the list of variants to be evaluated. But it applies only to a few variants.

Table 7.8 Statistics about structures and rules used for the detection of variants of top candidate terms in [EOL].

	De	En	Es	Fr	Ru
M	19/24	0	0	0	1/1
precision	79				100
S	38/48	96/102	123/164	78/104	117/126
precision	79	94	75	75	92
CP	9/9	1/1	0	0	1/1
precision	100	100			100
CT	1/1	1/5	0	1/3	0
precision	100	20		33	
A/R	47/62	94/96	123/164	77/101	116/125
precision	76	98	75	76	93
Jl	28/36	79/80	88/105	34/48	114/123
precision	78	99	84	71	93
Jr	0/2	10/11	35/59	39/49	0
precision	0	91	59	80	
I	19/24	4/4	0	4/4	2/2
precision	79	100		100	100
P	0	1/1	0	0	0
precision		100			

In all languages, variant detection rules that are commonly used are rules of right and left juxtapositions and insertions with typical modifiers of the term pattern. In German, morphological rules match one third of used syntagmatic rules. All morphological rules are insertion rules that break preliminarily the native compound and then insert elements. The resulting variant is a syntagmatic compound either made from split term elements and inserted elements, without compounding such as: *windstrom* 'wind power' → *wind generierten strom* 'wind generated power', or made from some split term elements and a new compound built from inserted elements and split term elements, at least one: *gaskraftwerke* 'gas plant' → *gasbetriebene kraftwerke* 'gas-powered plant'.

Table 7.9 Statistics about structures and rules used for the detection of variants of the top candidate terms in [CAN].

	En	Fr
M	1/1	0
precision	100	
S	93/104	105/137
precision	89	77
CP	1/1	0
precision	100	
CT	0/5	0
precision	0	
A/R	93/99	105/137
precision	94	77
Jl	84/90	58/76
precision	93	76
Jr	7/7	44/58
precision	100	76
I	3/3	3/3
precision	100	100
P	0	0
precision		

Table 7.10 Distribution of syntactically correct variants identified by augmented/reduced structures in the three categories of variants in [EOL] with D: denominative variants, C: conceptual variants, L: linguistic variants.

	D		C		L	
	T(%)	|T|(%)	T(%)	|T|(%)	T(%)	|T|(%)
Fr	0	0	53	159	24	54
			(70)	(75)	(30)	(25)
En	5	31	32	94	57	185
	(5)	(10)	(34)	(30)	(61)	(60)
Es	0	0	87	206	36	52
			(71)	(80)	(29)	(20)
De	2	2	44	59	1	7
	(4)	(3)	(94)	(87)	(2)	(10)
Ru	2	2	66	335	48	117
	(2)	(0)	(57)	(74)	(41)	(26)

The three types of structures, that is, competing, augmented/reduced, contextual, can be used for featuring the category of the variant. Denominative variants would be detected by rules of competing structures, with the exception of segmentation rules that pick up linguistic variants. Rules of augmented/reduced structures would detect conceptual variants, and contextual structures, linguistic variants. Examples of variants of the candidate term (EOL) En: *blade element* listed in Table 7.5 are identified by augmented/reduced structures. Three of them are conceptual variants but they show different relations: hypernymy for *annular blade element,* property for *Combined* blade element and meronymy for *element of an airscrew blade.* The forth variant with *ith blade element* is not a conceptual variant, but a linguistic variant.

Table 7.11 Distribution of syntactically correct variants identified by augmented/reduced structures in the three categories of variants in [CAN] with D: denominative variants, C: conceptual variants, L: linguistic variants.

	D		C		L	
	T(%)	|T|(%)	T(%)	|T|(%)	T(%)	|T|(%)
Fr	0	0	63 (68)	125 (64)	30 (32)	70 (36)
En	5 (5)	31 (10)	36 (34)	94 (30)	64 (61)	185 (60)

The heterogeneity of the variants detected by augmented/reduced structures leads us to perform an additional evaluation in order to estimate the distribution of the variants in our three categories. Native speakers have to assign a category to the variant as soon as they judge it as linguistically correct. It is not surprising that human categorisation matches the GGRV categorisation designed on our conceptualisation of variants. However, one can imagine that, for the first variant *combined blade element* presented in Table 7.5, another evaluator could judge differently, by categorising it as linguistic variant, or by considering that *blade element* was not a term.

All variants identified by competing structures are classified as denominative variants, with the exception of segmentation rules that detect linguistic variants reliably, and those identified by contextual structures are classified as linguistic variants. Variants identified by augmented/reduced structures are split into our three categories of variants. Tables 7.10 and 7.11 give the distribution of syntactically correct variants that are identified by the augmented/reduced structures into three categories of variants. Distribution strongly differs from one language to another. For French, Spanish and Russian, variants identified by the augmented/reduced structures are for 70% of conceptual variants, whereas they only constitute 35% for English As for German, they supply 95% of conceptual variants. Of course, this judgement only gives an approximation of the precision of rules.

Even if the precision of rules of augmented/reduced structures in order to identify the conceptual variants is reliable for French, Spanish and Russian and good for German, a margin of improvement is possible. Two types of clues can be used to improve the accuracy of the automatic classification of variants detected by augmented/reduced structures towards categories of conceptual or linguistic variants. The first concerns the nature of the morphological or syntagmatic rule. In German, all variants identified by morphological rules of augmented/reduced structures belong to the category of conceptual variants. Unfortunately, we have not checked this hypothesis for the other languages, because none of the examined terms had variants identified by morphological rules. The second clue is the adjective category that is added by right expansion or insertion for Romance languages. In Section 2.5.1, we have noted the remarkable character of relational adjectives. Table 7.12 gives the number of variants French and Spanish for [EOL] and [CAN] identified by the augmented/reduced structures where an adjective has been juxtaposed to the right or inserted. The examination of the adjective category shows that any relational adjective is not used in linguistics variants, with the exception of the occurrence for French of the adjective *typique* which is quite neutral. Symmetrically, all inserted adjectives and a third of the juxtaposed adjectives are relational. For example, in [EOL] for French, the adjectives *angulaire* 'angular', *inertiel* 'inertial', in Es: *marino* 'marine', and for [CAN] *ganglionnaire* 'lymph node'. For other adjectives, the composed adjectives Fr: *post-thérapeutique* 'post-therapeutic', *hormonosensible* 'hormonally-sensitive', En: *health-related* are only part of conceptual variants. The differentiation of rules of adjectival expansion and insertion depending on complex, relational and other types of adjectives provides an issue to improve the GGRV in its task of variants categorisation.

Table 7.12 Distribution of variants identified by augmented/reduced structures, thanks to the adjectival right juxtaposition (Er) or adjectival insertion (I), according to the categories of variants in [CAN] with C: conceptual variants and L: linguistic variants.

			C		L	
			T(%)	|T|(%)	T(%)	|T|(%)
EOL	Fr	Jr	13	45	11	17
		I	3	5	1	1
	Es	Jr	11	19	8	10
		I	0	0	0	0
CAN	Fr	Jr	23	38	19	51
		I	0	0	0	0

7.5 Summary of observations

This chapter focused on a state-of-the-art method for variants recognition, syntagmatic analysis, which is adapted to occurrences of variants where the term and the variant are inter-mixed. Syntagmatic analysis is performed with rules linking the term and the variant according to their patterns. A set of rules produces a grammar of variants for a language. We assumed the existence of a generic grammar of recognition of variants, the GGRV, performing operations of elemental editions on grammatical categories of constitutive elements of the complex term that is morphologically or syntactically constructed. The set of rules was divided into three subsets for the discovery of three types of structures: competing, augmented or reduced, and contextual structures. The GGRV is the first grammar that performs a unified treatment of morphological and syntagmatic compounds for five languages. The rules for each language are listed in Appendix D. The genericity of our grammar suggests a significant coverage of variant detection across languages. However, we do claim that the GGRV shares the exhaustivity and the precision of some of the grammars developed for a particular language, such as the variant recognition grammar of Jacquemin (2001) for English.

The application of the GGRV to the specialised corpus of the wind energy domain confirms the predominance of variants identified by the augmented/reduced structures for the central terms of the domain. These variants have few occurrences compared with the variants detected by segmentation rules and contextual structures. A great number of occurrences of a variant for a term gives a clue to a non-conceptual character of the variant. Conversely, a high number of different types of variants indicates the key position of the term within the domain terminology. This statement is not new, but it is confirmed for many languages.

We applied the GGRV to comparable corpora of two specialised domains and several languages, and we evaluated the precision of variant recognition. Our evaluation carried out by native speakers revealed a precision of variant detection between 75% and 94%. The rules of the GGRV have been hardly constrained. They need lexical or contextual filtering to improve their precision, such as those designed for English contextual structures suggested by Ville-Ometz et al. (2007). Even if we did not succeed in reaching a perfect isomorphism, the three types of structures correlate with the three categories of variants. Augmented/reduced structures identify mainly conceptual variants, contextual structures and segmentation rules of linguistic variants, and other competing structures of denominative variants.

Another observation is about the low quantity of denominative variants discovered by the GGRV. We believe that denominative variants, contrary to conceptual variants, derive mainly from synonymic substitution. Their detection, and more generally, the detection of synonymic variants of terms, requires a paradigmatic analysis. This task will be performed in the next chapter.

CHAPTER 8

Synonymic variants

The detection of denominative variants generated by synonymic substitution requires appropriate methods for the occurrence of those variants that might appear isolated from the term. Distributional analysis is based upon the idea of a correlation between the contexts in which the words appear and their semantic content. It supplies a theoretical framework allowing to perform a paradigmatic analysis, necessary for discovering synonymic variants of simple terms. This chapter details the distributional method briefly presented in Section 6.1.4 and introduces a new method, the semi-compositional method, adapted to the detection of synonymic complex terms.[1]

8.1 Distributional analysis

Distributional analysis is the most popular method for finding synonyms in corpora. It relies on the contextualist approach to word meaning: "You shall know a word by the company it keeps." (Firth 1957) Thus, the meaning of a word is defined by the set of contexts in which it occurs. Two words, generally two lexical units sharing similar contexts, are semantically linked. And words with similar meaning tend to occur in similar contexts (Harris 1954). The more similar the contexts, the more semantically close are the words. There have been many studies based on distributional paradigms (Hindle 1990; Grefenstette 1994b; Lin 1998; Hagiwara 2008; Ferret 2010, 2013). They differ according to the definition of the adopted context, the methods for comparing these contexts and the ranking of these words identified as semantically related. Lin (1998) for instance, introduced the idea that words sharing more syntactic relations are more likely to be synonyms. This idea has been extended to the syntactic path (Hagiwara 2008) in order to account for indirect syntactic dependencies. When a large number of semantically related words are detected, Ferret (2013) improves their ranking by detecting and by declassifying the more ambiguous of them.

1. This chapter is based on Hazem and Daille (2014), although the content has been substantially augmented.

Distributional analysis provides, for a lexical unit, a list of words potentially in semantic relation. A close word pair proposed by distributional analysis is not semantically featured. The semantic relation, if it exists, does not pick up synonymy or near-synonymy only; it also picks up other classical semantic relations such as antonymy, hypernymy, co-hyponymy, meronymy, and non-classic semantic relations such as action/agent (Morris and Hirst 2004). Morlane-Hondère (2013) exhaustively studied semantic relations generated by automatic distributional analysis for French in the general domain. The author confirms the broad set of semantic relations that have been identified.

Distributional analysis requires interpreting the semantic relation of a word pair, which causes many problems. Indeed, it is not obvious to make a clear distinction between, for example, synonyms and other semantically related words (Lin et al. 2003; Van der Plas and Tiedemann 2006). Resnik (1993: 18) states that: "It would seem that the information captured using distributional methods is not precisely syntactic, nor purely semantic – in some sense the only word that appears is *distributional*." Distributional relations cannot be precisely described.

8.1.1 Modelling of a distributional method

Distributional analysis assumes that two words are in a semantic relation if they share the same lexical contexts, so the aim of the distributional approach is to compare the contexts of words to find out similar words.

Modelisation of word contexts adopts the vectorial model: each element of a vector, called "context vector", is a word of the context to which a weight is associated, reflecting its importance towards the lexical unit that it features in a corpus (cf. Section 6.1.4). This weight is calculated thanks to an association measure. The context of each word is modelled in a vector, then a score of similarity is computed between all context vectors. The words having high similarity scores are retained as semantically related words.

Association measures

Association measures identify remarkable cooccurrences in corpus, i.e. pairs of words significantly associated. They compare the frequency of cooccurrences of two words with the frequency of occurrences of the one without the other and with the total number of words in the corpus. An association measure evaluates the strength of the bond between two words in a corpus. The underlying hypothesis to these measures is that lexical forms are randomly distributed in the corpus. Contingency tables used in statistics for measuring the association of two qualitative variables (Everitt 1992) can also be used for measuring the association between two lexical forms in a set C of contexts. A contingency table groups together two forms F_i and F_j, the number of their cooccurrences, and the number of cooccurrences of the one without the other, *nbocc*(F_i, F_j) is the number of cooccurrences of F_i and F_j, $\neg F_i$ represents all of lexical forms except F_i.

	F_j	$\neg F_j$	
F_i	$O_{11} = nbocc(F_i, F_j)$	$O_{12} = nbocc(F_i, \neg F_j)$	L_1
$\neg F_i$	$O_{21} = nbocc(\neg F_i, F_j)$	$O_{22} = nbocc(\neg Fi, \neg F_j)$	L_2
	C_1	C_2	N

	F_j	$\neg F_j$
F_i	$E_{11} = \frac{L_1 C_1}{N}$	$E_{12} = \frac{L_1 C_2}{N}$
$\neg F_i$	$E_{21} = \frac{L_2 C_1}{N}$	$E_{22} = \frac{L_2 C_2}{N}$

Point-wise mutual information

Point-wise mutual information introduced by Fano (1961) shows the quantity of information shared by two qualitative variables. Point-wise mutual information estimates and compares the number of occurrences observed with the number of cooccurrences expected from the two lexical forms:

$$MI = \log_2 \frac{O_{11}}{E_{11}} \tag{8.1}$$

When $O_{11} = E_{11}$, the association measure value is zero. When $O_{11} < E_{11}$, the two forms appear less frequently than expected, there is no association between the two forms. Point-wise mutual information tends to prefer rare events, so that mutual information will be identical for $O_{11} = 2$, $E_{11} = 1$ and $O_{11} = 100$, $E_{11} = 50$. To rebalance them in favour of the observation, two solutions are possible. One is to increase the weight of the observation and the other is to balance mutual information by the observation. The augmentation of the weight is carried out by putting the power:

$$MI^k = \log_2 \frac{O_{11}^k}{E_{11}} \tag{8.2}$$

The value of $k = 3$ gives the best results.

Local mutual information
Local mutual information balances mutual information by the observation:

$$MI_l = \sum_{ij} O_{ij} \log_2 \frac{O_{ij}}{E_{ij}} \tag{8.3}$$

It is then homogeneous to log-likelihood ratio.

Log-likelihood ratio
Log-likelihood ratio (Dunning 1993) evaluates in which measure it is likely to obtain such observation. It is less sensitive to low values of estimation but it does not cut, contrary to point-wise mutual information which makes a decision about a non-association.

$$LLR = 2\sum_{ij} O_{ij} \log \frac{O_{ij}}{E_{ij}} \tag{8.4}$$

Point-wise mutual information evaluates in which measure occurrence F_i determines occurrence of F_j whereas local mutual information and log-likelihood ratio evaluate in which measure the distribution of F_i governs the distribution of F_j.

Odds-ratio
Discounted log-odds was proposed by Evert (2008) for the detection of collocations.

$$LO = \log \frac{(O_{11} + \frac{1}{2}) \times (O_{21} + \frac{1}{2})}{(O_{21} + \frac{1}{2}) \times (O_{12} + \frac{1}{2})} \tag{8.5}$$

All contexts m_i of the word M are gathered together in a vector or ordered according to their association score *assoc(M, m_i)*, the context vector of the word v_M. Representations of terms as vectors provide a mathematical basis for assigning continuous values to the amount of similarity between two terms using different corpus-based similarity measures.

Similarity measures
Context vectors are created for all words of the corpus. In order to find out the closest words to the word M, the context vector v_M is compared to all context vectors associated with words of the corpus. Comparison is carried out by a similarity measure. Similarity measures explain how similar two terms are to each other by computing the distance between the context vectors. The most popular one is Cosine similarity (Salton and Lesk 1968) (COS) or weighted Jaccard index (JAC) (Grefenstette 1994b). Jaccard's coefficient is also known as Tanimoto coefficient. Candidates in semantic relation with M will be the words ranked according to their

similarity score. A higher similarity score between two words implies a semantically strong similarity.

Cosine similarity between two terms is based on the angular difference between the context vectors of the two terms. The range of the similarity value can be from −1 to 1, but the range can be and is usually made in the range [0,1] by normalising the context vector where 1 is the upper bound indicating that the two terms are identical, while 0 indicates that the two terms have nothing in common.

$$COS(V_M, V_k) = \frac{\Sigma_t\, assoc(M, m_t) \cdot assoc(K, m_t)}{\sqrt{\Sigma_t\, assoc(M, m_t)^2 \cdot \Sigma_t\, assoc(K, m_t)^2}} \qquad (8.6)$$

The range of values given by Jaccard's coefficient is 0 to 1 where no shared context words is zero and identical context vectors is 1. It can be defined as the proportion of contexts belonging to either of the words and shared by both words; i.e. the ratio between the size of the intersection of the context vectors and the size of the union of context vectors.

$$JAC(V_M, V_k) = \frac{\Sigma_t\, min(assoc(M, m_t)\,,\, assoc(K, m_t))}{\Sigma_t\, max(assoc(M, m_t)\,,\, \Sigma_t\, assoc(K, m_t))} \qquad (8.7)$$

8.1.2 Observations in specialised domains

The distributional approach has been used to find synonyms of words in large-sized corpora made of several hundreds of millions of words. For corpora of specialised languages of small size made of several hundreds of thousands of words, the distributional analysis does not supply probative results. For example, the classic implementation of distributional analysis modelling the context of terms by the help of a sliding window and using point-wise mutual information (MI Equation 8.1), as association measure, and cosine (COS Equation 8.6), as similarity measure supplies the results presented in Table 8.1 for three simple terms in French, English and Spanish for [EOL]. It is hard to interpret the pairs even if they appear at the first ranks. An interpretation for the first ranks would be, for French, a collocation *ferme éolienne* 'wind farm', for English, a hypernym *construction* being a type of *operation*, and, for Spanish, a holonym, *torre* 'tower' being an element of the *aerogenerador*. The pairs appearing at further ranks are semantically opaque in their majority. Candidates in bold will be kept by the semi-compositional approach during the intrinsic evaluation on [EOL] (cf. Section 8.4).

8.2 Compositional method

The compositional method is applied to create synonyms of a complex term. It is often preferred to the distributional method which is unsuitable for the processing of multi-word units and even more for complex terms belonging to a specialised domain. Most synonyms of complex terms are obtained by synonymic substitution. The compositional method relies upon the assumption of semantic composition to generate the synonyms of a complex term: one of the components of the complex term is substituted by one of its synonyms. The complex term generated is validated by searching it in the corpus. We propose to exploit the property of compositionality for identifying semantic variants of complex terms in corpora. We adopt the definition of synonymic variants of complex terms presented in Section 4.2.1.

Table 8.1 Example of results of distributional approach for Fr, En and Es on [EOL].

Rank	Fr: *ferme*	En: *construction*	Es: *torre*
1	*éolien*	*operation*	*aerogeneradores*
2	*horn*	*project*	*aerogenerador*
3	*aller*	*impact*	*pala*
4	*fréquence*	*road*	*rotor*
5	*puissance*	*require*	*estar*
6	*rev*	*aera*	***turbina***
7	*réseau*	*activity*	*altura*
8	***parc***	*plan*	*celosia*
…			
62		***tower***	

Hammon and Nazarenko (2001) defined three rules to detect synonymy relations. Given the complex candidate terms $CCT_1 = (T_1, E_1)$ and $CCT_2 = (T_2, E_2)$ with T_1 (respectively T_2) the head of the complex term and E_1 (respectively E_2) its expansion, and $syn(CT_1\ CT_2)$ a synonym relation between the candidate terms CT_1 and CT_2, the following inferences rules are used:

$$R_1\!: T_1 = T_2 \wedge syn(E_1,E_2) \supset syn(CCT_1, CCT_2)$$
$$R_2\!: E_1 = E_2 \wedge syn(T_1\ T_2) \supset syn(CCT_1, CCT_2)$$
$$R_3\!: syn(T_1, T_2) \wedge syn(E_1,E_2) \supset syn(CCT_1,CCT_2)$$

Rule R_1 means that heads are identical and expansions are synonymic, such as *general collector/common collector.* Synonym extraction of single-word terms such as *general* in this previous example is carried out using a dictionary of synonyms.

Jacquemin (2001) took up this idea by generalising the use of synonyms for different variants made by his English grammar of variants. The dictionary of general language synonyms, Wordnet 1.6 (Fellbaum 1998), was used. For example, if the term is *cell death,* Wordnet supplies for *death* the synonym *destruction,* the synonymic substitution can be applied for a rule expressing a variant of coordination such as *cell infiltrating and destruction,* for the term *cell death.*

8.3 Semi-compositional method

The semi-compositional method, like the compositional method, hypothesises compositionality of complex terms. But the nature of the relation between the substituted elements is no longer constrainted to the sole relation of synonymy.

Kraft (2007) notes that expressions and their parts are usually ambiguous and that a meaning can only be assigned to their analyses. We illustrate this remark with the analysis of multi-word term's synonyms that are recorded in term banks. Examining the parts of synonymic MWT of the wind energy domain sharing at least one common content part, we face miscellaneous relations:

1. Synonymy: *energy output/energy production,* the pair given by Termium[2] where *output/production* are synonyms;
2. Hypernymy: *turbine noise/turbine sound,* the pair given by Grand dictionnaire terminologique[3] where *sound* is a hypernym of *noise,* or *implantación de las máquinas / implantación de aerogeneradores,* the pair given by the Panlatin lexicon where *máquina* 'machine' is a hypernym of *aerogenerador;*
3. Undefined: *nuclear plant/nuclear station,* the pair given by Termium where *plant* and *station* are not related semantically or *arbre lent/arbre primaire* 'primary shaft', the pair given by Terminalf without semantic relation between *lent* 'slow' and *primaire* 'primary'.

The parts of a complex term and of its synonym do not necessarily share a relation of synonymy and can share other relations. The semi-compositional method that we intend to apply to the detection of synonymic variants of complex terms combines the compositional approach and the distributional analysis. We exploit the compositionality property and the synonymic substitution. But the latter is extended to all terms that are related by contextual semantic relations. The noisy character of synonyms produced by the distributional analysis for a simple term as seen at Section 8.1.2 will be reduced thanks to a syntagmatic constraint: the semantic relation between two terms must appear inside a pattern of a complex term and must occur in the corpus.

2. http://www.btb.termiumplus.gc.ca

3. http://www.oqlf.gouv.qc.ca/

The semi-compositional method has three steps:

1. The complex term is at first decomposed into constitutive elements;
2. For each of its parts, the distributional approach identifies simple terms that are semantically related to them;
3. The complex term of a synonymic candidate is generated with recomposing rules, and its validity is checked in the corpus.

For each complex term (TC), a rule of combination sets either its left part and substitutes its right part with a semantically related term supplied by the distributional analysis, or its right part and substitutes its left part with a term supplied by the distributional analysis. These two possible combinations match rules R_1^G and R_2^G:

$$R_1^G : T_1 = \mathrm{T}_2 \wedge sem(E_1,E_2) \supset sem(CCT_1,CCT_2)$$
$$R_2^G : \mathrm{E}_1 = \mathrm{E}_2 \wedge sem(T_1,T_2) \supset sem(CCT_1,CCT_2)$$

These rules allow to obtain the following synonymic terms:

(EOL) En: *wind turbine/wind machine, power supply/energy supply*
Fr: *énergie renouvelable* 'renewable energy'/*énergie durable* 'sustainable energy',
(SEIN) En: *invasive carcinoma/infiltrating carcinoma, adjuvant therapy/adjuvant treatment,*
Fr: *curage du ganglion* 'lymph node dissection'/*ablation du ganglion* 'lymph node ablation'.

The list of candidates of synonymic terms obtained by using rules R_1^G and R_2^G is checked either with n-grams or with complex terms extracted from the corpus. Candidates that do not occur in the corpus are removed from the list of candidates of synonymic terms.

8.4 Cross-lingual and cross-method observations

An intrinsic evaluation judges the quality of a method regardless of any application. It is based upon a reference compiled previously from terminological resources acknowledged and available for a specialised domain that inventories synonyms of complex terms. Of course, this type of judgement offers only a fragmented assessment of the performance of the method, because it is impossible to make a list of all possible synonyms of a term produced in various contexts.

Intrinsic evaluation allows us to compare compositional and semi-compositional methods for the detection of synonymic variants in specialised corpora. Compositional and semi-compositional methods are applied here only to syntagmatic compounds. They could be applied to German morphological compounds after using a splitting tool such as COMPOST (cf. Section 10.3.3). Indeed, we demonstrated that compositional and semi-compositional methods apply to

German native compounds after splitting were capable of identifying their English translations from comparable corpora (Morin and Daille 2012). But, handling all kinds of morphological compounds in distributional analysis remains a research topic that will be discussed in Chapter 11.

This evaluation is performed using [EOL] for French, English and Spanish, and [CAN] for French and English (cf. Section 5.2). The a priori lists of reference listing synonymic complex terms were compiled from existing terminological resources. We apply a standard implementation of the distributional analysis. We evaluate with common measurements used in distributional analysis.

8.4.1 Reference lists of synonyms

Reference lists have been built from various terminological resources. Only the resources that list synonymic terms in their terminological records have been examined. In such lists or databases, synonyms are not systematically present, and in records including them, there can be several synonymic variants. Most are terms related by other types of semantic relations, such as near-synonymy or hypernymy. Many variants of complex terms such as abbreviations, competing syntactic patterns, lexical reductions may also be listed in them. All these variants of complex terms are not included in our lists of reference because they can be detected thanks to a the GGRV presented in Chapter 7.

We build the reference list of [EOL] monolingually for each language. We note T the term, and V the variant.

For French, we selected syntagmatic compounds of the terminological list in the wind energy domain of Terminalf[4] and its 84 records. Synonyms are indicated under the domain competing form. 56 syntagmatic compounds accept between 1 and 3 synonymic variants, altogether 76 synonyms. To these 76 synonyms, 14 synonyms or near-synonyms are added after the reading of terminological records, especially by consulting the domains definition or genre. Content of the domain genre often makes a reference to a hypernym that can be used as a synonymic variant in the context. The synonymic variants listed in Terminalf which have not been included in our list are denominative or conceptual variants:

1. denominative variants obtained by compression upon the functional elements: T *rotor de Darrieus,* V *rotor Darrieus* 'Darrieus wind turbine';
2. conceptual variants obtained by anaphorical reduction: T *traînée aérodynamique* 'aerodynamic drag', V *traînée* 'drag', or T *coefficient de puissance du rotor* 'wind turbine power coefficient', V *coefficient de puissance* 'power coefficient'.

4. http://www.terminalf.scicog.fr

For Spanish, 64 syntagmatic compounds and their synonyms have been collected from the Panlatin lexicon of wind energy.[5] This lexicon includes 300 entries in eight languages. Some terms include synonyms available for Spanish in two different geographic zones: Spain and Mexico. For example, the Spanish term (Castillan) *aerogenerador de dos palas* 'two-bladed wind turbine' has its equivalent in Mexican Spanish *aerogenerador de doble aspa.* The geographic terminological variants are fully considered as synonyms. In comparison with Terminalf, which includes only simple terms or complex terms composed of two lexical units, the Panlatin lexicon makes a list of many terms of length higher than two full lexical units such as *aerogenerador de eje vertical con geometría variable* 'vertical axis wind turbine and variable geometry'. The listed synonyms include denominative and conceptual variants that we have not included in our list:

- denominative variants obtained by
  - synonymic substitution that substitute the preposition used inside the complex term: T *enfriamiento del aire,* V *enfriamiento por aire* 'air cooling'
  - compression: T *efecto de aceleración* 'effect of acceleration', V *efecto acelerador* 'accelerating effect' with *acelerador* derived from the noun *aceleración;*
  - competing patterns to those whose components at the position of expansion of the complex term have been permuted: T *aerogenerador para vientos de baja velocidad* 'lit. wind turbine for winds of low speed', V *aerogenerador para bajas velocidades de viento* 'lit. wind turbine for low speeds of wind';
  - lexical reduction: T *efecto de pérdida aerodinámica* 'effect of aerodynamic loss', V *efecto de* <u>*entrada en*</u> *pérdida aerodinámica* 'lit. entrance effect of aerodinamic loss'.
- conceptual variants obtained by expansion with the insertion of a morphological component: T *acoplamiento dinámico* 'dynamic coupling', V *acoplamiento* <u>*aero*</u>*dinámico* 'aerodynamic coupling'.

For English, we selected 84 syntagmatic compounds and their synonyms from the glossary of wind energy from the online part of the book (Gipe 2004) and from the terminological database Termium.[6] As for French and Spanish, we discard synonymic variants that can be identified by morphological or syntactic analysis.

Synonymic variants are less diversified than for French and Spanish. The most frequent synonymic variants are denominative variants obtained by lexical reduction such as the variant *wind plant* of the term *wind power plant.*

As a result of filtering and of corpus projection, our initial reference lists are reduced to 34 French, 26 Spanish, and 20 English syntagmatic compounds with their synonyms.

5. www.realiter.net/wp-content/uploads/2013/06/pan-energie-power.pdf

6. http://www.btb.termiumplus.gc.ca/tpv2alpha/alpha-eng.html?lang=eng

This method has been reiterated in order to build the lists of synonyms of complex terms in the breast cancer domain. Termium was used for this other domain. Here again, we discard the same types of variants as for (EOL). After filtering with [CAN] in each language, the reference lists of the breast cancer domain contain 20 French terms and 16 English terms associated with their synonyms.

The small size of reference lists, either for (EOL) or (CAN), can be explained by the small size of the specialised corpora which contains few specialised terms and few synonymic variants. But a more plausible explanation is that the majority of these synonymic variants are contextual. It is difficult for a terminologist to predict and to detect all synonymic variants that can be produced. Contextual synonymic variants do not generally appear in a dictionary resource (Kremer et al. 2014).

8.4.2 Experimental setup parameters

Experimental parameters are those of the distributional method, the dictionary of synonyms required by the compositional method, and the lists of candidate terms extracted from corpora for filtering synonymic candidates for the two methods we wish to test: compositional and semi-compositional methods.

Distributional method
A state-of-the-art implementation of the distributional method presented in Section 8.1.1 requires to set values for three major parameters and to decide upon a combination of measures as it has been recalled that it is an important factor:

1. size of the window used to build the context vectors;
2. size of the context vectors;
3. association measure to estimate the strength of the bond between two words occurring in a corpus;
4. similarity measure to calculate how close two words are by computing the distance between their context vectors.

To build the context vectors, we chose a 7-word span, i.e. 3 words before and 3 words after the word to be characterised. The size of the context vector is not constrained. Several measures are retained in order to explore several combinations of association and similarity measures. Association measures are point-wise mutual information (MI Equation 8.1), log-likelihood ratio (LLR Equation 8.4) and discounted log-odds (LO Equation 8.5). Similarity measures are cosine (COS Equation 8.6) and Jaccard (JAC Equation 8.7). Combinations investigated are LLR-JAC, MI-COS and LO-COS. Combination MI-COS is the state-of-the-art combination of the distributional approach (Ferret 2010).

Dictionaries of synonyms

The compositional method uses a dictionary of synonyms. One of the components of the term is substituted by its synonyms recorded in the dictionary. For French, we use the on-line dictionary DES[7] (Morel and François 2015) that record the synonyms of French words. DES contains 49,168 entries and 201,511 synonym relations. For English, we build a dictionary of synonyms from the lexical database WordNet[8] (Fellbaum 1998). WordNet contains approximately 117,000 English entries (synset). The main relation among words in WordNet is synonymy.

Filtering lists

Two lists extracted from the corpus are used: a list of n-grams and a list of candidate complex terms supplied by a terminology extraction tool. Synonymic candidates that do not belong to these lists will be ruled out. These two lists are built automatically from our preliminarily lemmatised corpus. N-grams allow us to eliminate combinations that do not occur in a contiguous way in the corpus. In addition, candidate terms supplied by TermSuite (cf. Section 10.3) ensure the syntagmatic correction of synonymic candidates.

8.4.3 Evaluation measures

To evaluate compositional and semi-compositional methods, we calculate precision on the first candidate synonym (P1), the first five synonymic candidates (P5), and the first ten synonymic candidates (P10). Precision P is the fraction of the candidate synonyms that belong to the reference list. In addition, we calculate *MAP* (Mean Average Precision) (Manning et al. 2008: 147–148), average of precisions computed at all positions. MAP is computed only for the semi-compositional method.

$$MAP = \frac{1}{|W|} \sum_{i=1}^{|W|} \frac{1}{Rank_i} \quad (8.8)$$

where $|W|$ is the size of the reference list and $Rank_i$ is the position of the synonym in the ranked list. If the synonym is not found in the reference list, MAP is equal to 0.

If the set of synonym candidates composed of the first, the first five, and the first ten candidates confirms the precision of the parameter setup at the top of the ranked candidates, MAP supplies the mean average of the parameter setup. Thus, a configuration A with a better precision at the first rank than a configuration B may have a smaller MAP if candidate synonyms ranked after the first position include less synonyms or synonyms at further positions than the configuration B.

7. http://www.crisco.unicaen.fr/des/synonyms

8. http://wordnetweb.princeton.edu/perl/webwn/

8.4.4 Results

Compositional method (*Comp*) and semi-compositional method (*Semi-Comp*) supply lists of synonymic candidates for each complex term of the reference lists. We propose to evaluate three rankings:

Association score: Synonymic candidates are ordered according to the decreasing value of the association score that weights the substituted component ($\text{Semi-Comp}_{\text{assoc}}$));
Count: Synonymic candidates are ordered according to the decreasing value of the number of occurrences of the substituted component in the corpus ($\text{Semi-Comp}_{\text{count}}$));
Frequency ratio: Synonymic candidates are ordered according to the decreasing value of the frequency ratio of the complex term for which synonyms have been sought and of the synonymic candidate ($\text{Semi-Comp}_{\text{ratio}}$).

Synonymic candidates are filtered by using two filtering lists: the list of n-grams, noted *without syntactic patterns,* that is written in the second column of each table of results, and the list of complex term candidates, noted *with syntactic patterns,* that is written in the third column of each table of results.

Three setups lead to three combinations of parameters. For each of them, the combination of an association measure and a similarity measure is explored. These three combinations constitute only a subset of the combinatory of association and similarity measures, but these are classically used in distributional analysis and have been distinguished comparatively to other combinations (Curran and Moens 2002; Panchenko and Morozova 2012). Configurations are written on the ordinate axis of tables. For instance, caption MI-COS means that the distributional approach provided by synonym components uses mutual information as the association measure and cosine as the similarity measure.

We show below examples of pairs of synonymic complex terms in French, English, and Spanish for [EOL] produced by the semi-compositional method using combined MI-COS and filtering thanks to syntactically-liked terms. These complex pairs have as components the simple terms for which we applied the distributional analysis presented in Section 8.1.2 and shown the results in Table 8.1.

Fr: *ferme éolienne* / *parc éolien* at rank 2 with *parc* proposed at rank 8 by the distributional analysis;
En: *lattice construction* / *lattice tower* at rank 1 with *tower* proposed at rank 62 by the distributional analysis;
Es: *torre éolica* 'wind turbine'/ *turbina éolica* at rank 1 with *turbina* proposed at rank 6 by the distributional analysis.

Quantitative analysis

For each configuration, the best results are written in bold in the table of results.

Table 8.2 gives the results of the compositional and the semi-compositional approaches on [EOL] for French. The results of the compositional approach are very low compared to the semi-compositional approach, regardless of the configuration. The dictionary of synonyms in French does not list all synonyms of terms belonging to specialised domains. The best results with a precision of 26.4% for the first candidate, 55.8% for the first five candidates and MAP of 38.5% are those of Semi-Comp$_{assoc}$ with the configuration MI-COS and with filtering by syntactic patterns. Best precision of 55.8% for the first five candidates is shared by all configurations with Semi-Comp$_{count}$ with any kind of filtering. Best precision for the first ten candidates is given by Semi-Comp$_{assoc}$ with the configuration LO-COS and with filtering by syntactic patterns.

Table 8.2 Results of compositional and semi-compositional approaches for Fr on [EOL].

	Method	without syntactic patterns				with syntactic patterns			
		P1	P5	P10	MAP	P1	P5	P10	MAP
	Comp	–	–	–	0.25	–	–	–	0.25
LLR-JAC	Semi-Comp$_{assoc}$	17.6	52.9	52.9	31.7	23.5	52.9	58.8	38.2
	Semi-Comp$_{count}$	14.7	**55.8**	64.7	31.2	17.6	**55.8**	64.7	34.8
	Semi-Comp$_{ratio}$	5.88	23.5	35.2	14.9	5.88	47.0	52.9	23.2
MI-COS	Semi-Comp$_{assoc}$	17.6	47.0	52.9	29.4	**26.4**	**55.8**	61.7	**38.5**
	Semi-Comp$_{count}$	14.7	**55.8**	64.7	31.2	17.6	**55.8**	64.7	34.8
	Semi-Comp$_{ratio}$	5.88	23.5	35.2	14.9	5.88	47.0	52.9	23.2
LO-COS	Semi-Comp$_{assoc}$	14.7	44.1	47.0	26.9	23.5	52.9	**70.5**	37.9
	Semi-Comp$_{count}$	14.7	**55.8**	64.7	31.2	17.6	**55.8**	64.7	34.8
	Semi-Comp$_{ratio}$	5.88	23.5	35.2	14.9	5.88	47.0	52.9	23.2

Table 8.3 gives the results of the compositional and the semi-compositional approaches on [EOL] for English. Results of the compositional approach are again very low compared to those of the semi-compositional approach.The best results of the semi-compositional approach with the first candidate of 45%, the first five candidates of 80%, the first ten candidates of 90% and MAP of 61.1% are obtained with Semi-Comp$_{count}$ and with filtering by syntactic patterns. Results are identical whatever the configuration. Filtering influences the results only marginally.

Table 8.3 Results of compositional and semi-compositional approaches for En on [EOL].

	Method	without syntactic patterns				with syntactic patterns			
		P1	P5	P10	MAP	P1	P5	P10	MAP
	Comp	–	–	–	3.63	–	–	–	3.63
LLR-JAC	$\text{Semi-Comp}_{\text{assoc}}$	20.0	55.0	65.0	36.1	15.0	60.0	70.0	38.2
	$\text{Semi-Comp}_{\text{count}}$	**45.0**	**80.0**	**90.0**	59.2	**45.0**	**80.0**	**90.0**	**61.1**
	$\text{Semi-Comp}_{\text{ratio}}$	20.0	40.0	40.0	28.2	15.0	40.0	45.0	26.7
MI-COS	$\text{Semi-Comp}_{\text{assoc}}$	15.0	55.0	65.0	32.8	15.0	60.0	70.0	35.8
	$\text{Semi-Comp}_{\text{count}}$	**45.0**	**80.0**	**90.0**	59.2	**45.0**	**80.0**	**90.0**	**61.1**
	$\text{Semi-Comp}_{\text{ratio}}$	20.0	40.0	40.0	28.2	15.0	40.0	45.0	26.7
LO-COS	$\text{Semi-Comp}_{\text{assoc}}$	15.0	40.0	55.0	27.2	10.0	40.0	60.0	26.8
	$\text{Semi-Comp}_{\text{count}}$	**45.0**	**80.0**	**90.0**	60.0	**45.0**	**80.0**	**90.0**	**61.1**
	$\text{Semi-Comp}_{\text{ratio}}$	20.0	40.0	40.0	28.3	15.0	40.0	45.0	26.7

Table 8.4 gives the results of the compositional and the semi-compositional approaches on [EOL] for Spanish. These results confirm the poor performance of the compositional approach for Spanish compared to the semi-compositional approach already seen for French and English. The results are close to those obtained for French but more clear-cut. The best results with a precision of 23% for the first candidate, 57.6% for the first five candidates, 65.3% for the first ten candidates, and MAP of 37% are those of $\text{Semi-Comp}_{\text{assoc}}$ with the configuration MI-COS and with filtering by syntactic patterns. The best precision of 65.3% for the first ten candidates is shared by $\text{Semi-Comp}_{\text{assoc}}$ with the configuration LO-COS and with filtering by syntactic patterns. The precision for the first five candidates with $\text{Semi-Comp}_{\text{count}}$ with any configuration and with filtering by syntactic patterns is inferior for 20% to the best results for Spanish.

Table 8.4 Results of compositional and semi-compositional approaches for Es on [EOL].

	Method	without syntactic patterns				with syntactic patterns			
		P1	P5	P10	MAP	P1	P5	P10	MAP
	Comp	–	–	–	8.09	–	–	–	8.09
LLR-JAC	$\text{Semi-Comp}_{\text{assoc}}$	7.69	38.4	42.3	19.7	11.5	50.0	61.5	29.8
	$\text{Semi-Comp}_{\text{count}}$	15.3	34.6	42.3	24.8	15.3	38.4	46.1	25.7
	$\text{Semi-Comp}_{\text{ratio}}$	3.84	11.5	15.3	7.90	11.5	30.7	42.3	23.1
MI-COS	$\text{Semi-Comp}_{\text{assoc}}$	15.3	38.4	42.3	25.3	**23.0**	**57.6**	**65.3**	**37.0**
	$\text{Semi-Comp}_{\text{count}}$	15.3	34.6	42.3	24.8	15.3	38.4	46.1	25.7
	$\text{Semi-Comp}_{\text{ratio}}$	3.84	11.5	15.3	7.90	11.5	30.7	42.3	22.5
LO-COS	$\text{Semi-Comp}_{\text{assoc}}$	0.0	30.7	42.3	14.4	19.2	53.8	**65.3**	32.6
	$\text{Semi-Comp}_{\text{count}}$	15.3	34.6	42.3	24.9	15.3	38.4	50.0	25.8
	$\text{Semi-Comp}_{\text{ratio}}$	3.84	11.5	15.3	7.90	11.5	30.7	42.3	22.5

To sum up, the semi-compositional approach outperforms the compositional approach for any configuration chosen. As for the ranking of the synonymic candidates, association score and frequency are to be favoured. Filtering by syntactic patterns performs better than n-grams. These three configurations involving different association measures and similarity measures yield close results that differ slightly according to language and ranking score. Ranking with frequency shows a great stability against the configuration chosen and for three languages. A possible explanation can be a strong correlation between the frequency of terms for which synonyms are searched and their synonyms. A similarity measure always favours a similar distribution (Weeds 2003).

Tables 8.5 and 8.6 show the results of the compositional and the semi-compositional approaches on the breast cancer corpus, respectively for French and English.

Unsurprisingly, the semi-compositional approach yields better results than the compositional approach. For French, best results with a precision of 31.5% for the first candidate, 73.6% for the first ten candidates, and MAP of 40.4% are obtained with Semi-Comp$_{count}$ by using the configuration LO-COS and with filtering without syntactic patterns. Nevertheless, precision of 31.5% for the first candidate is reached by all rankings whatever the configuration and the filtering, and precision of 52.6% for the first five candidates is given by Semi-Comp$_{count}$ with filtering with syntactic patterns whatever the configuration. Improvement of MAP for filtering without syntactic patterns appears between ranks five to ten only, which mitigates its interest. For English, best results with a precision of 26.6% for the first candidate, 53.3% for the first five candidates, 53.3% for the first ten candidates, and MAP of 38.1% are obtained with Semi-Comp$_{count}$ by using the configuration LLR-JAC or MI-COS and with filtering with syntactic patterns.

Table 8.5 Results of compositional and semi-compositional approaches for Fr on [CAN].

	Method	**without syntactic patterns**				**with syntactic patterns**			
		P1	**P5**	**P10**	**MAP**	**P1**	**P5**	**P10**	**MAP**
	Comp	–	–	–	4.92	–	–	–	4.92
LLR-JAC	Semi-Comp$_{assoc}$	5.26	15.7	47.3	13.9	26.3	47.3	57.8	34.7
	Semi-Comp$_{count}$	**31.5**	42.1	**73.6**	40.3	**31.5**	**52.6**	63.1	39.9
	Semi-Comp$_{ratio}$	0	15.7	31.5	8.6	15.7	47.3	47.3	30.3
MI-COS	Semi-Comp$_{assoc}$	10.5	36.8	52.6	19.9	21.0	**52.6**	57.8	35.7
	Semi-Comp$_{count}$	**31.5**	42.1	**73.6**	40.3	**31.5**	**52.6**	63.1	39.9
	Semi-Comp$_{ratio}$	0	15.7	31.5	8.6	15.7	47.3	47.3	30.3
LO-COS	Semi-Comp$_{assoc}$	15.7	42.1	52.6	27.1	26.3	57.8	57.8	38.5
	Semi-Comp$_{count}$	**31.5**	42.1	**73.6**	**40.4**	**31.5**	**52.6**	63.1	39.9
	Semi-Comp$_{ratio}$	0	15.7	31.5	8.6	15.7	47.3	47.3	30.3

Table 8.6 Results of compositional and semi-compositional approaches for En on [CAN].

	Method	without syntactic patterns				with syntactic patterns			
		P1	**P5**	**P10**	**MAP**	**P1**	**P5**	**P10**	**MAP**
	Comp	–	–	–	7.03	–	–	–	7.03
LLR-JAC	Semi-Comp$_{assoc}$	6.66	20.0	26.6	13.3	0	26.6	40.0	16.7
	Semi-Comp$_{count}$	20.0	46.6	46.6	29.0	**26.6**	**53.3**	**53.3**	**38.1**
	Semi-Comp$_{ratio}$	0.0	6.66	6.66	3.0	0	20.0	33.3	9.0
MI-COS	Semi-Comp$_{assoc}$	6.66	20.0	26.6	12.6	6.66	26.6	53.3	18.1
	Semi-Comp$_{count}$	20.0	46.6	46.6	29.0	**26.6**	**53.3**	**53.3**	**38.1**
	Semi-Comp$_{ratio}$	0.0	6.66	6.66	3.0	0	20.0	33.3	9.0
LO-COS	Semi-Comp$_{assoc}$	6.66	13.3	20.0	11.0	6.66	20.0	33.3	15.7
	Semi-Comp$_{count}$	20.0	40.0	40.0	25.7	**26.6**	46.6	46.6	34.8
	Semi-Comp$_{ratio}$	0.0	6.66	6.66	3.0	0	20.0	33.3	9.0

Results of Semi-Comp that ranks synonymic candidates according to frequency ratio are very low. This confirms the inefficiency of this type of ranking. The semi-compositional method yielding the best results in average on the first candidate, ranking according to frequency and filtering by syntactic patterns, is capable of identifying a synonym only once in four.

On the contrary, the semi-compositional method that ranks the candidate according to frequency, with the configuration MI-COS and filtering by syntactic patterns always gives the best results for the first five candidates for any domain or any language. The lowest score of precision for the first five candidates is 52.6% for French and the highest one is 80% for English on [EOL]. The examination of the first five synonymic candidates shows that two to three synonyms are supplied in average. The study of results of the first five candidates proposed by the semi-compositional method can help, with a tiny effort, to make a list of contextual synonymic variants that are not usually recorded in a dictionary resource (Kremer et al. 2014).

Qualitative analysis

It is interesting to complete the quantitative analysis of results supplied by the compositional and the semi-compositional methods with a qualitative analysis that examines the synonymic candidates proposed as well as the differences between rankings and filterings.

Rankings

For Spanish and (EOL), the best ranking is obtained very clearly with association measure while for French and English in (EOL) and (CAN) it is with frequency. We investigate Spanish results in order to understand this difference in behaviour.

The Spanish reference list includes peculiarities compared with other reference lists: longer complex terms and Spanish geographic variants. Many candidates at the first ranks are shared by the two rankings such as *torre eólica* 'wind tower' [ESP] / *turbina eólica* 'wind turbine' [ESP] or *flujo de viento* 'wind stream' [ESP] / *corriente de viento* 'wind flow' [ESP]. The inclusion of geographic variants of Spain [ESP] and of Mexico [MEX] does not cause particular problems. When they occur in the corpus, they appear at the highest positions in the two rankings such as *energía eólica* 'wind energy' [MEX] / *potencia eólica* 'wind capacity' [ESP] and *mapa de los vientos* 'lit. map of the winds' [ESP] / *mapa eólico* 'wind map' [MEX]. All synonyms at the first rank supplied by the rankings by frequency or by association measure are synonymic terms that are recorded by the Panlatin lexicon. Ranking differences concern some pairs of synonyms recorded in the Panlatin lexicon appearing at further positions with ranking by frequency rather than with ranking by association measures, such as *implantación máquina* 'machine installation' [ESP] / *implantación aerogeneradores* 'wind turbine installation' [ESP], or *implantación aerogeneradores* 'wind turbine installation' [ESP] / *instalación aerogeneradores* 'wind turbine establishment' [ESP] at rank 8 with ranking by frequency and at the first rank with ranking by association. There is a dubious pair in the reference list because it does not appear in the Panlatin lexicon nor in Termium: *abrigo de torre / sombra de torre* 'tower shadow' at first position with ranking by association and at rank 22 with ranking by frequency. The size of reference lists being small, these few facts explain the difference of results.

Filterings

Filtering by syntactic patterns supplies generally better results than filtering without syntactic patterns.

Let us examine the results for English on [CAN] for which this assertion is true. For example, filtering by syntactic patterns gives at rank 2 the pair *nipple prosthesis / nipple reconstruction,* and at rank 12 the pair *os biopsy / bone biopsy.* Both of them are ruled out with filtering without syntactic patterns. Filtering by syntactic patterns gives generally better ranks to synonymic pairs, such as *breast tissue / mammary tissue,* at rank 7 with filtering by syntactic patterns and at rank 29 with filtering without syntactic patterns. On the contrary, on [EOL] for English, filtering by syntactic patterns is equivalent to that proposed without syntactic patterns. The same pairs appear at the first rank such as *wind generator / wind turbine, lattice construction / lattice tower, drive train / power train.*

Of course, some synonymic pairs given by filtering without syntactic patterns are ruled out by syntactic patterns. For English, they are complex terms built with the present participle, such as *infiltrating carcinoma* in [CAN]. The pattern Vpresent participle N leads to too many wrong terms, and have been removed of our list of English term patterns. Similar remarks can be made for other languages. In French, the pairs *protocole radiothérapie* 'radiotherapy protocol'/ *protocole cmf* and *protocole chimiothérapie* 'chemotherapy protocol'/ *protocole cmf* are proposed respectively at the first rank and at rank 2 with filtering without syntactic patterns, and they are not part of the candidates given with filtering by syntactic patterns. This is without a doubt because of a tagging error upon *cmf*.

Table 8.7 Results for the semi-compositional approach to the identification of antonyms for Fr on [CAN].

	Method	without syntactic patterns				with syntactic patterns			
		P1	P5	P10	MAP	P1	P5	P10	MAP
LLR-JAC	Semi-Comp$_{assoc}$	**37.5**	37.5	37.5	39.7	25.0	**50.0**	**62.5**	37.2
	Semi-Comp$_{count}$	0	0	25.0	3.4	0	12.5	37.5	7.4
	Semi-Comp$_{ratio}$	0	0	0	2.0	0	25.0	37.5	8.4
MI-COS	Semi-Comp$_{assoc}$	25.0	**50.0**	50.0	34.5	37.5	**37.5**	50.0	40.0
	Semi-Comp$_{count}$	0	0	25.0	3.4	0	12.5	37.5	7.4
	Semi-Comp$_{ratio}$	0	0	0	2.0	0	25.0	37.5	8.4
LO-COS	Semi-Comp$_{assoc}$	12.5	37.5	50.0	27.8	**37.5**	37.5	**62.5**	**40.6**
	Semi-Comp$_{count}$	0	0	25.0	3.8	0	12.5	37.5	7.6
	Semi-Comp$_{ratio}$	0	0	0	2.0	0	25.0	37.5	8.4

To conclude, the different results for the two corpora and for the three languages confirm the effectiveness and the performance of the semi-compositional approach for detecting denominative variants of complex terms. The synonymic variants are due to the following two causes: competing geographic denominations such as for Spanish and contextual variants. The semi-compositional approach is not sensitive to these different categories of variants.

8.5 Towards the detection of antonymic variants

The semi-compositional method allows us to identify denominative variants of complex terms by exploiting the principle of compositionality. Synonyms of complex terms are not always composed of synonyms of their parts, and the use of semantically related words identified by a distributional analysis has shown its effectiveness. This method can be applied to any complex term with the rules R_1^G

and R_2^G. It identifies denominative variants obtained by synonymic substitution produced by various causes, such as the geographic denomination, discourse or unsettled nature of the concept. The ranking of synonymic candidates by frequency and with filtering by syntactic patterns supplies the best results when the classic distributional configuration combining an association measure and a similarity measure is adopted. Our previous experiment has shown that the ranking on the first five synonymic candidates includes half of correct synonyms, but there is still a margin of progress.

Besides the identification of complex term synonyms, we observe that distributional analysis can send back antonyms of simple terms, such as Fr: *fréquent/rare,* En: *dense/spark,* or opposites ones, such as Fr: *blanc/noir,* En: *light/dark.* We also wish to exploit the property of semantic compositionality for identifying near-antonyms of complex term as defined in Section 4.3, and to investigate how to distinguish between synonyms and antonyms. In the following part, we will use the term *antonym* in a broader sense including all near-antonyms.

Table 8.8 Results for the semi-compositional approach to the identification of antonyms for En on [CAN].

	Method	**without syntactic patterns**				**with syntactic patterns**			
		P1	**P5**	**P10**	**MAP**	**P1**	**P5**	**P10**	**MAP**
LLR-JAC	Semi-Comp_{assoc}	**25.0**	**25.0**	33.3	**27.6**	16.6	**25.0**	**41.6**	23.6
	Semi-Comp_{count}	8.33	8.33	16.6	10.8	8.33	16.6	25.0	12.8
	Semi-Comp_{ratio}	0	8.33	16.6	6.1	8.33	16.6	16.6	12.8
MI-COS	Semi-Comp_{assoc}	16.6	16.6	16.6	17.8	16.6	16.6	25.0	18.1
	Semi-Comp_{count}	8.33	8.33	16.6	10.8	8.33	16.6	25.0	12.8
	Semi-Comp_{ratio}	0	8.33	16.6	6.1	8.33	16.6	16.6	12.8
LO-COS	Semi-Comp_{assoc}	16.6	16.6	25.0	18.8	16.6	16.6	25.0	18.9
	Semi-Comp_{count}	8.33	8.33	16.6	10.8	8.33	16.6	25.0	12.8
	Semi-Comp_{ratio}	0	8.33	16.6	6.1	8.33	16.6	16.6	12.8

In order to evaluate the semi-compositional approach to the detection of complex term antonyms, we carry out another experiment on [CAN]. Antonymic candidates of complex terms are built according to rules R_1^G and R_2^G. Two complex terms are antonyms if their parts are. Reference lists for English and French in the breast cancer domain comprise respectively 12 and 9 pairs of complex term antonyms. These lists have been far more difficult to build than for synonymic terms. Antonyms are absent of all terminological resources used for the building of our reference lists of synonyms. They are linguistic resources for general language that record antonyms but not, to our knowledge, for specialised domains. Thus, we adopt a bottom-up approach: we identify in the corpus complex term antonyms to be included in the reference list of antonyms.

The general French linguistic resource, Trésor de la langue française (TLF), supplies antonyms of single words, such as *artificiel/naturel* 'artificial/natural'. The pairs of complex terms extracted from [CAN] that follow rules $R_1{}^G$ and $R_2{}^G$ with the antonymy relations recorded in TLF are included in the reference list, such as the pair Fr: *ménopause artificielle* 'artificial menopause' / *ménopause naturelle* 'natural menopause'.

For English, we translate the pair of French antonyms and check their occurrence in the corpus. Some antonyms lexically marked such as *malignant tissue/ non-malignant tissue* picked up in the corpus have been also added.

Looking at the results of Tables 8.7 and 8.8, the semi-compositional approach is also capable of identifying antonyms of complex terms. In the majority of cases, the ranking by association measure gives the best results with MAP of 40.6% for French (Semi-Comp$_{assoc}$ and LO-COS with filtering by syntactic patterns) and 27.6% for English (Semi-Comp$_{assoc}$ and LLR-JAC with filtering without syntactic patterns). Rankings by frequency and by frequency ratio give very weak results.

A first interpretation of these results is that, distributional analysis indeed identify simple term antonyms. But, antonyms are better classified than synonyms with ranking by association score. Therefore, ranking by frequency will favour the identification of synonymic variants of complex terms and ranking by association scores antonymic variants. This results strengthen the observation made by linguists (Morlane-Hondère 2013) that contexts shared by a term and its antonyms are scarce, and they are different from contexts shared by a term and its synonyms. Ranking by association scores highlights the remarkable nature, from the collocational point of view, of contexts shared by a term and its antonyms while ranking by frequency favours the importance of the number of contexts shared by a term and its synonyms.

This chapter explores the distributional analysis that supplies a theoretical and operational framework for the discovery of synonymic variants in specialised corpora. The distributional analysis that models the context of the term fits the discovery of the term variants whose occurrences are isolated from the term.

We presented the distributional method and its vector modelling, as well as its main parameters: context vectors, association measures and similarity measures. The distributional method applied to simple terms needs large corpora for probative results which hardly exist in specialised domains. Applied to our corpora, the results of distributional method, when it is used for the detection of synonymic simple terms, need to be filter out, and to be interpreted by a linguist. Such analysis is difficult to achieve.

For the detection of synonymic complex terms, the distributional method is still less conclusive than for simple terms. Its use requires elaborated modifications upon the setup, such as a contextual normalisation of the context vectors (Périnet and Hamon 2013). The state-of-the-art approach for detecting synonymic complex terms employs a compositional approach. We presented the compositional method, and we proposed a semi-compositional method for the discovery of synonymic complex terms. Exploiting the principles of distributionality and of compositionality jointly, this approach has shown significant improvements compared with the compositional approach. We carried out a cross-method evaluation of compositional and semi-compositional methods for the discovery of syntagmatic compounds in French, English and Spanish in the wind energy domain, and in French and English in a subdomain of the medical domain, the breast cancer domain. The compositional method, in spite of large resources for general language, proposes a very low numbers of synonyms, two or three synonymic complex terms for 25 complex terms in average. The semi-distributional method that ranks the candidate by frequency, with the configuration MI-COS and with filtering by syntactic patterns, supplies in average two to three synonyms for the first five candidates: the score of the weakest precision was 52.6% for French, and the highest was 80% for English in the wind energy domain.

The encouraging results of the semi-compositional approach confirm the benefit of combining distributional and compositional approaches to the identification of synonymic complex terms. Of course, this method of detection of synonymic variants of complex terms also need to be applied to morphological compounds and evaluated for the three languages used in our study on syntagmatic compounds, as well as on German and Russian, in order to demonstrate that it is as generic as syntagmatic analysis for these two categories of complex terms.

We also did a first experimentation to check if the semi-compositional method is capable of detecting antonyms, in the broader meaning, of complex terms. The first results show that the semi-compositional approach can also be used, but needs another ranking of candidates, a ranking by association score that favours remarkable collocational contexts.

The part dedicated to methods of discovery of variants in texts is now completed. We have presented and experimented different methods. Some of them such as n-grams can be easily implemented, and others such as the grammar of variants and the distributional analysis need specific programs. The next part is dedicated to integrated terminological extraction, i.e. terminology extraction and term variant detection accomplished at the same time, and to tools for variant detection. In particular, we will present a tool that implements the GGRV and the distributional analysis for denominative variant discovery.

PART III

Applications and tools

CHAPTER 9

Terminology extraction

Previously, we characterised and observed variants of terms in specialised corpora. We introduced the concept of variant, defined the main categories of variants, and listed the mechanisms that proceed to their creation thanks to linguistic operations. Then, we looked for variants exploiting different automatic methods. In Chapter 7, we created a generic grammar for the recognition of variants (GGRV) that has three sets of rules, each set is dedicated to the recognition of one category of variants. We measured the coverage of the grammar and evaluated its performance to predict the variant category correctly. All these experiments were conducted on several languages and specialised domains by means of comparable corpora. We concluded that the GGRV identifies:

1. Precisely and correctly denominative variants, but finds few of them. This observation has led us to explore another paradigm of analysis, the distributional analysis for the detection of synonymic variant of complex terms presented in Chapter 8.
2. Precisely linguistic variants but not correctly. Many sequences analysed as such are false positive, they are not variants;
3. Correctly conceptual variants but not precisely. Variants analysed as conceptual are spread over all categories of variants, and at equal part between conceptual and linguistic variants.

In order to complete our study about variants, we will pair the automatic detection of variant to a terminology acquisition application. We call it "integrated terminology extraction".

The objective of terminology extraction is to collect terms of a specialised domain which occur in a specialised corpus. First, we will explain the terminology extraction task and review the main methods. Then we will perform integrated terminology extraction in two domains and five languages. We will evaluate how useful it is comparatively to simple terminology extraction.

9.1 The core of terminology extraction

Identifying terms of a specific domain has been an active field of research since the early nineties (Bourigault and Jacquemin 2000). Twelve terminology extraction tools are described and compared by Cabré et al. (2001) determined by the need of various applications: information retrieval, information extraction, science and technology watch, and ontology acquisition. The core of terminology extraction involves various processing tasks on the input texts, from tokenisation to syntactic analysis, and on the output candidate terms, manual validation process through dedicated interfaces (Pazienza et al. 2005). Whatever the sophistication of the input or output processing steps, all the methods that are involved in the core of the extraction process are dedicated to compute the termhood and the unithood of a candidate term as defined by Kageura and Umino (1996). Two steps make up the core of the extraction process:

Collecting: Identification and collection of term-like units in the texts, mostly a subset of nominal phrases;
Filtering and sorting: Filtering of the extracted term-like units that may not be terms, syntactically or terminologically; sorting of the candidate terms according to their unithood, their terminological status and their usefulness for the target application.

Despite a high degree of similarity, methods may differ on several levels:

1. The complexity of the terminological unit, usually of the noun phrase, that is accepted: single noun, short noun phrase, maximal noun phrase. Considering the text sequence *low-temperature grain neutron diffraction*, some tools will only keep the simple term *diffraction* while others will extract the multi-word term *neutron diffraction*, *grain neutron diffraction*, or even the complete sequence.
2. The filtering mechanisms involved to accurately eliminate irrelevant candidate terms using statistical measures, predefined lexical sources, such as existing terminological resources and stop-term lists, embedding properties, or contextual information.
3. The sorting of candidate terms with a termhood measure. High values indicate high relevance for a given corpus (and for the domain of the corpus), and lower ones a lower relevance. In addition, such measures can carry out categorical filtering, given a threshold for accepting candidates as terms. There are two classes of termhood measures: the first scores the termhood from the specialised corpus, the second compares the distribution of the candidate terms in the specialised corpus and in a general language corpus.

9.2 Collecting candidate terms

The collection of candidate terms that are potentially relevant words or words sequences (most often noun chunks) makes use of part-of-speech patterns, a general phrase rule describing the nominal, phrase borders, a list of seed terms or samples of texts annotated with terms.

9.2.1 Patterns

Terms are selected according to their patterns. For simple terms, only nouns, sometimes adjectives, are term-like candidates. For complex terms, only nominal phrases are term-like candidates (L'Homme 2004). Patterns of complex terms vary depending on the language: in Section 2.5.2, we selected typical patterns of several languages listed in Chapter 2. When a sequence of part-of-speech tags merges several candidate term patterns, the longest pattern is kept. We will say that term recognition adopts a greedy strategy over term patterns. Thus, with the sequence Fr: *production primaire* épondique of N A A pattern, among the set of patterns: N A A, N A, N and A, only the N A A pattern will be kept.

Choosing the typical complex term patterns requires either linguistic competences of the language in order to provide hand-written patterns to identify candidate terms (Weller et al. 2011), or the help of data mining or machine learning techniques to identify term patterns from corpora (Guégan and De Loupy 2011).

9.2.2 Generic rules

Instead of listing the term-like patterns, a looser approach accepts any sequence of part-of-speech tags that occur in noun chunks, or lexicalisable noun phrases. A lexicalisable noun phrase rules out sentential arguments and modifiers.

French

For French, several generic rules for term-like candidates may be used:

> R1 Lexicalisable noun phrase: (N (R* A)+)* (P D? (R* A)* N (R* A)*)*
> R2 Constrained lexicalisable noun phrase (Hull 1998):
> (N+ A*) ((*de* | *à*) (*le* | *la* | *les* |*l'*)* ((N+ A*|A|V))+
> R3 Constrained lexicalisable adjectival or noun phrase: (N|A)+
> R4 Constrained noun chunk: N+ A?

The N P N pattern is more frequent than the N A pattern in French corpora. This result valid for general language, is also valid for specialised domains. We compute the two patterns in our corpora of different size and domains:

Corpus	Size	N (P D?)? N	NA
[SAT]	200,000	9,953	4,483
[CAN]	250,000	24,380	20,028
[EOL]	300,000	25,253	18,006
[TEL]	800,000	21,936	8,821

While the N P N pattern is the most frequent it is unreliable. Often N P N sequences are not candidate terms. Looking at the prepositions of the N P N pattern, the preposition *de* represents 70% of all prepositions, the preposition *à* 13%, all the single prepositions 13%, and N N pattern 5%. N *de* N is valid for half of its occurrences. This extremely high rate of ambiguity forces a term recognition program to ignore it in some applications in order to favour precision over recall. In key-phrase extraction, an information retrieval task, rules R3 and R4 that eliminate the N P N pattern are preferred to rules R1 or R2 that include it. The prenominal position of the adjective that holds an evaluative feature is ruled out in rules R1, R2 and R4. Rule R2 accepts the determiner inside the prepositional phrase which is an expansion of the head noun, but limited to the definite article.

English

For English, several generic rules of term-like candidates may be used:

R1 Lexicalisable noun phrase: (A R*)* N+ (P (A R*)* N+)*
R2 Constrained lexicalisable noun phrase TERMS (Justeson and Katz 1995): (A|N)+|(A|N)*(N P) (A|N)*)N
R3 Constrained lexicalisable noun phrase (Biber et al. 1999): C or N P C with C = noun syntagmatic compound patterns, such as A N, N N, A A N, A N N, N A N …
R4 Constrained lexicalisable adjectival or noun phrase (Hull 1998): (A|N)+

Rule R3 came from the Biber's corpus linguistic study about noun modifiers for the English language. Biber et al. (1999: 598) concluded by the following statement:

> In all registers, noun phrases with premodifiers are somewhat more common than those with postmodifiers … Proportionally, in academic prose, 60% of all noun phrases have some modifiers, 25% have a premodifier, 20% have a postmodifier, and additional 12% have both.

Burgos (2014: 33) analysed 3 specialised dictionaries and showed that 33,447 (92.8%) nominal syntagmatic compounds out of 36,040 did not include postmodifiers. Adverbs that are not a constituent of the term pattern are ruled out from generic noun phrase patterns. However, Burgos (2014: 102) included in the allowed part-of-speech the deadjectival adverbs ending by *-ly* restricted to the sole R A N pattern.

Spanish
Constrained lexicalisable noun phrase Herrera (2014: 102):

N ((R-*mente*? A)* P*de* N)*

This rule is similar to the French rule R2. Premodifiers are ruled out. With regards to prepositions, the analysis of Herrera (2014: 104) showed that for 62,767 entries in three Spanish specialised dictionaries, the preposition *de* appears in 46.5% of syntagmatic compounds. The other prepositions all together such as *en, por, a, con, para, sobre, sin, …* account for 12.8% of the entries. It also showed that only 11.2% of the dictionary entries include articles. Given that dictionary entries only include standard forms, a corpus study would increase the number of articles occurring inside syntagmatic compounds.

German
For German, a generic rule is:

Constrained lexicalisable noun phrase (Weller et al. 2011):
A* N (D|P A? N)

German has much syncretism as 80% of all noun phases are ambiguous with respect to case. German articles need to be restricted to the genitive case *der, des.*

Russian
For Russian, two generic rules of term-like candidates may be used:

R1 Constrained lexicalisable noun phrase (Mitrofanova and Zakharov 2009):
N P (A|V_p)* N N*
R2 Constrained lexicalisable adjectival or noun phrase (Bobyreva 2009):
(A|N)+

Rule R2 includes the two main patterns of terms that are A N and N N:---g. Rule R1 adds more complex pattern such as the N P A N and N P N N patterns.

9.2.3 Borders

Borders delineate noun phrase or terms. They are elements that do not belong to the nominal phrase. They are of miscellaneous nature: parts-of-speech, punctuation marks, words. For example, one of the natural boundary of a nominal phrase is a verb in an inflected tense. Borders identify noun phrase implicitly. For French, Bourigault (1994) provided the following list of borders of terms:

1. punctuation marks;
2. verbs;
3. pronouns;
4. determiner preceded by a verb or a punctuation mark.

9.2.4 Lexical expansion

Collecting candidate terms with lexical expansion is similar to a term variant recognition task, even if it is not claimed as such, to the exception of Jacquemin (2001). Lexical expansion relies on a list of seed terms that will be used to detect new terms. This method is language-independent and does not require linguistic pre-processing. Working on raw texts improves the recall of term collection as there is no filtering on part-of-speech tags. Errors in part-of-speech tags eliminate a significant quantity of good candidate terms.

Lexical expansion exploits first and second order co-occurrence analysis corresponding to the following two steps that are reiterated for a given number of iterations or until no new terms are discovered:

First-order co-occurrence analysis The nominal phrases that include occurrences of the seed terms are collected. Nominal phrase analysis is performed using one of the above methods: patterns or generic rules on part-of-speech analysed corpus, borders using punctuation marks, words, and eventually part-of-speech tags.

Second-order co-occurrence analysis The nominal phrase is split in order to shape the left and right expansions of the seed term. These expansions are new terms that are added to seed terms.

The size and nature of seed terms differ as well as the number of iterations. Nazar et al. (2012) chose a small list of terms as seed terms: 120 terms belonging to a specialised domain as Baroni and Bernadini (2004) did to build a specialised corpus from the web. Burgos (2014) decided to enlarge the size of the list of seed terms. He picked up the single nouns given by a domain glossary and all the nouns of English general language to create a list of 11,177 nouns. Jacquemin (2001) stopped after the first iteration: only term variants recognised by structural rules are kept, i.e. coordination, insertion and permutation rules introduced in Section 7.2.1.

Kageura (2012) demonstrated for Japanese that the number of native morphemes of a terminology heavily depends on the specialised domain. The domain with the highest number of morphemes is agriculture, the one with the lowest is computer science, and the other domains spread between these two boundaries. Considering that a morpheme in Japanese is roughly isomorphic to a lexical unit in Romance languages, the size of the seed terms highly depends on the specialised domain.

9.3 Filtering and sorting candidate terms

During terminology extraction, all term-like sequences are collected by one of the previous methods. Then they are ranked according to measures: the most likely terms should appear at the top of the list. The measures rely on term characteristic features. Some of them measure the centrality or the specificity of the candidate term in the specialised domain, others estimate the lexicalisation of the complex candidate term, or look at the candidate term neighbourhood, and so on. Features that are commonly used to rank the candidate term according to its more or less terminological character were split by Kageura and Unino (1996) between termhood and unithood criteria. We will see that drawing a line between them is not as easy as some criteria can be employed to measure indistinctly one or the other.

Sorting measures could also be used as filtering measures, keeping candidate terms above a given threshold. Sorting and filtering candidate terms are based on the specialised corpus alone from which they have been extracted, or both the specialised corpus and the general language corpus. These measures are calculated on the basis of the corpus, a textual instance of the specialised domain. They allow to hypothesise that the centrality and the specificity of a term in the corpus reflect those of the specialised domain. But the values that are calculated for a candidate term are only valid for a given corpus, and are not comparable to other values calculated from other corpora. Measure values rely on the corpus features that we have presented in Section 5.1. Without a normalisation procedure, it is not possible to decide about an a priori valid threshold, whatever the domain or the language of the corpus.

9.3.1 Frequency

The basic way to measure termhood is the frequency of the candidate term, assuming that relevant terms have a higher occurrence frequency than irrelevant ones. Frequency is classified as a measure of termhood.

Given a candidate term *t*, given a word *w*, the relative frequency *RF* is computed by dividing the absolute corpus frequency of *t* by the sum of all the frequencies of the corpus words *w*:

$$RF(t) = \frac{nbocc(t)}{\sum_m nbocc(w)} \tag{9.1}$$

The number of occurrences of a candidate term is calculated using its lemma in order to gain in representativeness. Stop words such as articles, prepositions, auxiliaries can be removed from the corpora as they are not candidate terms.

9.3.2 Association measures

Association measures test the strength of the bond between two words occurring in a corpus. They are fit to extract multi-word expressions, and thus syntagmatic compounds which are a subset of nominal multi-word expressions. The degree of lexicalisation of a nominal phrase is a clue to its terminological nature. It is thus a natural way to select the candidate syntagmatic compounds. Association measures are classified as unithood measures. Association measures derived from the mutual information (Equation 8.1) and the Log-likelihood ratio (Equation 8.4) have been presented in Chapter 8. These state-of-the-art measures help distinguish between free and idiomatic syntagmatic combinations.

Drouin (2003) carried out experiments that confirmed their usefulness to approximate the degree of stability of the syntagmatic combination. Of course, a strong bond between two or more words is only one feature of the syntagmatic compound. All prominent associations are not necessarily terms. Furthermore, many syntagmatic compounds selected by association measures look more like collocations than terms. Log-likelihood ratio and local mutual information seem more adapted to detect terms than point-wise mutual information, conversely point-wise mutual information looks more appropriate to discover collocations than the previous two measures.

Evert and Krenn (2005) observed that association measures applied to collocation extraction gave better results when their syntactic categories are distinguished. This result can be reused to estimate the unithood of each term pattern, such as the English pattern A N.

Several association measures are available in the reference tool for term extraction, TermoStat.[1]

Association measures may be used as termhood measures to rank the candidate terms. These measures performing corpus-inherent scoring are outperformed by those filtering with a general language corpus.

9.3.3 Specificity measures

Term frequency is a good clue to the centrality of a term in a specialised domain. But we have already pointed out that the frequency of candidate terms differs widely according to the specialised corpus. In order to extract terms, it is necessary not only to select the most frequent candidate terms but also to measure their relevance in the domain.

Domain specificity of a candidate term could be estimated by several termhood measures. The most popular one is the "weirdness ratio" (Ahmad et al. 1994) (WR). The weirdness ratio is the quotient of the relative frequency in both the domain specific corpus *C* and a general language corpus *G*:

$$\mathrm{WR}(t) = \frac{RF_S(t)}{RF_G(w)} \tag{9.2}$$

with $RF_G(t) > 0$
$\mathrm{WR(t)} \in [0, +\infty[$

The assumption is that domain relevant terms have a high occurrence frequency in corpora of their domain while they hardly ever occur in a general language corpus.

Table 9.1 provides the number of occurrences and WR score in [EOL] for a few terms.[2] We look at the terms: *wind, blade, wind energy* and *wind park* for German, English, Spanish, French and Russian in [EOL]. The term *wind,* even if it is central to the wind energy domain, is also very frequent in the general language corpus. Its WR score is low compare to the WR score of *blade.* This remark is valid whatever the language. We remark that De: *Blatt* is always agglutinated to *Rotor.* So only the specificity of *Rotorblatt* should be examined. Specificity scores provided by the WR should be comparable from one corpus to the other and from one language to the other. But because of the polysemy of simple terms, such as *blade,* this property is verified. Examining the two complex term *wind energy* and *wind park,* the

1. http://olst.ling.umontreal.ca

2. Figures of Table 9.1 are calculated using the lemma form of the terms. They differ slightly from those calculated upon the inflectional forms for the term *blade* in Chapter 5. These differences are not significant.

latter looks intuitively more specific to the energy domain than the former, but WR scores contradict it, to the exception of French We recall that [EOL] was built fully automatically by crawling using the seed term *wind energy* (cf. Section 5.2). The overrepresentation of the complex term *wind energy* arises from the way the corpus was built. For French, where a third of the corpus is made from manually picked up documents, this overrepresentation of the complex term *énergie éolienne* is not observed. So even if WR has proved more reliable than frequency to measure specificity of the term in a specialised domain, several factors could influence scores as polysemy of the term in the language, or corpus building. The variation of WR scores across languages, and we expect it will have the identical behaviours across domains, invalidates the setting of an a priori threshold despite a frequency normalisation.

Table 9.1 Examples of number of occurrences and WR scores for simple terms and complex terms in [EOL] and in general language corpus.

	t	$nbocc_S(t)$	$nbocc_G(t)$	WR(t)
De	Wind	117	941	17
En	wind	4,431	1,164	296
Es	viento	2,687	3,978	232
Fr	vent	1,272	2,896	89
Ru	ветер	1,761	388	65
De	Blatt	13	1,224	45
De	Rotorblatt	103	13	1,073
En	blade	1,425	175	634
Es	pala	838	211	1,280
Fr	pale	477	0	96,018
Ru	лопасть	743	4	2,675
De	Windenergieanlage	578	4	19,578
En	wind energy	394	0	30,692
Es	energía eólica	437	27	5,216
Fr	énergie éolien	219	0	44,083
Ru	энергия ветра	213	0	3,067
De	Windpark	175	19	1,248
En	wind farm	465	24	1,509
Es	parque eólico	8	0	2,578
Fr	parc éolien	276	0	55,557
Ru	ветряная электростанция	1	0	14

Ranking of candidate terms by frequency and by weirdness ratio are usual sorts proposed by concordance tools such as WordSmith, Antconc,[3] IMS Open Corpus Workbench,[4] and term extraction tools such as TermoStat.[5]

Observation of the *WR* scores shows that it correctly ranks simple terms, but it is less adapted to complex terms, as many of them are fully specific to specialised domains and do not occur in a general language corpus. Two adaptations for calculating have been proposed based on their properties: first the collection of all complex term occurrences in a general language corpus, second the collection of single words only in a general language corpus.

Judea et al. (2014) propose a simplified approach in estimating WR that examine the distribution of the head of the MWT *h(t)*. *biais(h(t))* measures the deviation between the expected frequency of the head of *t* estimated in a general language corpus and the specialised corpus. The basic idea behind is that a noun without a specialised meaning will share a similar frequency across domains and communication levels, resulting in a lower biais.

$$biais(h(t)) = \frac{nbocc_G(h(t))nbocc_S}{nbocc_G}) - nbocc_S(h(t)) \quad (9.3)$$

Collecting complex terms can be carried out by using a generic rule (cf. Section 9.2.2) as there is no need to distinguish between specific term patterns.

Another point of view will consider that specificity is the expansion of the complex term. So, WR is calculated by keeping the maximal score of one of its components:

$$WR(mwt) = argmax_c WR(t_c) \quad (9.4)$$

with t_c the component of subscript *c*.

Alternatively to the weirdness ratio, Rayson and Garside (2000) adapted the loglikelihood ratio (Equation 8.4) to contrast the use of a term with two corpora:

3. www.laurenceanthony.net/software/antcone/

4. cwb.sourceforge.net

5. http://olst.ling.umontreal.ca

$$LLR(t) = 2((nbocc_S(t) \log \frac{nbocc_S(t)}{E_1}) + (nbocc_G(t) \log \frac{nbocc_G(t)}{E_2})$$

$$E_1 \frac{nbocc_S(nbocc_S(t) + nbocc_G(t)}{nbocc_S + nbocc_G} \tag{9.5}$$

$$E_2 \frac{bocc_G(nbocc_S(t)+ nbocc_G(t)}{nbocc_S + nbocc_G}$$

with:
$\mathcal{C}$ a specialised corpus,
$\mathcal{G}$ a general language corpus,
$nbocc_S$ the number of occurrences of m in $\mathcal{C}$: $\Sigma_m\, nbocc(m)$,
$nbocc_G$ the number of occurrences of w in $\mathcal{G}$: $\Sigma_w\, nbocc(w)$.

Specificity scores provide an estimation of how the term is specific to the specialised domain. Calculation of specificity measures requires the collection of large specialised corpora because the correlation between specificity and frequency becomes stable only with a significant volume of data. This could pose problem for a specialised domain or a language if it is not possible to collect enough data. The collection of occurrences of simple terms circumvents homonymy and polysemy problems, part-of-speech tagging errors that lead to erroneous lemmatisation, the fact that many candidate terms are not valid or not autonomous linguistic units, i.e. they are only substrings of complex terms. The collection of occurrences of complex terms is submitted to part-of-speech tagging errors and of their erroneous linguistic status, but marginally to homonymy and polysemy problems. The main problem is that they often do not occur in a general language corpus. Lastly, the collection of occurrences from a specialised corpus and a general language corpus needs to be done with the same procedure. This could raise critical barriers to scale up large corpora during the collection of all candidate terms.

9.3.4 Filtering by removing nested terms

During the candidate term collection, specific or generic patterns are applied only to pick up syntactically term-like candidates. However partial analysis that was introduced in Section 6.1.3 makes many errors. Candidates terms can be incorrect: incomplete when a part of the term is missing, or on the contrary too long when expansions are not part of the term. For example, given the term patterns, N, A, A N, N N, A N N, and the occurrence *offshore wind turbine* ANN, candidate terms collected are: *offshore* A, *wind* N, *turbine* N, *offshore wind* A N, *wind turbine* N N, *offshore wind turbine* A N N. Among them, the nested sequence *offshore wind* A N although syntactically correct is not a valid candidate term. Conversely, given the occurrence *horizontal axis wind turbine* A N N N, the candidate term *axis wind turbine* N N N although syntactically correct is incomplete, and furthermore not valid. At least, the French sequence *aérogénérateur en énergie électrique* 'aerogenerator in electric energy' N P N A, is incorrect because the expansion P N A does not depend upon *aérogénérateur*. C-value (Frantzi and Ananiadou 2000: 150) defined nested terms as candidate terms "that appear within other longer terms, and may or may not appear by themselves in the corpus." Originally defined as a term extraction method, it is now used to filter wrong candidate terms. C-value keeps nested terms as candidate terms only if one of the following conditions are observed:

1. the nested substring occurs in the corpus by itself, without being nested in other candidate terms;
2. the nested substring occurs as a nested substring of several candidate terms.

Whatever the condition, the length of the substring is taken into consideration in order to favour long sequences over short ones. The underlying hypothesis is at equal distribution, the longer candidate term will be more domain specific.

$$C\_value(t) = \begin{cases} \log_2 |t|\, nbocc(t) & t \text{ not nested} \\ \log_2 |t| \left(f(t) - \frac{1}{nb(Et)} \Sigma_{Et}\, nbocc(Et)\right) & \text{otherwise} \end{cases}$$

with:
$|t|$ length of the candidate string
nbocc(t) number of occurrences of the candidate string
Et a candidate term that contains *t*
nbocc(Et) number of occurrences of candidate terms that contain *t*
nb(Et) number of candidate terms that contain *t*.

9.3.5 Contextual filtering

Contextual filtering relies on the contextual neighbourhood of a term in a specialised corpus. Two types of neighbourhood are examined: internal context which only observes the candidate term, or external context which observes the surroundings of the term without looking at the term itself. Distinguishing between internal or external context depends on the nature of the candidate term, simple or complex. For simple terms or morphological compounds, only external contexts are examined. For syntagmatic compounds, the definition of neighbourhood is shallower and involves sometimes a mixture of internal and external contexts. The contextual filtering we are dealing with only relies on the external context of the candidate term.

The first assumption is that the term is gregarious. When a term occurs in a document, it comes along with other terms. Thus, if other terms or candidate terms occur in the neighbourhood of a candidate term, it is a good clue to the terminological character of the candidate term.

The second assumption is that terms share terminologically-marked contexts contrary to noun phrases. Such terminologically-marked contexts include knowledge-rich contexts as coined by Meyer (2001). Knowledge-rich contexts identify a relation between two terms. For example, given *t* a term, given *ct* a candidate term, given the generic-specific knowledge pattern, *is a type of,* the occurrence: *ct is a type of t* or *t is a type of ct* characterises a definitory context, and affirms the terminological character of *ct.* A terminological marker occurring in the candidate term neighbourhood confirms it as a term. To identify the occurrences of terminological markers, list of makers are required that were developed by linguists, such as the lexicon of conceptual relation markers, in particular hierarchical or definitory markers by Marshmann et al. (2002). Lexicons of markers are commonly built for a language and a specialised domain and they are not very reliable when they are transposed from one specialised domain or text genre to another (Condamines 2002), or even translated to be used in other languages.

The academic lexicon lists words and multi-word expressions that are specific to the communication level about scientific objects and procedures. The academic lexicon includes words that describe scientific procedures such as the verb *to describe,* evaluations such as the verb *to conclude,* scientific objects such as *assumption.* Academic lexicons were built for English (Paquot 2010), French (Tutin 2007), Russian (Bolshakova 2008). Jacquet et al. (2013) observed that a subset of the entries of the academic lexicon can be used as terminological markers. Nouns denoting a scientific processes such as *study, research* and scientific objects are reliable contextual markers of terms. But they need to be distinguished from other academic entries denoting observable nouns such as *results,* and relation nouns such as *cause.*

There are other methods that perform contextual filtering without the help of external lexical resources. NC-value (Frantzi and Ananiadou 2000) exploits the gregarious property of the term in discourse. The assumption is that the neighbours of a term, that are also likely to be terms, are shared with other terms. To detect terms in the neighbourhood of candidate terms, NC-value performs a distributional analysis. The neighbours of terms are nouns, adjectives or verbs and are juxtaposed before or after terms. A candidate term will be a term if term neighbours occur in its neighbourhood. NC-value is computed in two stages:

1. The neighbours of the candidate terms *vct* appearing at the top of the list of candidate terms ranked thanks to the C-value are collected. The terminological weight of *vct* is estimated from the number of *ct* sharing the neighbour. A weight is assigned to each context *vct* of a candidate term *ct*. *weight (vct)* is estimated by comparing frequencies of *vct* in the neighbourhood of terms with its overall frequency *v:*

$$weight_S(tv) = \frac{nboccs_S(vct)}{nboccs_S(v)} \quad (9.6)$$

2. The C-value is then weighted with the scores assigned to neighbours. The NC-value is calculated by summing the weights of the candidate term neighbours computed at the first stage, zero otherwise, multiplied by their frequency.

$$NC - value(ct) = 0.8C - value(t) - 0.2 \sum_{tv} nboccs_S(vct) weight_S(vct) \quad (9.7)$$

9.3.6 Supervised learning methods

All the preceding filtering and ranking methods are unsupervised. They do not need to rely on terms previously identified in a document. There are few corpora where terms have been identified and tagged in the public domain. The GENIA corpus[6] (Kim et al. 2003) gathers 2,000 MEDLINE abstracts (400,000 words) and almost 100,000 annotations for biological terms. For French, a sub-part of the Scientext corpus[7] (Billami et al. 2014) gathers 62 articles belonging to linguistics (400,000 words). All texts are divided into 47 articles of conferences (75.81% of documents and 57.06% of occurrences), and 15 articles of journals (24.19% of documents and 42.94% of occurrences).

There are other corpora that have been developed by researchers but which are not publicly available such as the patent corpus where terms have been tagged by Judea et al. (2014). For this corpus, the inter-annotator agreement calculated on 16 patents was of 0.76 (Fleiss' Kappa). Such annotated corpora are used as training corpora to learn a classifier that will be capable of making a decision on the terminological status of an occurrence of a candidate term in the test corpus. Features used by Judea et al. (2014) are:

6. www-tsujii.is.s.u-tokyo.ac.jp/GENIA

7. apps.atilf.fr/smarties

1. mean string similarity of *t* with one of the terms that precedes a figure reference;
2. $nbocc_S(t)$ as a term that precedes a figure reference;
3. $tf - idf(t)$;
4. *t* in uppercase (boolean);
5. *t* is followed by a figure reference (boolean);
6. $tf - idf(h(t))$;
7. $nbocc_S(h(t))$ as a term that precedes a figure reference in the test corpus;
8. $biais(h(t))$;
9. number of sentences of captions of figures in which *t* occurs;
10. *C_value(t)*;
11. $nbocc_S(h(t))$ in the train corpus.

These features were best selected by the classifier from among a set of 74. These features are corpus and document statistics (features 3, 6, 8, 9), the type of characters of the term (feature 4), and the exploitation of the patent layout: patents typically contain figure references that are preceded by terms (features 1, 2, 4, 5, 7).

Other linguistic features might be added such as contextual filtering features presented above, concerning syntagmatic compounds, occurrences of relational adjectives (cf. Section 2.5.1), concerning morphological compounds, occurrences of Latin or Greek roots (Estopà et al. 2000).

9.4 Evaluation

Evaluating one or several tools for terminology extraction is not an easy task: generally tools include low-level processes using various lexical resources which act upon the quality of the extraction (Kageura et al. 2000). Moreover, evaluation focuses on the quality of the candidate terms without taking into account other parameters such as speed, portability, robustness or partial structuring of candidate terms.

Lastly, terminology extraction relies upon the specialised domain and the application, each application requiring different terms. Evaluation of an application oriented terminology extraction needs to be carried out by the end-users of the application by measuring their satisfaction and the accuracy of candidate terms.

These evaluating methods rely on resources and measures similar to other NLP evaluations.

9.4.1 References

In order to build a terminology of a specialised domain from scratch, the two main evaluation directions are the human evaluation and the reference list. Chaudiron (2001) suggests another direction involving end-users, close to real-life conditions. But such evaluations which assess the candidate terms, the tool and the user-interface, are extremely difficult to organise and carry out. Precise assessment protocols are required, such as the one we designed to evaluate a tool for machine-aided indexing by expert librarians (Jacquemin et al. 2002). We detail below human evaluation and reference lists regardless of any application.

Human evaluation
Human evaluation consists in presenting a list of candidate terms to humans, experts of the specialised domain. The expert has to judge the terminological character of candidate terms within the specialised domain, and decide whether they are syntactically valid candidate terms. Vivaldi and Rodriguez (2007) gave three experts a list of 326 candidate terms, automatically extracted from medical records, for evaluation. They computed the inter-annotator agreement between experts. They observed that the three experts only agreed on 37% of candidate terms, that two experts agreed on 26%, and 37% of candidate terms were only acknowledged by one expert. There are several causes of disagreement. One of them is to establish the perimeter of the domain: if some terms are central to the domain, others are more peripheral (Uchiyama 2011). Term evaluation is a difficult task that could be even more complicated if several lists of candidate terms have to be evaluated generated by several term extraction tools or different versions of a given tool. Sincc several tools are evaluated, and since the expert looks at several lists, it is impossible to judge if the expert has not been influenced by the prior results. Ideally, an identical number of experts and tools or versions of one tool would be necessary and all the systems should be evaluated by all the experts. Expert evaluation is so costly that it is usually restricted to samples. Morevover, human experts are reluctant to examine long lists, are influenced by the presentation and are likely to change their opinion. Moreover, this method is not capable of measuring silence, except if the protocol specifies that experts should pick up missing terms not extracted by the system.

A priori / a posteriori reference lists
The list of candidate terms can be compared with the reference list of terms (RTL). An a priori RTL is built from a known terminological database or from a specialised dictionary. When a multi-domain terminological database is used, only terms belonging to the specialised domain reflected by the corpus are kept. The a priori

RTL is compiled independently from the output provided by the term extraction tool. Thus, it is useful to compare one tool over several tools. It allows us to calculate recall and silence of the term extraction tool. In order not to introduce a bias in the evaluation, it is necessary to take out of the RTL terms that do not occur in the corpus. Indeed, terms which are not in the corpus but in the RTL will never be proposed. If they are kept, it is not the precision of the tool that is evaluated, but rather the corpus representativeness towards the specialised domain.

An a posteriori RTL is built from the specialised corpus by experts. If no experts are available, the terminological status of the candidate term could be checked by examining several multilingual terminological database such as Termium or IATE. The terms of the RTL should reflect the capabilities of the extraction tool, and of course the properties of the target technical terminology. Thus, the a posteriori RTL is useful to estimate the performance that can be expected from the terminology extraction tool on the specialised corpus. The a posteriori RTL is often richer in terms of term patterns and types than an a priori RTL.

A reference list built from corpora seems to be a priori more suitable than human evaluation: cheaper, done for once, it allows repetition of the experiment and guarantees objective results. Of course, RTL lists only offer a fragmentary view of the extraction tool performance, as RTL could never be exhaustive.

Matches

Comparison between a term of the RTL and a candidate term is based on full match. Thus, the form of the elements of the RTL should be compatible with the form of the candidate term submitted for evaluation. This method imposes a precise format to terms and masks numerous good candidate terms. In order to loosen the match between a candidate term and a term of the RTL, metrics have been proposed by Kageura et al. (2000) and Nazarenko et al. (2009). They deal with fuzzy matches corresponding to subsets of term variants: graphical and morphological variants and expansion variants.

Within the NTCIR'1 workshop's term recognition task, Kageura et al. (2000) chose not to limit the term patterns and defined different types of alignments: where T_R, T_{R1}, T_{R2} are terms of the reference list, T_E is a candidate term proposed by one of the systems:

- **F** T_R fully matches T_E if and only if T_R is strictly equal to T_E ;
- **I** T_E is included in T_R if and only if T_E is a sub-string of T_R ;
- **P** T_R is included in T_E if and only if T_R is a sub-string of T_E ;
- **B** (T_E is included in T_{R1}) and (T_{R2} is included in T_E) ;
- **A** *(all inclusive)* (T_R is included in T_E) or (T_R fully matches T_E) or (T_E is included in T_R).

These different types of alignment allow us to infer that some systems show a tendency to extract only sub-strings of terms belonging to the reference list. These alignments are not fully satisfactory because they are only based on string length and do not treat all kinds of term variants. The integrated term extraction that performs in parallel term extraction and variant recognition no longer requires fuzzy matches since either the candidate term or the variant has to match the term of the RTL.

9.4.2 Measures

Measures generally used for term extraction evaluation are precision and recall. Given RTL, the reference term list:

$$Precision = \frac{number\ of\ candidate\ terms\ included\ in\ RTL}{number\ of\ candidate\ terms} \tag{9.8}$$

$$Recall = \frac{number\ of\ candidate\ terms\ included\ in\ RTL}{number\ of\ terms\ of\ RTL} \tag{9.9}$$

Precision evaluates the number of correctly extracted terms. Recall evaluates the rate of correct candidate terms (vice versa the rate of correct terms which have not been extracted).

F-measure combines precision and recall. It is a weight harmonic mean which penalises diverging values between precision and recall.

$$F\alpha = \frac{1}{\alpha\frac{1}{precision} + (1-\alpha)\frac{1}{recall}} \tag{9.10}$$

with α a weight. A compromise between precision and recall gives an equal weight of both of them ($\alpha = 0.5$):

$$F_1 = \frac{2 \cdot precision \cdot recall}{precision + recall} \tag{9.11}$$

Other measures can be calculated such as noise and silence:

$$Noise = \frac{number\ of\ candidateterms\ not\ in\ RTL}{number\ of\ candidateterms} \tag{9.12}$$

$$Silence = \frac{number\ of\ candidateterms\ not\ in\ RTL}{number\ of\ terms\ in\ RTL} \tag{9.13}$$

9.5 Comparing term extraction without and with variant recognition

Variant recognition is interesting from a terminological point of view and for several applications. The aim of this section is to check if variant recognition is useful for classical terminology extraction. We propose to extract terms from several corpora and languages. The evaluation will be fully automatic. It will compare the number of terms and their rank in the list of candidate terms to an a priori and an a posteriori reference term lists (RTL). We believe variant recognition will improve the performance of term extraction for two reasons. First, it will increase the number of term occurrences. We saw that the number of occurrences of a given term is an input parameter for specificity measures, so specificity scores should raise accordingly. Second, the set of variants allows to increase the number of matches with the RTL since it offers more options.

Table 9.2 Size expressed in number oftokens of comparable corpora [EOL] and [MOB].

	De	En	Es	Fr	Ru
[EOL]	358,602	313,954	454,095	314,551	323,946
[MOB]	474,316	303,972	474,534	437,505	318,225

This study will be performed for five languages and two specialised domains. We will describe successively data, integrated terminology extraction, protocol of comparison and results for the two types of RTL.

9.6 Experimental setting

Term extraction is performed on two comparable corpora available in five languages. Candidate terms are compared to two a posteriori RTL for two specialised domains, and to two a priori RTL for one specialised domain.

9.6.1 Corpora

Comparable corpora reflect two specialised domains: renewable energy and mobile technologies. The building of the comparable corpora of renewable energy domain ([EOL]) has been described at Section 5.2. The corpus of mobile technology ([MOB]) was built in the same way. Both are available in five languages.

Table 9.2 indicates for each language and each domain the size of the corpus on which the terminology extraction is performed. These corpora are small specialised corpora.

A posteriori RTL

Two a posteriori RTL were built to evaluate term extraction on the basis of corpora related to the domains of renewable energy and mobile technology in German, English, Spanish, French and Russian. RTL were built monolingually by native speakers of each language. For the sake of homogeneity across languages and domains, common requirements about each monoligual corpus were defined initially and were reviewed during the building (Loginova et al. 2012). As an example, a fixed distribution of different term types was set: 20% of simple terms, 20% of morphological compounds and 60% of syntagmatic compounds. This requirement was difficult to comply with due to the differences between the languages under study. Another requirement was a minimal number of occurrences of ten for simple terms and for morphological compounds, and five for syntagmatic compounds. All the terms of the RTL were chosen monolingually with no guaranty that they were translations of each other. All specialised languages show a gradient of domain-specificity: most domains are interdisciplinary, with terms from other domains interfering, En: *solar energy* or Fr: *géothermie* 'geothermy' occur commonly in [EOL]. So the inclusion of relevant terms from adjacent domains was authorised.

Table 9.3 shows one record of the English RTL for (EOL). A record lists the term lemma, its part-of-speech, for syntagmatic compound, its pattern, all the inflectional forms occurring in [EOL], and the number of occurrences. Table 9.4 gives the number of terms in the RTL for each language.

Table 9.3 Extract of English RTL for [EOL].

Language	
term lemma	sustainable energy
Simple term/complex term	complex term
pattern	AN
morphophological tag	A—s- Nc-s-
origin	
inflected forms (IF)	
frequency	39
most frequent IF	sustainable energy
frequency of mfIF	39

Table 9.4 Number of terms in RTL for (EOL) and (MOB).

	De	En	Es	Fr	Ru
$RTL_{[EOL]}$ – Terms	132	128	136	126	107
$RTL_{[MOB]}$ – Terms	159	140	137	130	103

A priori RTL

We selected two RTL from the wind energy domain available on the web. Both of them are multilingual and cover several languages of our variant study.

Terminalf[8] contains 84 terminological records in the wind energy domain in French, English and Spanish (Carey 2004). All terms are nouns, either simple or complex terms. They cover components of the wind turbine, natural constraints of a wind park, technological background of the wind energy system and different kinds of wind turbines.

The Danish wind industry association[9] provides a Wind Energy Reference Manual of twelve chapters that answers most questions which students ask. It comes along with a wind energy glossary (DAG) of 133 terms in French, English, German, Spanish and Danish (DWID 2003). Terms are nouns or adjectives, either simple or complex terms. Concepts are about wind energy technology and industrial wind production.

We observed that Terminalf and DAG RTL share 34 terms: 41% of the Terminalf terms are in DAG, 26% of DAG terms are in Terminalf.

9.6.2 Our integrated terminology extraction

Candidate terms and variants are collected from corpora altogether with the terminology process. The collecting of candidate terms and term variants is carried out with TermSuite, a tool dedicated to terminology extraction and variant recognition that will be fully presented in Chapter 10. Candidate terms and variants are linked with the syntagmatic rules of the GGRV. As patterns were used to collect them, the GGRV could be applied without any further treatment. If borders had been used instead of patterns to collect candidate terms and variants, an additional treatment would have been necessary to compute candidate term and variant patterns.

Table 9.5 Size of TCL and TCL_V extracted from [EOL] and [MOB] without hapaxes.

		De	En	Es	Fr	Ru
[EOL]	TCL	15,426	16,656	31,370	16,022	15,143
	TCL_V	17,939	24,288	34,409	19,849	17,344
[MOB]	TCL	17,957	16,547	20,506	17,306	12,965
	TCL_V	20,605	26,574	32,431	24,013	14,899

8. www.terminalf.scicog.fr

9. http://windpower.org/en/knowledge/windpower_wiki.html

Collecting terms

Collecting candidate terms includes the extraction of simple and complex terms that can be nouns or adjectives. Syntagmatic compounds are extracted with patterns provided in Section 2.5.2. Filtering is limited to the removing of hapaxes that consists of half of candidate terms. Results of term extraction process appear as a list of candidate terms (TCL), which are lemmatised and ordered according to (cf. Section 9.3.3). The following example shows the beginning of the TCL for English on [EOL]:

Rank	Lemma of the term candidate
1	wind project
2	wind energy project
3	aerodynamic
4	wind energy
5	wind turbine energy
6	onshore wind energy
7	energy from wind
8	small-scale wind energy

Collecting term variants

Term variants are of all variant categories. We used the GGRV whose rules by language are described in Section 7.2. We also applied string distance measures with a constrained threshold to the detection of graphical variants (cf. Section 6.2).

The list of candidate terms with variants TCL_V is ordered according to WR, in the same way as *TCL*. But for each term, variants that have been detected appear at the same rank as the candidate term. The following example shows the top of the TCL_V for English on [EOL]:

Rank	Term/variant	Lemma of the candidate term or variant
1	T	wind project
1	V	wind energy project
2	T	aerodynamic
3	T	wind energy
3	V	wind turbine energy
3	V	onshore wind energy
3	V	energy from wind
3	V	small-scale wind energy

Table 9.5 gives the size of TCL and TCL_V in terms of number of terms for each language and each corpus. The size of TCL_V is larger than TCL. As the number of occurrences of each variant is added to the number of occurrences of the candidate

term, many candidate terms that were hapaxes and removed in TCL are kept in TCL_V because of their variants.

Table 9.6 Maximum recall of RTL in the comparable corpora [EOL] and [MOB].

	De	En	Es	Fr	Ru
$RTL_{[EOL]}$	43.61	95.31	67.65	92.06	49.46
$RTL_{[MOB]}$	71.07	96.43	89.05	97.69	75.73
TERMINALF	–	42.17	59.52	59.76	–
DAG	40.3	55.64	74.07	51.11	–

9.6.3 Comparison protocol

The protocol specifies how to compare terminology extraction with or without variant recognition. Measures are precision and recall, which are calculated for TCL and TCL_V. A candidate term that belongs to TCL or TCL_V will be judged correct if a full match with a term of the RTL is found. Match is calculated with the lemma form. Two configurations are distinguished:

1. If the candidate term belongs to TCL, we observe the match between the candidate term and the term of the RTL. If the match succeeds, the rank of the candidate term in TCL is returned. For example, the term *onshore wind energy* of TCL belongs to RTL, rank 5 is returned.
2. If the candidate term belongs to TCL_V, we observe the match between the candidate term or term variant, and the term of the RTL. If the match succeeds, the rank of the candidate term in TCL_V is returned. For example, the term *onshore wind energy* of TCL_V belongs to RTL, it is proposed as a term variant of the candidate term *wind energy* of rank 2, so rank 2 is returned.

Precision and recall are calculated for the first 50 candidate terms in TCL and TCL_V, then for the first 100, 500, 1,000, 5,000 candidate terms. We decided not to look at the candidate terms after the first 5,000 ranks. Indeed, recognition of variants should be useful for first ranks and not at the end of the list. With the first step set at the first 50 candidate terms, top first ranks are not evaluated. We will add commentaries about them when results will be presented.

9.6.4 Maximum recall

Maximum recall gives the number of terms of TCL that belong to RTL. Table 9.6 indicates for each RTL its maximum recall for candidate terms extracted from [EOL] and [MOB].

Maximum recall should be close to 100 for the a posteriori RTL. But reading the scores of maximum recall computed with the a posteriori $RTL_{[EOL]}$ and $RTL_{[MOB]}$, this is not the case, especially for Spanish, German and Russian for [EOL]. A score of maximum recall that is inferior to 50 for the a posteriori RTL is comparable to a score of maximum recall for the a priori RTL. We can observe that, for Spanish and [EOL], the maximum recall of 74 using the a priori DAG RTL is superior of the maximum recall of 67.5 for the a posteriori $RTL_{[EOL]}$. After investigation, the a posteriori RTL have been compiled on corpora of larger sizes than the [EOL] corpora, thus many terms of $RTL_{[EOL]}$ do not occur in [EOL]. But for [MOB], the corpora used for collecting reference terms and candidate terms was much the same, and we observe that the maximum recall is 71 for German and 75.7 for Russian. The explanation comes from an incorrect lemmatisation that makes the match unsuccessful.

Concerning the a priori TERMINALF and DAG RTL, the scores of maximum recall are the one we expected. They are quite good given that comparable corpora were compiled automatically by thematic crawling on the web.

The two following sections will be devoted to the results of the comparison of two terminology extraction configurations, without or with variant recognition. Scores of precision and recall are calculated. Precision indicates the number of terms of the RTL that occur in the subset of candidate terms. Recall indicates the ratio of terms of the RTL that occur in the subset of candidate terms. Scores of precision and recall calculated for each extraction configuration and each language are visualised in a graphic where the x-axis is the number of candidate terms, and the y-axis, the score of precision or recall, the maximum value of the y-axis being the maximum recall of the RTL. Our aim is to evaluate the faculty of term extraction to rank at first ranks the terms of the RTL. Each graphic includes four curves: two for the precision without and with variant recognition, two for recall without and with variant recognition. Broken lines show the terminology extraction precision and recall scores without variant recognition. Solid lines show the terminology extraction precision and recall scores with variant recognition. White circle lines are for precision. Black circle lines are for recall.

9.6.5 Observations with a posteriori RTL

A posteriori RTL allow us to investigate how useful variant recognition is for a term extraction application on two specialised corpora and five languages. Table 9.1 and Table 9.2 show results respectively in [EOL] and in [MOB]. We observe that terminology extraction with variant recognition always outperforms terminology extraction on its own. However, improvement differs according to language and domain. It is slightly larger in [EOL] than in [MOB], with the exception of Russian where discrepancies are consistently higher in the two domains. An explanation has to be sought in specialised domain features and specialised corpora. [MOB] gathers numerous technical documents of three main genres: telephony standards, transmission protocols, mobile phone user guides. For these genres, documents are often translated and terminology is controlled. Simple terms are preponderant, as for French *serveur* 'server', *protocole* 'protocol', *paquet* 'packet', *routage* 'routing', and many of them are borrowed terms, as English, French, German, Spanish *roaming, streaming bluetooth, proxy.* Term variants are less numerous. In [EOL], precision improves significantly up to the first 500 candidate terms and recall improves constantly from the top first and up to the first 5,000 candidate terms.

Improvement of results on the top first ranks when variant recognition is performed is due to the re-ranking of terms belonging to the RTL at first ranks. These terms are analysed as term variants:

1. Either of a candidate term that is recorded in the RTL:
   En: *offshore wind turbine, domestic wind turbine, onshore wind turbine* $\in$ $RTL_{[EOL]}$ and are variants of candidate term *wind turbine* $\in$ LC_V rank 1, *wind turbine* $\in$ $RTL_{[EOL]}$, *offshore wind turbine* $\in$ TCL rank 110, *domestic wind turbine* $\in$ TCL rank 239, *onshore wind turbine* $\in$ TCL rank 7,948;
   Ru: кинетическая энергия ветра 'kinetic energy of the wind' $\in$ $RTL_{[EOL]}$ and is a variant of the candidate term энергия ветра 'wind energy' $\in$ LC_V rank 4, энергия ветра $\in$ $RTL_{[EOL]}$, кинетическая энергия ветра 'kinetic energy of the wind' $\in$ LC rank 157;
2. Either of a candidate term that is not recorded in the RTL:
   De: *Geräusch von Windenergieanlage* $\in$ $RTL_{[EOL]}$ and is a variant of the candidate term *Anlagengeräusche* $\in$ LC_V rank 591, *Anlagengeräusche* $\notin$ $RTL_{[EOL]}$, *Geräusch von Windenergieanlage* $\notin$ TCL;
   Es: *caja multiplicadora de velocidad* $\in$ $RTL_{[EOL]}$ and is a variant of the candidate term *caja multiplicador* $\in$ LC_V rank 37, *caja multiplicador* $\notin$ $RTL_{[EOL]}$, *caja multiplicadora de velocidad* $\in$ TCL rank 4,999;
   Fr: *gaz à effet de serre* 'greenhouse gas' $\in$ $RTL_{[EOL]}$ and is a variant of the candidate term *effet de serre* 'greenhouse' $\in$ LC_V rank 125, *effet de serre* $\notin$ $RTL_{[EOL]}$, *gaz à effet de serre* $\in$ TCL rank 13,607;
   Ru: средняя скорость ветра 'average wind speed' $\in$ $RTL_{[EOL]}$ and is a variant of the candidate term скорость ветра 'wind speed' $\in$ LC_V rank 14, скорость ветра $\notin$ $RTL_{[EOL]}$, средняя скорость ветра $\in$ TCL rank 63.

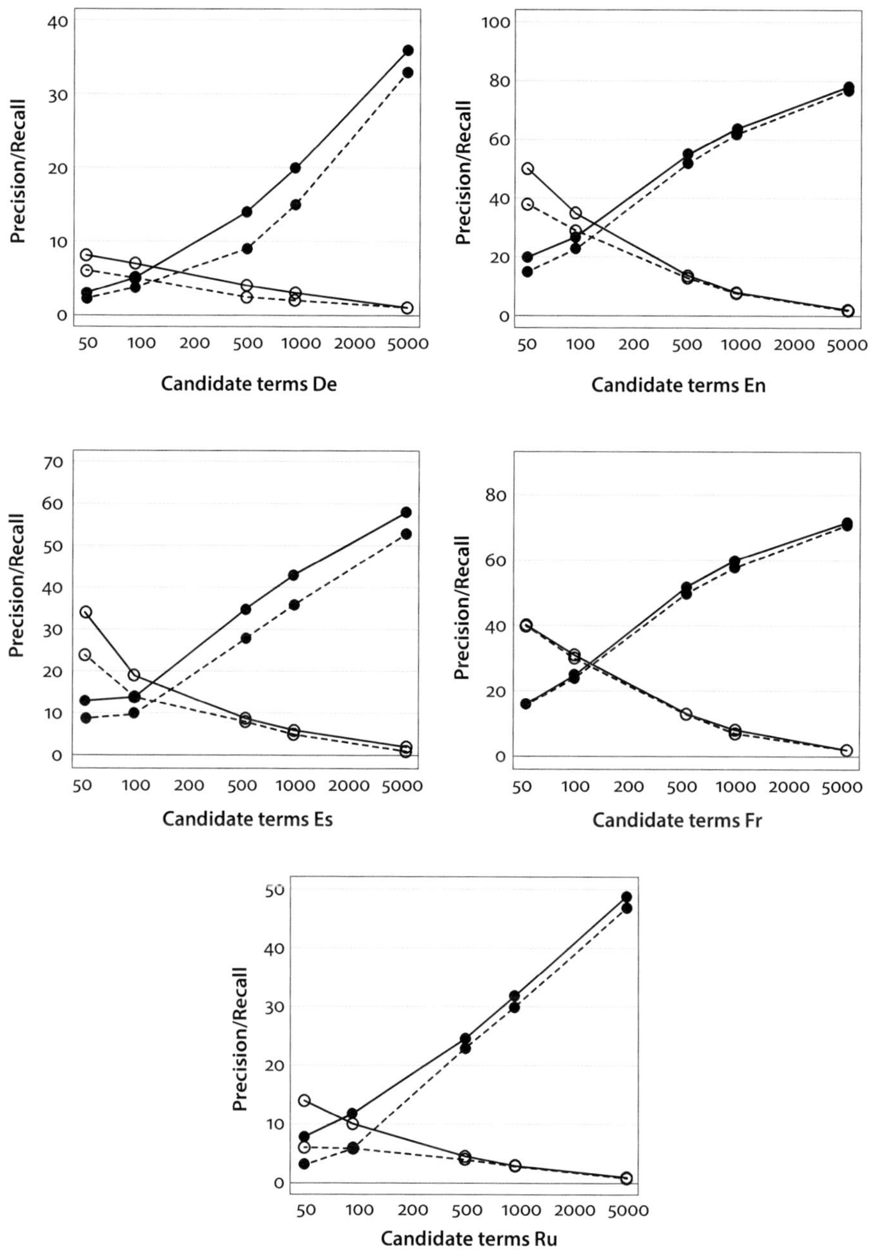

Figure 9.1 recall in [EOL] with RTL$_{[EOL]}$ (white circle: precision; black circle: recall; broken line: precision; solid line: recall).

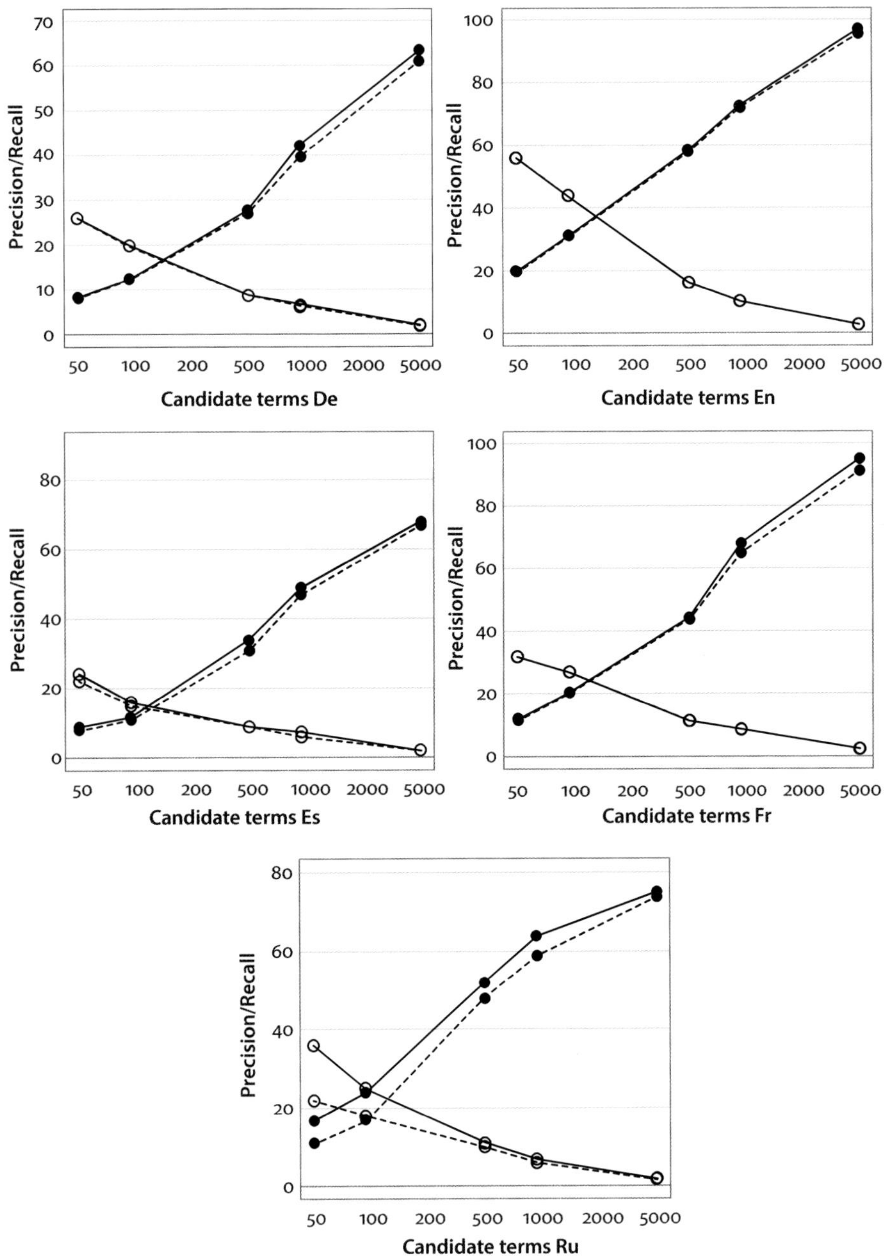

Figure 9.2 Precision/recall in [MOB] with RTL$_{[MOB]}$ (white circle: precision; black circle: recall; broken line: precision; solid line: recall).

Variant recognition improves recall because many terms of the RTL that were ranked after the 5,000th position are classified as variants of a candidate term appearing before the 5,000th position.

However, these results have to be taken cautiously as there are average numbers calculated for an interval of candidate terms. Even if the numbers for an interval are similar, they encompass different realisations. It is not the same terms of the RTL that are extracted and the rank of a candidate term may vary inside the interval. For instance, for French, where the results look the same, there are discrepancies with regards to the candidate terms ∈ $RTL_{[EOL]}$ when examining rankings of TCL_V and TCL:

1. *calage de pale* 'blade setting' ∈ TCL_V rank 118, ∈ TCL rank 8,428. The high difference of ranks between the two RTL can be explained by the large number of variants of the term *calage de pale* that have been detected such as: *calage de la pale* 'setting of the blade', *calage variable du pale* 'variable blade setting';
2. *éolienne à axe horizontal* 'horizontal-axis wind turbine' ∈ TCL_V rank 167, ∈ TLC rank 306.

9.6.6 Observations with a priori RTL

A priori RTL allow us to investigate how useful variant recognition is for a term extraction application for [EOL], in three languages with Terminalf RTL and four languages with DAG RTL. These RTL record the same numbers of terms whatever the language because they were designed multilingually. Table 9.3 shows results for [EOL] with Terminalf and Table 9.4 with DAG. We observe the same trend as for the a posteriori RTL, the overall tendency of variant recognition to improve the results of term extraction, here again both for precision and recall. The discrepancy is greater with Terminalf than with DAG. Precision improves considerably until the first 500 candidate terms and recall improves constantly whatever the interval of candidate terms.

We can make similar remarks for the a priori RTL as for the a posteriori RTL: variant recognition allows candidate terms as conceptual variants to be re-ranked at first ranks because they are analysed as term variants of either a candidate term that belongs to the RTL or a candidate term that does not belong to the RTL. For example, the term En: *wind turbine* ∈ TERMINALF, ∈ DAG occurs ∈ TCL_V at rank 1, variants of *wind turbine* ∈ TERMINALF that have been identified are: *two-bladed wind turbine* ∉ TCL, *three-bladed wind turbine* ∈ TCL at rank 1,263, *wind turbine generator* ∈ TCL at rank 313, and the variant ∈ TERMINALF and ∈ DAG that has been identified: *offshore wind turbine* ∈ TCL at rank 110. The term *mean wind speed* ∈ TERMINALF and ∈ TCL at rank 501 is analysed as a variant of *wind speed* ∈ TERMINALF and ∈ TCL_V at rank 4.

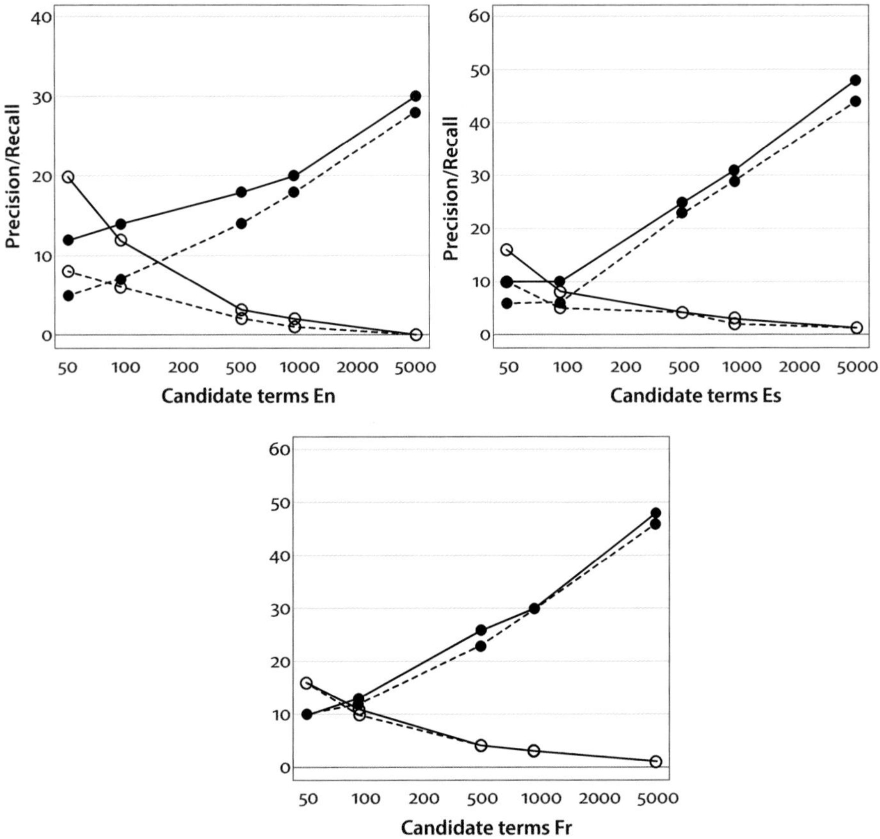

Figure 9.3 Precision/recall on [EOL] with TERMINALF (white circle: precision; black circle: recall; broken line: precision; solid line: recall).

Detection of denominative variants thanks to the competing structures (cf. Section 7.2.1) re-ranks at the first ranks candidate terms that belong to the RTL, as for En: *density ofair* ∈ DAG and ∈ TCL at rank 2,553 but which is analysed as a denominative variant of *air density* ∈ TCL_V at rank 229.

A few terms ∈ DAG, such as En: *downwind machine*, are not extracted from [EOL] because they occur under a synonymic variant, *downwind rotor* or *downwind turbine*, and both of them are ∈ TCL. Synonymic variant recognition as performed and presented in Chapter 8 will also be helpful to improve terminology extraction.

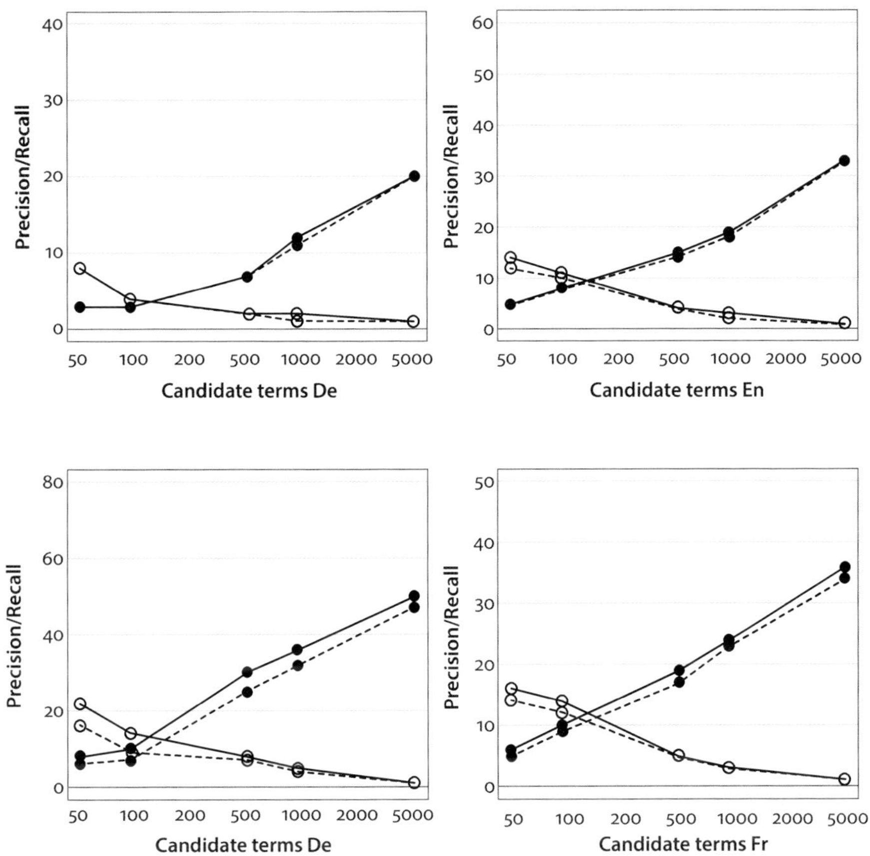

Figure 9.4 Precision/recall on [EOL] with DAG (white circle: precision; black circle: recall; broken line: precision; solid line: recall)

9.7 Summary of observations

This chapter has been dedicated to terminology extraction, a natural language processing application which aims to collect the terms of a specialised domain by exploiting a corpus made from textual documents of this same domain. Terminology extraction comprises two steps: selection of words and phrases that best fit term patterns, and filtering and ranking of candidate terms.

There are several ways to select candidate terms that are generally language dependent: by elaborating a list of patterns of term-like candidates, by relying on generic rules that describe nominal phrase structure, by identifying noun phrase borders, or by operating lexical expansion from a set of seed terms. Filtering and sorting of candidate terms, whatever the selection method, rely on various statistical measures that are frequencies, association measures or specificity measures. Filtering can rule out nested candidate terms. It can also examine the context of the candidate terms to discover clues as to their terminological status. Lastly, all term properties, either linguistic, statistical or contextual collected for each term occurrence in a corpus can be used as features of a classifier in order to make decisions about each candidate term occurrence in a corpus. This last method requires a corpus where term occurrences have been firstly identified and annotated. The output of term extraction is ideally a list of syntactically correct candidate terms, without redundancies, and as central to the domain as possible. Ranking of candidate terms should reflect the centrality of the term with regards to the specialised domain, the most specific should appear at the top of the list.

There are also several ways to evaluate the output of terminology extraction. The list of candidate terms might be examined by a human who determine the terminological status of each candidate term, generally for a given application. This list can used as such as input of an application; an end-user will evaluate the terminology extraction results through the application. Lastly, the list can be compared to a reference list compiled elsewhere or elaborated from the same corpora on which the terminology extraction will be performed. The evaluation of term extraction is conducted by calculating the state-of-the-art precision and recall metrics. They can be adapted to be more flexible toward various forms of candidate terms, a subset of term variants.

The terminology extraction task that we introduced was a preparation for the examination of the terminology extraction enhanced with variant recognition that we called the integrated terminology extraction. With the integrated terminology extraction, terms and variants are identified in parallel from corpora. For the term extraction task, we defined term patterns for each language and ranked them according to a specificity score without any additional post-treatment, with the exception of removing hapax occurrences. For the variant recognition task, we use the GGRV that performs syntagmatic analysis (cf. Chapter 7.2) and discovers denominative, conceptual and linguistic variants, as well as distance measures (cf. Section 6.2) for graphical variant detection. We compare the results of terminology extraction without or with variant recognition for two domains and five languages exploiting a posteriori or a priori reference lists. We observed on our data that our assumption that variant recognition improved the outputs of term extraction was justified. Improvement concerns both precision and recall: the ranking of the candidate terms is more accurate and more terms are detected. This improvement on both sides, precision and recall, is quite remarkable in natural language processing, improvement of one leading generally to decreasing of the other. Variants are handled differently depending on their category and do not play the same role with regards to the improvement of term extraction:

1. Denominative variants detected by the GGRV are merged. The pilot term that will be selected among the set of denominative and inflectional variants is the most frequent form. This merging increases the number of occurrences of the candidate terms and improves its ranking, as for the term (EOL) *air density* that gathers the denominative variants *air density* and *density of air;*
2. Conceptual variants that are detected by the GGRV are merged with the candidate term, but also kept as candidate terms. We recall that conceptual variants recognised by the GGRV are only variants of this category at 70% for all languages, and only at 35% for English. Merging does not increase significantly the number of occurrences of the candidate terms; indeed, conceptual variants are obtained by expansion process by 90%, but each of them occurs once, or very few times (cf. Section 7.4). The grouping of the term and its variants constitutes a first structuring of the output of term extraction. As an example, terms as *two-bladed wind turbine* and *wind turbine* that occur far from each other in the list of candidate terms proposed by the terminology extraction program are analysed as variants and clustered by the integrated terminology extraction program;
3. Linguistic variants like coordinative variants and graphical variants are occurrences of the candidate term similar to inflectional variants. Then the misspelled form *wind tubine* is analysed as one occurrence of the candidate term *wind turbine, off-shore wind farm* is one occurrence of the candidate term *offshore wind farm.* The number of occurrences of linguistic variants is merged with the number of occurrences of the candidate terms, as denominative variants they are taken out of the list of candidate terms. For a number of applications, they are not interesting as such and might not been recorded.

In the next chapter, we will review a few applications where variant recognition has been demonstrated to be useful, e.g. information retrieval and technology watch, as well as some tools that have been designed for their detection, in particular Termsuite that performs integrated terminology extraction and has been used for our experiments.

CHAPTER 10

End-user applications and tools

In the previous chapter, we confirmed that variant detection benefits terminology acquisition for the building of terminological resources. This chapter describes two further end-user applications where variation recognition has been demonstrated to be useful and for which tools are associated. We will end this review of tools designed for variant detection by presenting the framework TermSuite and several of its components that have been used for this study and that perform terminology extraction and variant recognition.

10.1 Machine-aided indexing and FASTR

Document indexing allows the user to access the documents that best fit his query. To perform accurate indexing close to human indexing, information retrieval might use key-phrases that represent the main content of a document. In specialised domains, many key-phrases chosen to describe the document content are terms. There are two ways of selecting key-phrases for a document:

1. free indexing which extracts the most important words or phrases occurring in a document;
2. controlled indexing which assigns key-phrases from a domain-specific terminology, such as a thesaurus or a knowledge organisation system.

Variant recognition is used differently according to the kind of indexing. For free indexing, key-phrases are extracted from documents using the generic rules that were introduced in Section 9.2.2 and then key-phrases and their variants are clustered to form a single entity. The approach is close to integrated terminology extraction but not identical, as it is not a corpus that is processed but a single document, often limited to a abstract. Variants are rare in short texts, so shallow techniques such as those introduced in Section 6.3 that are too noisy on corpora can be quite efficient. Bougouin et al. (2013) group key-phrases that share at least 25% of overlapping using a hierarchical agglomerative clustering with an average linkage strategy. Grouping key-phrases and variants improves the results of graph-based ranking algorithms up to 16 points of f-measure on short texts.

For controlled indexing, the key-phrases are known. They have to be identified in the document either in the linguistic form in which they are registered in the thesaurus or in a variant form of the term. The reference tool to perform controlled indexing is FASTR (Jacquemin 2001) designed for French and English, and with implementations in Japanese. FASTR performs automatic indexing from a list of controlled terms. This list might be enriched using lexical expansion (see Section 9.2.4). Variant recognition is at the heart of FASTR:

> In creating an automatic information-processing system that deals with scientific or technical texts, close attention must be given to term variability. Ignoring term variability may lead to the conception of inefficient indexing engines that are unable to relate conceptually close but linguistically different occurrences.
> (Jacquemin 2001: 3)

FASTR was used for an indexation task to assign terms among other from:

1. MESH thesaurus, English biomedical literature in MEDLINE (Aronson 2001; Névéol et al. 2007) or French medical texts (Pereira et al. 2008);
2. UMLS concepts, clinical texts (Zou et al. 2003).

It was also used to structure terminologies in cross-language environments (Dupuch et al. 2013).

FASTR adopts a unification-based grammar that implements the morpho-syntactic transformations from term into term variants. It accounts for denominative and linguistic variants of syntagmatic compounds of two content words. Denominative variants are adjectivation, adverbialisation, or verbalisation, labelled as morpho-syntactic variants, and synonymic substitution (see Section 3.2.1) at fixed position, labelled as paradigmatic variants. Linguistic variants are coordination variants. From the set of conceptual variants, only denominalisation and modifications by insertion are retained.

10.2 Thematic cartography and TermWatch

TermWatch has been designed by Ibekwe-SanJan and SanJuan (2006) for scientific science and technological watch for English. It performs a thematic cartography of a corpus. It is a text mining system with three main steps:

1. Term candidates are collected by lexical expansion (see Section 9.2.4). The seed terms are single words that occur in the corpus. When several seed words occur in a noun phrase, splitting rules are used. As an example, the following phrase pattern for English:

(D|A)* N+ of (D|A)* N+ P V (D|A)* N+

extracts two term candidates:

(D|A)* N+ of (D|A)* N+ and (D|A)* N+

2. Links between term candidates are established when a variant relation is acknowledged. Two categories of variants are handled: denominative variants and conceptual variants. Denominative variants are subsets of our denominative variants. They include term candidates that accept competing patterns, and synonymic variants obtained by substitution at word level in fixed position. Words that can be substituted belong to the same Wornet synset. Conceptual variants are obtained by expansion eventually associated with permutation at word level;
3. Aggregation takes groups constituted by a candidate term and its variants. When a variant is common to two groups, a link is inferred. Then an algorithm performing classification by preferential clustered link is used to calculate the strength between linked groups.

Term Watch gives as output a graph of terms visualised through a graphical interface. Term variant recognition is at the heart of TermWatch for topic detection. In order to establish links between different groups, detection of conceptual variants is crucial. To detect conceptual variants, TermWatch relies on left and right expansion rules, but also on rules than combine both left and right expansions, and expansion and insertion. Furthermore, expansion rules are not bounded to a fixed number of modifiers on the contrary of the GGRV that limits it to one or two, depending on the variant rule. So, variant may induce a conceptual gap from the term such as: *nuclear factor* → *AP($_2$ like nuclear factor binding* (Ibekwe-SanJuan 2007). The underlining assumption is that conceptual gaps reflect the domain evolution.

10.3 TermSuite

TermSuite is a term extraction tool that extracts terminology from corpora. It is multilingually designed, scalable, and handles term variants. It also capable of aligning terms across languages when multilingual corpora are available. TermSuite is implemented in Java and executed with a command-line or within the graphical interface. It is based on the Unstructured Information Management Architecture (UIMA) framework which supports applications that analyse large volumes of unstructured information and is designed to manage multilingualism. UIMA was developed initially by IBM (Ferruci and Lally 2004) but is now an Apache project.[1]

1. http://uima.apache.org

UIMA enables such applications to be decomposed into components (and components into sub-components) and to aggregate the latter easily. Below, we present only the part of TermSuite that is dedicated to terminology extraction and variant recognition, the multilingual alignment part being beyond the scope of this study. First, we briefly present the general architecture of TermSuite, and the input and output formats. Then, we will detail UIMA TokenRegexp, a tool to define term and variant patterns using word annotations within the UIMA framework, and Compost, the multilingual compound splitter, a grouping tool to cluster terms and variants.

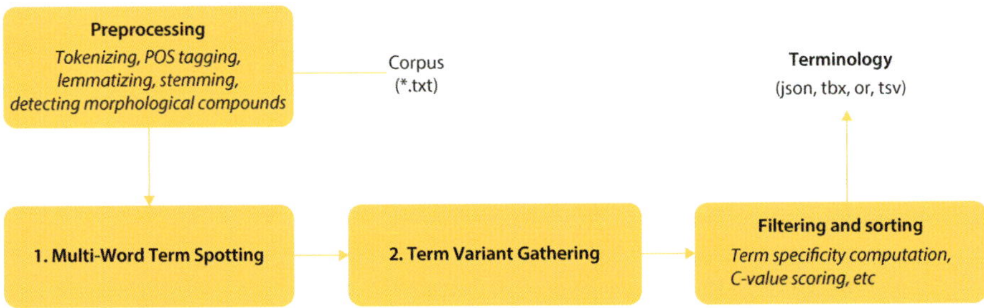

Figure 10.1 TermSuite NLP pipeline.

10.3.1 Architecture

TermSuite computes the termhood and the unithood of a term candidate. It adopts the two core steps of the terminology extraction process (cf. Section 9.1). Term-like units are collected with the following NLP pipeline that is summarised in Figure 10.1. They are ranked according to the most popular termhood measure.

The output Terminology is available under several formats: a Tab-separated values (tsv) format, a TermBase eXchange XML Schema (TBX) [ISO 30042:2008] compliant with the TMF (Terminological Markup Framework) meta-model [ISO 16642:2001], and a Jason input/output format, internal to TermSuite.

10.3.2 Token Regex

Candidate terms and their variants are extracted with Token Regex, a concise and expressive language coupled with an efficient rule engine. Token Regex allows the user to define rules over a sequence of UIMA annotations, i.e. over tokens of the corpus, each rule being in the form of a regular expression. Compared to RUTA (Kluegl et al. 2016), UIMA Token Regex operates only on annotations that appear sequentially, which is the case for word annotations. The occurrence recognition engine has been implemented as a finite-state machine with linear complexity. Token Regex syntax is formally defined by an ANTLR[2] grammar that is inspired by Stanford TokensRegex (Chang and Manning 2014).

A regular expression applying over annotations shares the syntax of the regular expressions over strings. UIMA Token Regex support the following features:

1. three operators: the space between two symbols indicates that the first symbol is followed by the second, the *or* operator |, and the *and* operator &;
2. four quantifiers of regular expressions are available: ?, +, *, and {*m*, *n*});
3. main anchors: initial position ^ and string final position $;
4. parentheses are used for grouping.

In a token sequence, individual tokens are bracketed by [and]. A token sequence is a boolean expression over the features and the values of the annotation. It is an expression of type `feature comparator value`, with six comparators available: ==, ! =, >=, >, <=, <. A string sequence is delimited by /.

The metacharacter . denotes any character in regular expression over strings. The metacharacter [ ] denotes any annotation in regular expressions over annotations.

Token Regexp rules

A rule formulated in UIMA Token Regex language consists of:

1. key-word `term`
2. rule name (string epression between double quotes (“))
3. separator :
4. annotation utterance written as a regular expression,
5. semicolon ;

In the type system of TermSuite, the values of the feature `category` are the part-of-speech (POS) tags. Rule `an` below extracts MWT composed of one or several adjectives followed by a noun.

```
term "an": [category=="adjective"] + [category=="noun"];
```

Rule `an`, below, extracts terms of A N pattern, such as *blade radius.*

2. http://www.antlr.org/

Macros

For the sake of readability, UIMA Token Regex supports definition of macros introduced by the keyword `matcher` which can be used latter in regular expressions. Thus, Rule can be expressed concisely as `A + N` using the matchers `N` and `A`:

```
matcher N: [category=="noun"];
matcher A: [category=="adjective"];
matcher C: [category=="conjunction"];
matcher P: [category=="adposition" & subCategory=="preposition"];
term "an": A+ N ;
term "npn": N P D? N ;
term "acan": A C A N ;
```

The quantifier `?` expresses an optional determiner. Rule `npn` can extract both MWT: *energy of wind* and *energy of the wind.* Rule `acan` extracts coordination variants that match the "adjective conjunction adjective noun" pattern, such as *onshore and offshore locations.*

A macro can be renamed or completed with additional required annotations with the keyword `as`. In the following macro, a new macro `Pde` is defined from the previous macro `P`

```
matcher Pde as P: [P & lemma=="de"];
```

Categories and subcategories are annotation features. Annotation features available in UIMA Token Regex are `category`, `subCategory`, `lemma`, and `stem` and inflectional features such as `mood`, `tense`, `case`, `number`, or `gender`. The verb inflection at past participle is defined by the macro:

```
matcher Vpp: [V & mood=="participle" & tense=="past"];
```

and the noun case in genitive case by:

```
matcher Ng: [N & case=="genitive"];
```

Lexical filtering

Regular expressions on tokens can be enhanced with lexical filtering expressing either positive or negative lexical constraints. On the lemma feature, an example of a positive constraint is the following statement that will only match the prepositions *of* and *with:*

```
matcher P: [category=="adposition"
& subCategory=="preposition"
& (lemma=="of" | lemma=="with")];
```

On the lemma feature, an example of negative constraint is the following statement that will match all lemma to the exception of *same, other* and *several:*

```
matcher A: [category=="adjective" & lemma!="same"
& lemma!="other" & lemma!="several"];
```

Contextual filtering

In order to improve the precision of term patterns, contextual filtering is useful to describe adjacent contexts of term patterns. Context annotations that are not part of term patterns should be preceded by tilde character ~.

The term variant rule expressing coordination for the base term of N A pattern in French requires as a left context a determiner in order to reduce false positive:

```
matcher D as D: [(category=="determiner" | category=="article") &
subCcategory != "possessive"];
matcher N: [category=="noun"];
matcher A1 as A: [category=="adjective"];
matcher A2 as A: [category=="adjective" | category=="numeral"];
matcher C: /^(et|ou)$/;
term "naca": ~ DN A1+ C A2+;
```

Annotation search

UIMA Token Regex engine parses the list of rules and creates for each of these rules a finite-state automaton. The engine provides automata with the sequence of UIMA annotations of the preprocessed input document.

Sequential search

UIMA Token Regex engine looks at the set of annotations that tag each token or each sequence of tokens sequentially following the linear order of the text. An annotation can be shared by *k* automata. For example, the part-of-speech *N* is shared by several rules at initial position: *NN, NPN, NA,* and so on. The match of the part-of-speech annotation generates *k* instances of automata. An instance of an automaton corresponds to a partial match where several elements have still to be recognised. When an instance has recognised all its elements, a term candidate occurrence or a term variant occurrence is recorded. If the instance succeeds, the engine looks at the next token occurring after the sequence of tokens that was matched. If the instance fails, the motor looks at the next token after the token that has raised the instance. For example, given the sequence 1-N 2-P 3-N 4-A and the rules (1) N P D? N, (2) N N, from the reading of , two instances of automaton are created I1 and I2 corresponding to rules (1) and (2) respectively for which there is a partial match on , the instance I1 succeeds, matches the sequence 1-N 2-P 3-N and tries to find another match from the position 4-A; the instance I2 fails and tries to find another match from the position 2-P 3-N 4-A.

Behaviour of the engine
UIMA Token Regex engine implements the default behaviour of a regular expression engine. It is *greedy, backtracking,* picking out the *first alternative,* and *impatient:*

Greedy
As long as there are annotations that can be matched and that the quantifier allows it, the engine adds annotations to the occurrence to be matched;
Backtracking
If the engine fails on one annotation, then the engine backtracks to the first fork of type `or` (eg. (A | *Vpp)* in the rule *N (A | Vpp) P N* is a fork of type `or`) and tries the following fork (*Vpp);*
Impatience
The motor looks at the token at the first left position following the linear order of the text;
First alternative
When a rule includes a fork expressed by `or`, the engine chooses the first element of the fork (*A*) and then tests the next annotations of the rule. The second element of the fork will only be chosen (*Vpp)* if the first fork fails during the exploration of the elements following it (*P* or *N*).

Every time an automaton (i.e. a *rule*) matches, TermSuite generates a rule *occurrence* and stores the offset indexes of the matched text.

10.3.3 Compost

All simple terms and term components of syntagmatic compounds are submitted to Compost. Compost is a compound splitting tool that works at word level without looking at the neighbourhood of the term occurrence. Compost has been integrated to TermSuite and default values have been set depending on each language for its optimisation. Splitting of the morphological compound is required for the detection of morphological variants of terms.

Compost *"Compound Splitting Tool"*[3] (Loginova-Clouet and Daille 2014) was designed to be applied to different languages, but also to be able to integrate linguistic knowledge. For a given word, the system makes the decision as to whether it is a compound, and for compounds it gives one or several candidate analyses ranked by their scores. The compound splitting method emcompassing Compost:

3. https://logiciels.lina.univ-nantes.fr/redmine/projects/compost

1. is language-independent and, therefore, multilingual;
2. can exploit linguistic knowledge provided by the user;
3. is designed for specialised domains, but usable also with general language texts;
4. includes manual parametrisation to control the precision/recall ratio;
5. copes with various compound types including neoclassical, native, loan and parasynthetic compounds, as well as prefixed words.

Such a large scope requires dedicated resources and ranking methods. We observed that the use of the list of neoclassical roots and prefixes generally improves splitting quality, as well as the use of domain specificity measure instead of corpus frequency. The specificity measure allows us to boost the in-domain segmentation candidates ranked first.

Segmentation strategy
To split a candidate compound, we start by generating all its possible two-part segmentations beginning with the components of minimum permitted length: we used the minimum length of 3 characters, which is a frequent choice for compound splitting systems (Koehn and Knight 2003; Dyer 2009).

DE *Traktionsbatterie* 'traction battery':
Traktionsbatterie → tr|aktionsbatterie
Traktionsbatterie → tra|ktionsbatterie
...
Traktionsbatterie → traktion|batterie
...
Traktionsbatterie → traktionsbatter|ie

If we can provide rules for this language to transform components into independent lexemes, we apply them to the component candidates. In the German example above, the rule *"s"* → "" can be applied: *Traktions* → *Traktion.* If rules are not available or not sufficient to cover all transformation cases, potential lemmas are proposed using a similarity measure.

For each candidate segmentation, lemmas for both components are matched with a lexicon and with a monolingual corpus. The lexicon contains a monolingual dictionary filtered by part-of-speech and combined with a list of neoclassical roots and prefixes. In this work, we only kept nouns, adjectives, verbs and adverbs in the lexicon to reduce prospective errors, even though we are aware that compound components can belong to other parts-of-speech (pronouns, numerals), but in the languages that we investigated such formations are scarce. The corpus allows us to calculate word frequency, which enables the algorithm to choose more plausible component candidates if several variants are possible. Then, the segmentation score is calculated (see below).

When this is done, we try to split the right side component further in a recursive manner, and so on up to a given level. This level is a parameter corresponding to the maximum expected number of components:

Ru: килоэлектронвольт ‘kiloelectronvolt’:
‘kiloelektronvolt’ → ‘kilo’|‘elektronvolt’
‘elektronvolt’ → ‘elektron’|‘volt’

Finally, the algorithm returns the N best segmentations ordered by their score. For De: *Traktionsbatterie* the output is:

traktion|batterie 0.85
trakt|ion|batterie 0.82
transaktions|batterie 0.78
traut|ion|batterie 0.77
traktat|ion|batterie 0.75

At each level of segmentation recurrence (at the first level the word is divided into 2 components, at the second level into 3 components and so on), the segmentation score is calculated as follows:

$$Score(segm) = \begin{cases} \dfrac{Score(compA) + Score(compB)}{2} & \text{if exact match} \\ \dfrac{Score(compA) + Score(compB)}{nbComp} & \text{otherwise} \end{cases}$$

where *nbComp* is the number of components in the word at this level of recurrence. “Exact match” means that all components are found “as they are” in the dictionary or corpus. We consider that two-part segmentations are more frequent and more plausible than those containing three and more parts, which is why we favor splits into two components.

Ru: ветроколеса ‘windwheel (plural)’:
Correct split: vetro|kolesa = veter ‘wind’|koleso ‘wheel’

$$Score(vetro + kolesa) = \frac{Score(veter) + Score(koleso)}{2}$$

Incorrect split: vetro|ko|lesa = veter ‘wind’|ko ‘co’ (prefix)|les ‘wood’

$$Score(vetro + ko + lesa) = \frac{Score(veter) + \frac{Score(ko) + Score(les)}{2}}{3}$$

An exception occurs for splits where components exactly match the dictionary or corpus. These splits are realistic and we do not penalise them dividing by *nbComp.*

$$Score(kilo + elektron + volt) = \frac{Score(kilo) + \frac{Score(elektron) + Score(volt)}{2}}{2}$$

This way of calculating the segmentation score at each splitting level also corresponds to the theoretical principle defended by Benveniste (1974) and that we share: a compound word is always formed by two components. Among these two components, one can be a compound itself, but only two components take part in a compound formation. The score obtained in such a way is rather close to the arithmetic mean of component scores.

The score of a component is calculated by a linear interpolation:

$$Score(comp) = \alpha\ sim(comp, lemma) + \beta\ inDico + \gamma\ inCorpus + \delta\ dataCorpus \quad (10.1)$$

where *sim(comp,lemma)* means similarity between the component and a candidate lemma (from 0 to 1), *inDico* and *inCorpus* indicate the existence of the lemma in the lexicon and in the corpus (0 or 1), *dataCorpus* equals either domain specificity (if we deal with specialised vocabularies), or general language corpus frequency. The sum of coefficients α, β, γ and δ is 1.

If a lemma in the lexicon is neoclassical, which implies that it does not occur individually in the corpus, we assign it the value $inCorpus = 1$; otherwise the score would be penalising for all neoclassical compounds.

To calculate the similarity between components and their potential lemmas found in the dictionary or in the corpus, we use "normalised edit distance" based on edit distance (for a detailed outlook of algorithms of strings see Section 6.2):

$$sim(comp, lemma) = 1 - \frac{nbEditOper}{max(length(comp), length(lemma))} \quad (10.2)$$

where *nbEditOper* is the minimum number of edition operations (substitutions, deletions, insertions) needed to transform a component into a lemma and *comp* a compound component.

Coefficients α, β, γ and δ are parameters and should be learned for each language using a small amount of training data (about a hundred of compounds per language).

Depending on the language and on the domain, we obtained a recall of between 77% and 90% for first segmentation, and between 86% and 94% for five first candidate segmentations. Precision was between 48% and 77% for first segmentation and between 53% and 88% for five first candidate segmentations.

10.3.4 Variant grouping

TermSuite is capable of gathering terms according to morphological and syntactic variant patterns that are defined with YAML syntax (Ben-Kiki et al. 2005). Occurrences of term-like and variant-like patterns are collected with UIMA Token Regex. The variant grouping engine pairs term and variant candidates. Variant rules implement the generic grammar for the recognition of variants (GGRV) that we designed in Chapter 7 in the Groovy language.

Variant rules
A variant rule states a set of conditions that two term candidates must fulfil to be paired. It consists of:

> **a rule name** a string expression between double quotes ("), ended by a colon (:),
> **a source pattern** and **a target pattern**, which are sequences of `matcher` labels,
> **a boolean expression** a logical expression on source and target term features, denoted by `rule`. The field `rule` is interpreted by a Groovy engine and must be defined in valid Groovy syntax.

The field `source` defines the pattern of the term to which the transformation applies. The field `target` defines the pattern of the variant resulting from the transformation applied. Rule can be applied to several source and target patterns, if so they have to be separated by a comma. The tag `[compound]` added to a part-of-speech tag indicates that the word or the word component has been identified as a compound by Compost. By convention, the field `source` holds the term and the field `target`, the variant, but any patterns of any term or variant occurrences collected by UIMA Token Regex can be indicated.

Finally, the field `rule` is expressed with the Groovy language boolean expression. A boolean expression is made of one or several equations combined with *and* (& &) and *or* (||) operators. The boolean expression accesses words and their elements with their positions inside the source or the target patterns. Two word properties are also reachable with their positions: `lemma`, which is the default property and could be omitted, and `stem`. The `compound` property is also reachable and returns `true` if the word is a compound, `false` otherwise. Description of pattern position is as follows:

1. `s[i].lemma (ors[i])` reaches the lemma of the ith component of the source pattern;
2. `s[j].stem` reaches the stem of the jth component of the target pattern;
3. `s[i]s[j]. lemma (ors[i][j])` reaches the jth element of ith the component of the source pattern. Of course, the component `s[i]` of the source pattern has to be a compound otherwise the rule returns `false`.

We exemplify the rule syntax with syntactic and morphological variant rules for English:

Syntactic variant

```
"S-I-NN-(N|A):
    source: N N
    target: N N N, N A N
    rule: s[0]==t[0] && s[1]==t[2]
```

This rule is named S-I-NN-(N|A): it is a syntactic rule *(S)* that describes an insertion *(I)* applying to the term of N N pattern *(NN),* and the element that is inserted is either a noun (N) for an adjective (A); | is use for the alternative. So, one term candidate (the source) must be of N N pattern, and the second term candidate (the target) of N N N or N A N pattern.

The `rule` field states that the `lemma` property of *s*[0], the first noun of the *source,* has the same lemma as *t*[0], the first noun of the `target`. Likewise *s*[1] and *t*[2] must share the same lemma. For example, this variant grouping rule will be satisfied for the two terms *turbine structure* and *turbine base structure.*

- `source`: *turbine structure*
- `target`: *turbine base structure*
- the pattern of the term `source` is *NN*
- patterns of the variant `target` are either *NNN* or *NAN;* for *turbine base structure* it is *NNN*
- the lemma of the first component of the term `source` *(wind)* equals the lemma of the first component of the term `target` (coefficient numbering starts with 0)
- the lemma of the second component of the term `source` *(energy)* equals the lemma of the third component of the term `t`

We indicated that a rule may operate upon the features `lemma` and `stem`, for example:

```
"S-PI-NN-P":
    source: N P N
    target: A N, N N
    rule: s[0]==t[1] && s[2].stem==t[0].stem
```

This rule will detect the variant pair *effect of rotation* ↔ *rotational effect.* Lemmas of the third component of the term `s` *(rotation)* and of the first component of the term `t` *(rotational)* differ, but these components share the same stem.

Morphological variants
TermSuite implements Compost that makes the decision as to whether the term composed of one graphic unit, is a simple term or a compound, and for compounds, the best split is kept. Compound elements are reachable when TermSuite comes to apply the variant grouping rules. The syntax of YAML variant rules allows the user to define compound properties for term or term components, for example `[compound]` or `t[0].[compound]` and to express morphological variants between two terms:

```
"M-I-EN-N|A":
   source: N [compound]
   target: N N, A N
   rule: s[0][0]==t[0][0] && s[0][1] == t[1]
```

In the rule M-I-EN-N|A above, the tag `[compound]` after the source pattern states that the source has to be a morphosyntactic compound. In the `rule` field, we access the component features with the second index of the two-based indexing arrays, the first index referring to the POS position in the source or target patterns. This rule will match variants such as *windfarm* ↔ *windmill farm* and *hydropower* ↔ *hydro-electric power.* As well as simple terms, compound components have `lemma` and `stem` properties.

Engine
Term variant grouping applies to term pairs with a complexity of O(n^2), where n is the number of term candidates extracted by UIMA Token Regex. TermSuite copes with this issue by pre-indexing each term candidate with all its pairs of single-word lemmas. For example, the term of length 3 *offshore wind turbine* has three indexing keys: `(offshore, wind)`, `(offshore, turbine)`, and `(turbine, wind)`. The grouping engine operates over all terms sharing the same indexing key, for all indexing keys. Therefore, the $O(n^2)$ complexity applies to small subsets of term candidates, and the weight of variant grouping in the overall terminology extraction process is quite reasonable.

Table 10.1 Figures of $\mathcal{G}$: size expressed in megabytes and gigabytes, and number of tokens expressed in million.

Newspaper	Language	Size	Nb tokens
Die Speigel	De	382*M*	60M
Glasgow Herald	En	302*M*	28M
Agencia EFE	Es	1.1*G*	171M
Le Monde	Fr	1.1*G*	82M
Izvestia	Ru	66*M*	5.8M

10.3.5 Ranking by termhood

Candidate terms are ranked according to their termhood that is measured with the *weirdness ratio* (WR Equation 9.2) introduced in Section 9.3.3. WR requires a domain specific corpus $\mathcal{C}$ and a general language corpus G for its computation.

General language corpora

General language corpora are part of the compilation of newspapers provided by CLEF 2004 (Jones et al. 2005). These corpora cover numerous and miscellaneous topics, which are useful to obtain a corpus representative of the general language. Figures of general language corpora that we use to compute frequencies of candidate terms are given in Table 10.1.

WR computation

The first problem that we faced while calculating WR is when a term candidate does not occur in $\mathcal{G}$. The relative frequency *RF* (Equation 9.1) is not calculable as there is zero quotient. We use the smoothing suggested by Gale and Church (1991) which assigns to an unknown word the normalised frequency $RF^0{}_{norm}$ given by the following equation:

$$RF^0_{norm}(ct) = \frac{1000 \times 0.5}{nboccS(ct)} \tag{10.3}$$

In other words, the frequency of 0.5 is assigned to a term candidate that does not occur in G.

The number of term candidates collected from $\mathcal{G}$ is huge. We decide to shorten the list of term candidates because of memory capacity, but also because of calculation efficiency, by applying a frequency threshold that removes term candidates with low frequency. The frequency threshold relies on the size of $\mathcal{G}$, as an example, it was set to 10 for French and 3 for English. It follows that the set of term candidates extracted from $\mathcal{G}$ will not include candidate terms below the threshold. As a consequence, WR will not be capable of discriminating between low frequency candidate terms.

WR behavior

Figure 10.2 gives WR distribution on the English part of [EOL]. The x-axis of Figure 10.2 is set to WR base-10 logarithm, hence a value of 2 means that the term candidate is a 100 times more frequent in the specific corpus $\mathcal{C}$ than in $\mathcal{G}$.

We distinguish two sets of terms on Figure 10.2. The first one, starting around 0 until $log(wr) \simeq 2$, contains the terms that are not domain specific since they occur in both $\mathcal{C}$ and G. The second set, from the peak at $log(wr) \simeq 2$ to the upper bound, contains both the terms that appear much more frequently in $\mathcal{C}$ than in $\mathcal{G}$ and the terms that never occur in $\mathcal{G}$. Actually, the first peak at *log(wr)* $\simeq$ 2 refers to terms that occur once in $\mathcal{C}$ and never in $\mathcal{G}$, the second lower peak refers to terms that occur twice in $\mathcal{C}$ and never in $\mathcal{G}$ and so on.

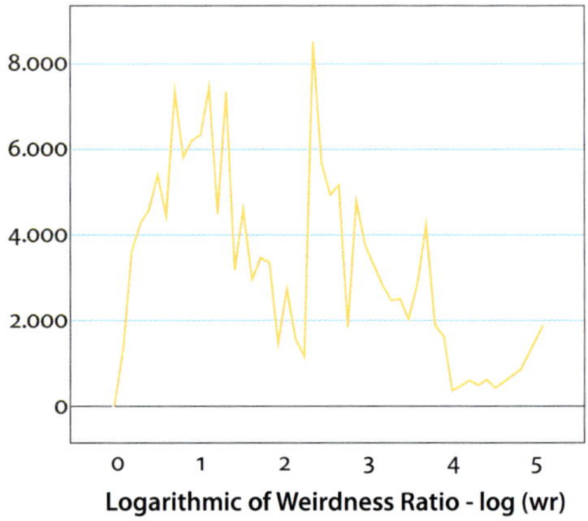

Figure 10.2 Distribution of WR base-10 logarithm over all terms extracted by TermSuite on English [EOL].

We did not provide the distributions for other [EOL] languages nor for other corpora, because their WR distributions are similar. For all configurations, the first peak always appears at WR $\simeq$ 2 and the upper bound at WR $\simeq$ 5. As a result of the analysis of WR distribution, we set 2 as default value of *log*(WR) threshold for accepting candidates as terms.

10.3.6 Performance

TermSuite executed on English [EOL] operates in 11 seconds with the technical configuration: Ubuntu 14.04, 16Go RAM, Intel (R) Core(TM) i7-4800MQ (4×2, 7Ghz). We detail the execution times of each main component with the use of two part-of-speech taggers TreeTagger[4] and Mate:[5]

4. http://www.cis.uni-muenchen.de/~schmid/tools/TreeTagger/

5. https://code.google.com/p/mate-tools/

	TT	Mate
Tokeniser	1.3s	*idem*
POS/Lemmatiser	2.4s	81s
Stemmer	0.67s	*idem*
MWT Spotter	4.8s	*idem*
Morph. Compound Finder	0.14s	*idem*
Syntactic Term Gatherer	0.23s	*idem*
Graphical Term Gatherer	0.27s	*idem*
Total (without UIMA overheads)	**9.8s**	**88.5s**

10.3.7 Release

TermSuite is under license Apache 2.0. The source code of TermSuite and all its components are released on Github at https://github.com/termsuite.

The github site gathers source codes, documentation, resources, and a graphical user interface. Sources of the core of TermSuite, which includes java API and scripts to launch TermSuite with a command line interface and documentation, are available under the sub-directory `termsuite-core`. All resources required by TermSuite are separated from the source codes. It means that the user bas to provide its resources and to indicate to TermSuite where to find them. This choice to separate resources from code has many advantages. The set of components of TermSuite is simplified and of reduced size. Then, users can modify the resources as they wish and make their own improvements. Of course, we provide all the resources that we have developed for the five languages, which include term and variant patterns as input to UIMA Token Regex, the GGRV as input for variant grouping, the list of terms and variants compiled from the general language corpora.

The lastest compiled version of TermSuite is also available on Maven Central.

This chapter presented two end-user applications for variant detection which have demonstrated to be useful: machine-aided indexing and thematic cartography, and the associated tools FASTR and TermWatch. Then, we presented TermSuite, the framework that we design to perform both terminology extraction and variant recognition and that encodes our variant specifications and integrates our generic grammar for the recognition of variants. TermSuite is a JAVA and UIMA-based toolkit. The main features of TermSuite are syntagmatic and morphological compound term detection, compound splitting, term variants detection and term specificity computation, among others.

PART IV

Conclusions

CHAPTER 11

Term variants and their discovery

This study described various aspects of the concept of term variants for their linguistic processing. It has proposed a unified theoretical framework under which all types of term variants can be situated for the five languages being considered: French, English, German, Spanish and Russian.

11.1 Summary of the present study

This book makes three main contributions to the study of term variants: on the aspects of their linguistic specifications, on the automatic methods for their detection and on applications. These three aspects are closely linked.

11.1.1 A unified typology of term variants

First, we introduced the linguistic and terminological foundations on which our study of variants is based. In Chapter 2, we defined the term, recalled its properties and the main linguistic mechanisms that are used to form it. We then identified, for several languages, the most current patterns of simple and complex terms. The complex term regroups two linguistic realities: the complex term that is morphologically built, i.e. the morphological compound, and the one that is syntactically built, i.e. the syntagmatic compound. We estimated the frequency of these terms both in existing terminologies and in several corpora, and confirmed the preponderance of nominal complex terms constituted of two words that adopt specific patterns. Our study of term variants concentrates on these complex terms. We then recalled our definition of a term variant and introduced the two main categories of variants: denominative variants that are other means to name a concept, and conceptual variants that place the term in the terminology of the domain.

Chapter 3 detailed the linguistic specifications of variants depending on their category and the main mechanisms leading to the formation of term variants. Linguistic operations enlarge those that we proposed in the defined typology for English and for an information retrieval application (Daille et al. 1996). A mechanism uses one of many linguistic operations. We made a description and illustrated these mechanisms as well as their linguistic operations associated with orthography and grammar of a language depending on the variant category. Some linguistic operations are preferred for a category of variants, others are shared. Some only generate a variant for articulating the term in the language system. The category of linguistic variants was added to denominative and conceptual variants We postulated a hierarchy of variants: a conceptual variant accepts denominative variants, and a denominative variant accepts linguistic variants. In the description of language mechanisms, we treated morphological compounding and syntagmatic expansions in the same way. In Chapter 4, we approached the semantics of denominative and conceptual variants by characterising the link between the term and the variant. We defined the fundamental relations, synonymy and hierarchical relations, and proposed some complex relations that were already introduced in the literature for describing the link between two terms, or the internal link of components of the complex term. We added to these semantic relations the relation of predication and the instance.

Our linguistic and semantic specifications of variants have been designed to be exhaustive and to overcome the language barrier. Many examples in the various languages considered are included, even if French and English predominate. These specifications must be applied to data: the second part of this study focused on semi-automatic and automatic methods for discovery and categorisation of variants.

11.1.2 A variety of methods for the discovery of variants

A term variant is at first a linguistic phenomenon that is observed in texts and registered in a discourse inside a specialised domain. The automatic recognition of variants requires various methods.

In Chapter 5, we carried out a linguistic corpus analysis by using a simple method, the n-grams, on three comparable corpora of three specialised domains in five languages. We checked empirically the precedence of the conceptual variant over the denominative variant, and the latter over the linguistic variant. This study showed that variants are shared across languages. They are associated with similar semantic paradigms that are expressed differently depending on languages. These differences highlighted by this contrastive study show the artificial character of the separation between morphological compounds and syntagmatic compounds, and between compounding and prefixation. These blurred borders have already been pointed out in Part I.

Chapter 6 reviewed several methods to be used for detecting the variants. Rough methods such as n-grams and clustering were treated quickly and more importance was given to natural language processing methods, namely morphological, syntactic, and distributional analyses. Some variants such as graphical variants are identified with traditional string searching algorithms. Edit distances are powerful mechanisms that can be used for updating morphological variants and, when they are developed to the level of constituents of the complex term, for detecting syntactic variants. Finally, the updating method for detecting such variants depends on the way in which the term and the variant co-occur. Three situations were identified, namely one in which the variant is isolated from the base term, one in which the variant and the term are inter-mixed, and one in which the variant and the term co-occurred separately locally.

Chapters 7 and 8 exploited linguistic processing for detecting variants. The generic grammar for the recognition of variants (GGRV), applied to occurrences where the term and the variant are inter-mixed, was described in Chapter 7 and was adjusted for five languages. The GGRV is composed of elementary morphological and syntactic operations that apply to the terms of each language and generate term variants. It includes three sets of rules: competing, augmented or reduced, and contextual structures. We chose to observe the global behaviour of the GGRV rather than evaluate each rule separately. We provided the number of detected variants and, for each language, the most pervasive rule and the most frequent triplet <Base term, Variant, Rule>, i.e. the Variant of the Term obtained by the Rule. Unsurprisingly, we observed that augmented/reduced structures generate the largest number of variants: between 80% and 90% of <Term, Variant> pairs, and between 60% and 70% of <Term, Variant> occurrences. We noticed that the frequently used rules belong to the augmented/reduced structure set, but each variant only has a few occurrences of <Term, Variant> pairs. By contrast, frequent triplets <Term, Variant, Rule>, i.e. a rule with many occurrences but which only applies to a few triplets <Term, Variant, Rule>, belong to the contextual structure set. This rule behaviour could be used to change the assignment of a rule from a set to another without further qualitative evaluation. We designed the three sets of rules in the aim of pairing denominative variants with competing structures, linguistic variants with contextual structures and conceptual variants with augmented/reduced structures. The human scanning of detected variants for some central terms of three specialised domains confirms the isomorphism for the first two cases, but not for the third case. Indeed, variants detected by augmented/reduced structures divide almost equally between conceptual and linguistic variants. This empirical observation correlates the linguistic specifications of the production of variants presented in Chapter 3.

The last linguistic analysis we carried out is the distributional analysis. The goal was to check whether this theoretical framework when applied to specialised corpora was adapted for discovering denominative variants generated by synonymic substitution. Synonymic variants are difficult to identify, firstly because they appear isolatedly from the term, and secondly because term synonyms are strongly related to specialised domain and to discourse. We described distributional analysis and its main implementations. We proposed a semi-compositional method for the discovery of synonymic variants of complex terms. A multilingual observation of this method for several languages and for several specialised domains has shown that, with a specific setting, the semi-compositional method supplies in average 2 to 3 synonyms in the five first candidate synonymic variants.

11.1.3 A terminology-resource building application

The detection of term variants, despite its genuine interest, is part of many applications. For natural language applications, conceptual variants have proven to be useful for the building of structured terminological resources. For other applications directly related to the user, such as information retrieval, detection of term variants helps perform accurate indexing close to human indexing, whether this indexation relies on repositories or not. Generally, the application chooses the categories of variants that are useful for it.

Chapter 9 was dedicated to a natural language application, terminological extraction. The objective of terminological extraction is to identify terms of a specialised domain that occur in a specialised corpus. Terminological extraction consists of two main steps, namely collecting term candidates, then sorting them according to their usefulness for the target application. Some candidate terms may be filtered out according to syntactic and terminological criteria. Criteria for the detection and the sorting of candidate terms are paired in a classical way with criteria of recognition of the linguistic unit (unithood) and criteria of recognition of the terminological unit of a specialised domain (termhood). We reviewed these criteria and showed that there is not always a clear distinction between criteria of unithood and termhood. For example, morphological or syntagmatic compounding characterise the linguistic unit, but also the terminological unit. Furthermore, the scores of association measures that reflect the strength of the bond between two words occurring in a corpus are useful to measure both unithood and termhood. We performed an integrated terminology extraction where terms and variants are identified in parallel from corpora, in five languages and two specialised domains by means of two comparable corpora. We observed with these data and these languages that the results of terminology extraction with variant recognition are always better than results of terminology extraction alone. For terminology extraction, all variants are useful, as it is crucial to identify exhaustively all candidate terms. But they are handled differently depending on their category and do not play the same role with regards to the improvement of term extraction. In particular, conceptual variants constitute a first structuring of the output of term extraction and allow the user to handle extracted terminological data more conveniently.

In Chapter 10, we described further end-user applications where variation recognition plays an important role, and for which tools were developed: machine-aided indexing and thematic cartography. We concluded this study by the framework that we designed to perform both terminology extraction and variant recognition and that encodes our variant specifications and integrates our generic grammar for the recognition of variants. TermSuite is a generic and modular tool, usable for many languages. It is a Java and command-line UIMA-based toolbox. The main features of TermSuite are syntagmatic and morphological compound term detection, compound splitting, term variant detection and term specificity computation, among others. We used TermSuite all along this study.

11.2 Remaining issues and direction for further research

Several issues were left unaddressed throughout the study, mainly concerning automatic methods of variant recognition.

11.2.1 Semantic analysis of variations

In Chapter 7, we proposed a generic grammar for the recognition of variants, the GGRV, whose aim was to proceed to a first classification of variants into three main categories, namely denominative, conceptual and linguistic. The classification for conceptual variants has yet to be improved since they only reach a precision of 70% for French, Spanish and Russian, and 35% for English. We mentioned a first track that retains for the expansions by modification, relational adjectives, deadjectival adverbs and adjectival compounds.

However, our categorisation of variants in three categories constitutes a first step for the structuring of terminology in a specialised domain. A more detailed categorisation of conceptual variants identified by augmented/reduced structures would be necessary. In Chapter 4, we listed the main semantic relations that can characterise the relation between terms and variants. For some variants obtained by derivation, the semantic relation might be directly inferred by the semantics of the affix. For other variants, such as variants obtained by predication, it would be interesting to distinguish the collocations of the term that reveal the term's properties from regular predications. For example (EOL) Fr: *implantation du parc éolien* 'construction of wind park' is an interesting collocation whereas *description du parc éolien* 'description of the wind park' is not. Jacquey et al. (2013) filtered spurious candidate terms proposed by TermSuite thanks to the transdisciplinary scientific lexicon. Such a lexicon could be useful to filter out spurious variants. Finally, for variants of expansion obtained by modification, the term instances that are interesting only in the case of a discourse analysis should be identified as such.

11.2.2 Distributional analysis at the morpheme level

In Chapter 7, we detected denominative variants obtained through synonymic substitution by performing a distributional analysis. In our specification of variants described in Chapter 3, we noted that synonymic substitution could be performed on all the components of terms, namely elements or words in morphological or syntagmatic compounds. However, we reduced distributional analysis to the sole detection of synonymic syntagmatic compounds. Processing all kinds of term compounds is not only a technical issue, but also requires theoretical consideration.

Distributional analysis assumes that two words are in a semantic relation if they share the same lexical contexts. The semi-distributional method calculates the contexts of each word of the syntagmatic compound. The modelling of the context relies on words occurring in the term neighbourhood. Therefore, for the sequence: Fr: *Pour les connexions des parcs éoliens au réseau* 'For the connection of wind parks to the network' and the syntagmatic compound *parc éolien* 'wind park', the contexts of *parc* 'park' are: *connexion, éolien* and *réseau* and those of *éolien* 'wind': *parc, connexion, réseau.* For a morphological compound, the modelling of the context based on words is no longer trivial. Context can be expressed by lexical contexts, as for syntagmatic compounds, but also by morphological contexts or a combination of the two, knowing that, in this latter case, the distribution of morphemes and of words differs in a corpus. With the sequence *From a biodiversity conservation standpoint* and the morphological compound *biodiversity,* there are several possibilities for modelling the contexts of *bio* and of *diversity.* If we take a span of 3 around these elements, the context may include:

1. Only lexical contexts: for *bio* and *diversity,* contexts are identical and are constituted by *conservation, standpoint;*
2. Only morphological contexts provided by the application of a morphologival analyser on morphological compounds. These morphological contexts can be collected from the compound only, or enlarged to the other morphemes occurring in a textual sequence. For *bio: diversity* only, or *diversity, conservation, stand,* and for *diversity: bio* only, or *bio, conservation, stand, point;*
3. A mixture of lexical and morphological contexts that only keeps morphological contexts of the compound. For *bio: diversity, conservation, standpoint* and for *diversity: bio, conservation, standpoint.*

Another more sophisticated way of modelling the context would differentiate context units depending on the nature of the morphological element, native, neoclassical or prefix. But such modelling depends on the availability of a morphological analyser capable of performing such analysis in spite of the difficulty of the task. We actually noted in Section 2.3 the fuzziness of the borders between native compounds and neoclassic compounds, and between compounding and derivation.

Distributional analysis applied to morphological compounds raises problems of compound splitting, of compound categorisation, but also of context modelling that we could not solve in this study. We will leave this topic for future works.

11.2.3 Recognition of other variants

A variety of methods is required for recognising the broad range of variants that occur in texts. We integrated several of these methods in TermSuite. The generic and modular architecture of Termsuite allows us to handle many languages in a homogeneous way. Language is an input parameter.

Therefore we privileged generic natural language processing tools that are either language independent, such as the Porter's stemmer, or available for numerous languages, such as TreeTagger. Our main concern was to treat in a uniform way variants of simple terms, morphological compounds and syntagmatic compounds.

We integrated string algorithms for graphical variant recognition. We adapted the distributional method to the detection of denominative variants for syntagmatic compounds obtained by synonymic substitution. Some work was carried out but we are far from recognising all variants. Acronyms, abbreviations and anaphoric variants are missing. Their detection as well as their integration in TermSuite will be considered for future work.

11.3 Implications for related studies

11.3.1 Variants and paraphrases

Term variation has often been assimilated to the phenomenon of paraphrase. On the one hand, term variation is a broader phenomenon than paraphrase, at least based on our definition of term variant. Only denominative variants and a subgroup of linguistic variants could be defined as paraphrases. Paraphrases gather:

1. lexical paraphrases matching our denominative variants obtained by synonymic substitution;
2. syntactic paraphrases including our other denominative variants obtained by simplification, exemplification, or allowing competing structures;
3. paraphrases combining lexicon and syntax.

Syntactic paraphrase applies to all syntagmatic units of the sentence, as well as the sentence itself. On the other hand, paraphrase is a much larger phenomenon than term variation. Paraphrases ease the understanding of texts, and their automatic acquisition has been a recurrent topic in natural language processing (Madnani and Dorr 2010).

The study of paraphrases in specialised domains will allow us to complete our typology of variants, from the phrase to the sentence level. The GGRV includes some paraphrase detection rules such as the English competing patterns: N_1 N_2 and N_2 P N_1. More sophisticated paraphrases might be recognised with the use of a morphological analyser or a syntactic parser. Déléger (2009) paraphrased neoclassic morphological compounds as syntagmatic compounds with the help of the French morphosemantic analyser DERIF (Namer 2003). DERIF splits neoclassical compounds and pairs the neoclassical root with its lexical French equivalent such as: (MED) Fr *gastrite* 'gastritis' with *inflammation de l'estomac* 'stomach inflammation'. The extreme diversity of competing syntactic structures at the sentence level rather advocates the use of empirical methods such as those proposed by Fujita and Isabelle (2015) which learn variation rules from pairs of terms and variants.

11.3.2 Variants and translation

We have shown the interest of variants for terminology extraction, machine-aided indexing and thematic cartography, but variants are also useful in translation. Even if translators usually translate into their mother tongue, the fact that they master the current language does not mean that they master the terminology, nor that know the linguistic behaviour of the specialised domain. Technical translation requires a in-depth prior understanding of the domain. Durieux (2010) points out two difficulties, namely access to the good term, and knowledge for using it in discourse, in particular by associating it to its proper collocations. Scurtu (2008) deplores the absence of available computational resources for the translator that should be richer than common term lists supplied without knowledge or linguistic contexts.

Variants of terms can contribute to a better comprehension of the concept conveyed by the term and to see how the term behaves in discourse. Regarding of comprehension, denominative variants obtained by the mechanism of exemplification help the translator to understand the meaning of the source term in his mother tongue, and conceptual variants, to apprehend the structure of the specialised domain. Conceptual variants can also provide a better picture of typical contexts in which terms appear and thus become reliable clues for collocations. Variants allow the user to understand and correctly use terms.

In the area of automatic construction of multilingual terminological resources, compositionality-based methods have been introduced to generate translations of source terms. The compositionality-based approach consists in decomposing source terms into sub-units holding a meaning, translating these sub-units and reordering the translated items so as to generate a candidate translation. Candidate translations are then filtered out with the target specialised corpora. Source terms are morphological or syntagmatic compounds. The compositionality-based approach supplies few translations, but these translations are of good quality (precision between 42% and 99% observed by Harastani et al. 2012; Morin and Daille 2012). For most conceptual variants, the property of compositionality between the term and the added element is also valid. For example, (EOL) Term Fr: *effets sur la santé/En: health effect,* Variant Fr: *effets dommageables sur la santé* and Fr: *dommageable/En: adverse,* the compositional translation will generate the collocation: En: *adverse health effect.* The alignment of conceptual variants will provide richer bilingual terminological resources including not only term translations but also translations of term collocations. It can help explain the meaning of terms that designate complex technical or scientific concepts and also to adapt the translation to a specific readership.

Bibliography

S. Abney. Partial parsing via finite-state cascades. *Natural Language Engineering*, 2(4): 337–344, 1996. doi:10.1017/S1351324997001599

K. Ahmad, A. Davies, H. Fulford, and M. Rogers. What is a term? The semiautomatic extraction of terms from text. *Translation Studies: An Interdiscipline*, pages 267–278, 1994.

D. Amiot and G. Dal. Integrating neoclassical combining forms into a lexeme-based morphology. In *Proceedings of the 5th Mediterranean Morphology Meeting (MMM5)*, 2007.

D. Amiot and G. Dal. La composition néoclassique en français et l'ordre des constituants. *La composition dans les langues*, pages 89–113, 2008.

A. Aronson. Effective mapping of biomedical text to the UMLS metathesaurus: The metamap program. In *Proceedings of the 25th Annual Symposium of the American Medical Informatics Association (AMIA 2001)*, pages 17–21, 2001.

M. Baroni and S. Bernardini. BootCaT: Bootstrapping corpora and terms from the web. In *Proceedings of the 4th conference on International Language Resources and Evaluation (LREC 2004)*, pages 1313–1316, 2004.

M. Baroni and A. Lenci. Distributional memory: A general framework for corpus-based semantics. *Computational Linguisics*, 36(4):673–721, 2010. doi:10.1162/coli_a_00016

C. Barrière. Recherche contextuelle d'équivalents en banque de terminologie. In *Actes de la 17ème conférence sur le Traitement Automatique des Langues Naturelles (TALN 2010)*, 2010.

L. Bauer. *English word-formation*. Cambridge University Press, Cambridge, 1983. doi:10.1017/CBO9781139165846

L. Bauer. *Morphological productivity*. Cambridge University Press, Cambridge, 2001.

L. Bauer and A. Renouf. A corpus-based study of compounding in english. *Journal of English Linguistics*, 29:101–123, 2001. doi:10.1177/00754240122005251

H.-D. Béchade. *Phonétique et morphologie du français moderne et contemporain*. Presses Universitaires de France, Paris, 1992.

O. Ben-Kiki, C. Evans, and B. Ingerson. Yaml ain't markup language (yaml^{TM}) version 1.1. *yaml. org, Tech. Rep*, 2005.

M. Benson. Collocations and general-purpose dictionaries. *International Journal of Lexicography*, 3(1):23–25, 1990. doi:10.1093/ijl/3.1.23

É. Benveniste. *Problèmes de linguistique générale*, chapter Formes nouvelles de la composition nominale, pages 163–173. Gallimard, Paris, 1966.

É. Benveniste. *Problèmes de linguistique générale*. Gallimard, Paris, 1974.

D. Bergmark, C. Lagoze, and A. Sbityakov. Focused crawls, tunneling, and digital libraries. In M. Agosti and C. Thanos, editors, *Research and Advanced Technology for Digital Librairies – 6th European Conference, ECDL 2002*, volume 2458 of *Lecture notes in computer science*, pages 91–106. Springer, New York, 2002.

D. Biber. A Typology of English Texts. *Linguistics*, 27(1):3–43, 1989. doi:10.1515/ling.1989.27.1.3

D. Biber, S. Johansson, G. Leech, S. Conrad, and E. Finegan. *Longman Grammar of Spoken and Written English.* Longman, London, 1999.

M.-B. Billami, J. Camacho-Collados, E. Jacquey, and L. Kister. Semantic annotation and terminology validation in full scientific articles in social sciences and humanities (annotation sémantique et validation terminologique en texte intégral en shs). In *Actes de la 21e conférence sur le Traitement Automatique des Langues Naturelles (TALN 2014)*, pages 363–376, 2014.

L. Bloomfield. *Language.* Allen and Unwin, London, 1935.

N. N. Bobyreva. Syntactic way of term-building in terminological system of rhytmic gymnastics in the Russian and the English languages. *TCHGPU*, 12, 2009.

E. Bolshakova. Common scientific lexicon for automatic discourse analysis of scientific and technical texts. *International Journal "Information Theories & pplications"*, 15: 189–195, 2008.

B. Bommier-Pincemin. *Diffusion ciblée automatique d'informations : conception et mise en œuvre d'une linguistique textuelle pour la caractérisation des destinataires et des documents.* PhD thesis, Université Paris IV, Sorbonne, 1999.

A. Bosredon. Un adjectif de trop : l'adjectif de relation. *Information grammaticale*, 37: 3–7, 1989. doi:10.3406/igram.1988.2048

A. Bosredon. Prédicativité et lexicalisation. *Studia Romanica Posnaniensia*, 16:85–100, 1991.

A. Bougouin, F. Boudin, and B. Daille. TopicRank: Graph-Based Topic Ranking for Keyphrase Extraction. In *Proceedings of the 8th International Joint Conference on Natural Language Processing (IJCNLP 2013)*, pages 543–551, 2013.

D. Bourigault. *LEXTER : un logiciel d'EXtraction de TERminologie. Application à l'extraction des connaissances à partir de textes.* Mathématiques, informatique ap-pliquée aux sciences de l'Homme, École des Hautes Études en Sciences Sociales, Paris, 1994.

D. Bourigault and C. Jacquemin. Construction de ressources terminologiques. In J.-M. Pierrel, editor, *Ingénierie des langues*, pages 215–234. Hermes, Paris, 2000.

D. Bourigault and M. Slodzian. Pour une terminologie textuelle. *Terminologies nou-velles*, 19:29–32, 1999.

L. Bowker and S. Hawkins. Variation in the organization of medical terms – exploring some motivations of term choice. *Terminology*, 12(1):79–110, 2006. doi:10.1075/term.12.1.05bow

L. Bowker and J. Pearson. *Working with Specialized Language: A Practical Guide to Using Corpora.* Routledge, London, 2002. doi:10.4324/9780203469255

D. A. Burgos Herera. *Towards an Image-Term Co-occurrence Model for Multilingual Terminolog Alignment and Cross-Language Image Indexing.* PhD thesis, Universitat Pompeu Fabra, 2014.

G. Burnage. *CELEX: A Guide for Users.* Center for Lexical Information, Univerty of Nijmegen, 1990.

H. Bussmann. *Routledge Dictionary of Language and Linguistics.* Routledge, London, 1996.

M. T. Cabré. *La terminologie: théorie, méthodes et applications.* Armand Colin, Paris, 1998.

M. T. Cabré. *La terminologia. Representación y communicación. Una teoría de base communicativa.* Universitat Pompeu Fabra, Barcelona, 1999.

M. T. Cabré. Do we need an autonomous theory of terminology? *Terminology*, 5(1): 2–20, 2000.

M. T. Cabré and J. Sager. *Terminology: Theory, Methods, and Applications.* John Benjamins, Amsterdam, 1999. doi:10.1075/tlrp.1

M. T. Cabré, R. E. Bagot, and J. V. Platresi. Automatic term detection: A review of current systems. In D. Bourigault, C. Jacquemin, and M.-C. L'Homme, editors, *Recent Advances in Computational Terminology*, volume 2 of *Natural Language Processing*, pages 53–88. John Benjamins, Amsterdam, 2001.

E. Carey. L'énergie éolienne. Master's thesis, Maitrise LEA. Université Paris III, 2004.

R. Chaffin and D. J. Herrmann. The similarity and diversity of semantic relations. *Memory and Cognition*, 12(2):134–141, 1984. doi:10.3758/BF03198427

A. X. Chang and C. D. Manning. TokensRegex: Defining cascaded regular expressions over tokens. Technical Report CSTR 2014-02, Department of Computer Science, Stanford University, 2014.

S. Chaudiron. *L'évaluation des systèmes de traitement de l'information textuelle : vers un changement de paradigme*. Mémoire pour HDR, Université de Paris X, Paris, 2001.

G. Ciapuscio. *Textos especializados y terminología*. PhD thesis, Institut Universitari de Lingüística Aplicada, Universitat Pompeu Fabra, Barcelona, 2003.

T. Collet. La réduction des unités terminologiques complexes de type syntagmatique. *Meta : journal des traducteurs / Meta: Translators' Journal*, 42(1):193–206, 1997. doi:10.7202/002348ar

CollinsDictionary. Collins dictionary, 2013.

G. Colpron. Les anglicismes au québec : essai de classification et de numération comparative. Master's thesis, Université de Montreal, Faculté des lettres, 1965.

A. Condamines. Corpus analysis and conceptual relation patterns. *Terminology*, 8(1): 141–162, 2002. doi:10.1075/term.8.1.07con

A. Condamines. L'expression de la méronymie dans les petites annonces immobil-ières ; comparaison français, anglais, espagnol. *Journal of French Language Studies (JFLS)*, 19:3–23, 2009. doi:10.1017/S0959269508003554

M. Creutz and K. Lagus. Unsupervised morpheme segmentation and morphology induction from text corpora using morfessor 1.0. In *Computer and Information Science, Report A81*, Helsinki University of Technology, 2005.

M. Crochemore, C. Hancart, and T. Lecroq. *Algorithmique du texte*. Vuibert, Paris, 2001.

K. Crowston, B. Kwaśnik, and J. Rubleske. Problems in the use-centered development of a taxonomy. In A. Meher, S. Sharoff, and M. Santini, editors, *Genres on the Web*, volume 42 of *Text, Speech and Language Technologies series*, Chapter 4. Springer, New York, 2010.

D. A. Cruse. *Lexical Semantics*. Cambridge University Press, Cambridge, 1995.

D. A. Cruse. *Meaning in Language: An Introduction to Semantics and Pragmatics*. Oxford University Press, Oxford, 2004.

J. R. Curran and M. Moens. Improvements in automatic thesaurus extraction. In *Proceedings of the Workshop on Unsupervised Lexical Acquisition associated to the 40th Annual Meeting of the Association for Computational Linguistics (ACL 2002)*, pages 59–66, 2002.

B. Daille. Variations and application-oriented terminology engineering. *Terminology*, 11 (1): 181–197, 2005. doi:10.1075/term.11.1.08dai

B. Daille, B. Habert, C. Jacquemin, and J. Royauté. Empirical observation of term variations and principles for their description. *Terminology*, 3(2):197–257, 1996. doi:10.1075/term.3.2.02dai

B. Daille, C. Enguehard, C. Jacquin, R. Raharinirina, B. Ralalaoherivony, and C. Lehman. Traitement automatique de la terminologie en langue malgache. In K. Chibout, J. Mariani, N. Masson, and F. Néel, editors, *Ressources et évaluation en ingénierie des langues*, Actualité scientifique – Universités Francophones, pages 225–242. De Boek & Larcier, Bruxelles, 2000.

J. Dancette and M.-C. L'Homme. Building Specialized Dictionaries using Lexical Functions. *Linguistica Antverpiensa*, 3:113–132, 2004.

C. de Groc. Babouk: Focused web crawling for corpus compilation and automatic terminology extraction. In *Proceedings of the 2011 IEEE/WIC/ACM International Conferences on Web Intelligence and Intelligent Agent Technology (WI-IAT 2011)*, pages 497–498, 2011.

L. Déléger and P. Zweigenbaum. Extracting lay paraphrases of specialized expressions from monolingual comparable medical corpora. In *Proceedings of the 2nd Workshop on Building and Using Comparable Corpora: from Parallel to Non-parallel Corpora*, pages 2–10, Suntec, Singapour, 2009. doi:10.3115/1690339.1690343

A. Depierre. Souvent HAEMA varie ...: Les dérivés du grec HAEMA en anglais : Étude de cas de variation. *Terminology*, 13(2):155–176, 2007. doi:10.1075/term.13.2.03dep

P. Drouin. Term extraction using non-technical corpora as a point of leverage. *Terminology*, 9(1):99–117, 2003. doi:10.1075/term.9.1.06dro

T. Dunning. Accurate methods for the statistics of surprise and coincidence. *Computational Linguistics*, 19(1):61–74, 1993.

M. Dupuch, T. Hamon, and N. Grabar. Groupement de termes basé sur des régularités linguistiques et sémantiques dans un contexte cross-langue. In *Actes de la 20e conférence sur le Traitement Automatique des Langues Naturelles (TALN 2013)*, pages 62–75, 2013.

C. Durieux. *Fondement didactique de la traduction technique*. La maison du dictionnaire, Paris, 2010.

P. Dury. Les indices d'évolution diachronique dans les dictionnaires de langue générale : une étude de cas autour de carbon. In F. Maniez and P. Dury, editors, *Lexicologie et terminologie : histoire des mots*, Travaux du CRTT, pages 269–284. Presse universitaire de l'Université Lumière-Lyon 2, Lyon, 2007.

P. Dury and P. Drouin. L'obsolescence des termes en langues de spécialité : une étude semi-automatique de la "nécrologie" en corpus informatisés, appliquée au domaine de l'écologie. In *Proceedings of the XVII European LSP Symposium 2009*, pages 1–11, 2010.

DWIA. *Wind Energy Reference Manual*. Danish Wind Industry Association, 2003.

C. Dyer. Using a maximum entropy model to build segmentation lattices for MT. In *Proceedings of the Human Language Technologies: The 11th Annual Conference of the North American Chapter of the ACL (HLT-NAACL 2009)*, pages 406–414, 2009.

R. Estopà, J. Vivaldi, and M. T. Cabré. Use of greek and latin forms for term detection. In *Proceedings of the 2nd conference on International Language Resources and Evaluation (LREC 2000)*, 2000.

R. Estopà Bagot. Les unités de signification spécialisées élargissant l'objet du travail en terminologie. *Terminology*, 7(2):217–237, 2001. doi:10.1075/term.7.2.06est

B. S. Everitt. *The Analysis of Contingency Tables*. Chapman & Hall, London, 1992.

S. Evert. Corpora and Collocations. In A. Lüdeling and M. Kytö, editors, *Corpus Linguistics: An International Handbook*, pages 1212–1248. Mouton de Gruyter, Berlin, 2008.

S. Evert and B. Krenn. Using small random samples for the manual evaluation of statistical association measures. *Computer Speech & Language*, 19(4):450–466, 2005. doi:10.1016/j.csl.2005.02.005

L. Faigley and S. Witte. Analyzing revision. *College Composition and Communication*, 32(4):400–414, 1981. doi:10.2307/356602

R. M. Fano. *Transmission of Information: A statistical Theory of Communications*. MIT Press, Cambridge, MA, 1961.

C. Fellbaum, editor. *WordNet: An Electronic Lexical Database*. MIT Press, Cambridge, MA, 1998.

O. Ferret. Testing semantic similarity measures for extracting synonyms from a corpus. In *Proceedings of the 7th conference on International Language Resources and Evaluation (LREC 2010)*, 2010.

O. Ferret. Identifying bad semantic neighbors for improving distributional thesauri. In *Proceedings of the 51st Annual Meeting of the Association for Computational Linguistics (ACL 2013)*, pages 561–571, 2013.

D. Ferrucci and A. Lally. UIMA: an architectural approach to unstructured information processing in the corporate research environment. *Natural Language Engineering*, 10:327–348, 2004. doi:10.1017/S1351324904003523

J. Firth. A synopsis of linguistic theory 1930–1955. In F. R. Palmer, editor, *Selected Papers of J. R. Firth 1952–1959*, pages 168–205. Longman, London, 1968.

T. Fontenelle. Dictionnaires et outils de correction linguistique. *Revue française de linguistique appliquée*, X(2):119–128. 2005.

P. Forchini and A. Murphy. N-grams in comparable specialized corpora: Perspectives on phraseology, translation, and pedagogy. *International Journal of Corpus Linguistics*, 13(3):351–367, 2008. doi:10.1075/ijcl.13.3.06for

B. Fradin. *Nouvelles approches en morphologie*. Presses Universitaires de France, Paris, 2003. doi:10.3917/puf.fradi.2003.01

K. Frantzi and S. Ananiadou. The C-Value/NC-Value domain independent method for multi-word term extraction. *Journal of Natural Language Processing*, 6(3):145–179, 2000. doi:10.5715/jnlp.6.3_145

J. Freixa. *La variació terminològica: Anàlisi de la variació denominativa en textos de diferent grau d'especialització de l'àrea de medi ambient*. PhD thesis, Institut Universitari de Lingüística Aplicada, Universitat Pompeu Fabra, Barcelona, 2002.

J. Freixa. Causes of denominative variation – A typology proposal. *Terminology*, 12 (1):51–77, 2006. doi:10.1075/term.12.1.04fre

O. Frunza and D. Inkpen. Identification and Disambiguation of Cognates, False Friends, and Partial Cognates Using Machine Learning Techniques. *International Journal of Linguistics*, 1(1), 2009.

A. Fujita and P. Isabelle. Expanding paraphrase lexicons by exploiting lexical variants. In *Proceedings of the 2015 Conference of the North American Chapter of the Association for Computational Linguistics: Human Language Technologies*, pages 630–640. Association for Computational Linguistics, 2015.

W. A. Gale and K. W. Church. Identifying word correspondences in parallel texts. In *Proceedings of the Workshop Speech and Natural Language*, pages 152–157, 1991. doi:10.3115/112405.112428

F. Gaudin. *Socioterminologie. Une approche socioterminologique de la terminologie*. De Boeck/Duculot, Bruxelles, 2003.

A. Gelbukh and G. Sidorov. Approach to construction of automatic morphological analysis systems for inflective languages with little effort. In A. Gelbukh, editor, *Computational Linguistics and Intelligent Text Processing – 4th International Conference, CICLing 2003*, volume 2588 of *Lecture Notes in Computer Science*, pages 215–220. Springer, New York, 2003.

P. Gipe. *Wind power: renewable energy for home, farm, and business*. Chelsea Green, Chelsea, VT, 2004.

G. Grefenstette. Corpus-derived first, second and third-order word affinities. In *Proceedings of the 6th International Congress of the European Association for Lexicography (EURALEX 1994)*, pages 279–290, 1994a.

G. Grefenstette. *Explorations in Automatic Thesaurus Discovery*. Kluwer, Boston, MA, 1994b. doi:10.1007/978-1-4615-2710-7

G. Gross. Degré de figement des noms composés. *Langages*, 90:57–72, 1988. doi:10.3406/lgge.1988.1991

M. Guégan and C. de Loupy. Knowledge-poor approach to shallow parsing: Contribution of unsupervised part-of-speech induction. In G. Angelova, K. Bontcheva, R. Mitkov, and N. Nicolov, editors, *Proceedings the Recent Advances in Natural Language Processing (RANLP 2011)*, pages 33–40, 2011.

M. Hagiwara. A supervised learning approach to automatic synonym identification based on distributional features. In *Proceedings of the HLT Student Research Workshop associated to Workshop on the 46th Annual Meeting of the Association for Computational Linguistics (ACL 2008)*, pages 1–6, 2008.

T. Hamon and A. Nazarenko. Detection of synonymy links between terms: experiments and results. In D. Bourigault, C. Jacquemin, and M.-C. L'Homme, editors, *Recent Advances in Computational Terminology*, volume 2 of *Natural Language Processing*, pages 185–208. John Benjamins, Amsterdam, 2001.

Y. Haralambous and E. Lavagnino. La réduction de termes complexes dans les langues de spécialité. *Traitement automatique des langues (TAL)*, 52(1):37–68, 2011.

R. Harastani, B. Daille, and E. Morin. Neoclassical compound alignments from comparable corpora. In *Proceedings of the 13th International Conference Computational Linguistics and Intelligent Text Processing (CICLing 2012)*, pages 72–82, 2012.

Z. S. Harris. Distributional structure. *Word*, 10(23):146–162, 1954. doi:10.1080/00437956.1954.11659520

B. Hauer and G. Kondrak. Clustering semantically equivalent words into cognate sets in multilingual lists. In *Proceedings of the 5th International Joint Conference on Natural Language Processing (IJCNLP 2005)*, pages 865–873, 2011.

E. Haugen. The analysis of linguistic borrowing. *Language: Journal of the Linguistic Society of America*, 26:210–231, 1950. doi:10.2307/410058

F. J. Hausmann. Kollokationen im deutschen wörterbuch. ein beitrag zur theorie des lexikographischen beispiels. In H. Bergenholtz and J. Mudgan, editors, *Lexikographie und Grammatik. Akten des Essener Kolloquiums zur Grammatik im Worterbuch*, volume 3 of *Lexicographica Series Maior*, pages 118–129. Niemeyer, Tübingen, 1985.

A. Hazem and B. Daille. Semi-compositional Method for Synonym Extraction of Multi-Word Terms. In *Proceedings of the 9th edition of the Language Resources and Evaluation Conference (LREC 2014)*, 2014.

U. Heid. On the representtion of collocational phenomena in sublanguage lexicons. In *Proceedings of the Third International Congress on Terminology and Knowledge Engineering (TKE 1993)*, pages 343–353, 1993.

D. Hindle. Noun classification from predicate-argument structures. In *Proceedings of the 28th Annual Meeting of the Association for Computational Linguistics (ACL 1990)*, pages 268–275, 1990. doi:10.3115/981823.981857

D. Hull. A practical approach to terminology alignment. In *Proceedings of the First Workshop on Computational Terminology (COMPUTERM 1998)*, pages 1–7, 1998.

F. Ibekwe-SanJuan. *Fouille de textes*. Hermès Sciences – Lavoisier, Paris, 2007.

C. Jacquemin. *Spotting and Discovering Terms through Natural Language Processing*. MIT Press, Cambridge, MA, 2001.

C. Jacquemin, B. Daille, J. Royauté, and X. Polanco. In vitro evaluation for a program to machine-aided indexing. *Information Processing & Management (IPM)*, 38(6):765–792, 2002. doi:10.1016/S0306-4573(01)00050-4

M.-P. Jacques. Emploi de termes réduits comme révélateur de la centralité dans le domaine. In *Actes des spetièmes journées scientifiques du réseau Lexicologie, Terminologie, Traduction (LTT) : Mots, termes et contextes*, pages 299–308, Paris, 2005. Archives Contemporaines.

E. Jacquey, A. Tutin, L. Kister, M.-P. Jacques, S. Hatier, and S. Ollinger. Filtrage terminologique par le lexique transdisciplinaire scientifique : une expérimentation en sciences humaines. In *Proceedings of the 10th International Conference on Terminology and Artificial Intelligence (TIA 2013)*, pages 121–128, 2013.

G. J. F. Jones, M. Burke, J. Judge, A. Khasin, A. Lam-Adesina, and J. Wagner. Experiments in monolingual, bilingual and multilingual retrieval. In C. Peters, P. Clough, J. Gonzalo, G. J. F. Jones, M. Kluck, and B. Magnini, editors, *Multilingual Information Access for Text, Speech and Images: 5th Workshop of the Cross-Language Evaluation Forum, CLEF 2004*, pages 207–220. Springer, Berlin, 2005. doi:10.1007/11519645_22

A.-L. Jousse and M. Bouveret. Lexical functions to represent derivational relations in specialized dictionaries. *Terminology*, 9(1):71–98, 2003. doi:10.1075/term.9.1.05jou

A. Judea, H. Schütze, and S. Bruegmann. Unsupervised training set generation for automatic acquisition of technical terminology in patents. In *Proceedings of the 25th International Conference on Computational Linguistics (COLING 2014)*, pages 290–300, 2014.

D. Jurafsky and J. H. Martin. *Speech and Language Processing: An Introduction to Natural Language Processing, Speech Recognition, and Computational Linguistics*. Prentice-Hall, Upper Saddle River, NJ, 2009.

J. S. Justeson and S. M. Katz. Technical terminology: some linguistic properties and an algorithm for identification in text. *Natural Language Engineering*, 1(1):9–27, 1995. doi:10.1017/S1351324900000048

K. Kageura. *The Quantitative Analysis of the Dynamics and Structure of Terminologies*. John Benjamins, Amsterdam, 2012. doi:10.1075/tlrp.15

K. Kageura and B. Umino. Methods of automatic term recognition: a review. *Terminology*, 3(2):259–289, 1996. doi:10.1075/term.3.2.03kag

K. Kageura, M. Yoshioka, K. Takeuchi, K. Koyama, K. Tsuji, and F. Yoshikane. Recent advances in automatic term recognition: Experiences from the NTCIR workshop on information retrieval and term recognition. *Terminology*, 6(2):151–173, 2000. doi:10.1075/term.6.2.03kag

J.-D. Kim, T. Ohta, Y. Tateisi, and J. Tsujii. Genia corpus – a semantically annotated corpus for bio-textmining. *Bioinformatics*, 19(suppl 1):1180–1182, 2003. doi:10.1093/bioinformatics/btg1023

L. Kister. Is it possible to predetermine a referent included in a French n de n structure? In S. P. Botley and A. M. McEnnery, editors, *Corpus-Based and Computation Approches to Discourse Anaphora*. John Benjamins, Amsterdam, 2000.

G. Kleiber and I. Tamba. L'hyperonymie revisitée : inclusion et hièrarchie. *Langages*, 98:7–32, 1990. doi:10.3406/lgge.1990.1578

P. Kluegl, M. Toepfer, P. Beck, G. Fette, and F. Puppe. UIMA ruta: Rapid development of rule-based information extraction applications. *Natural Language Engineering*, 22 (1):1–40, 2016. doi:10.1017/S1351324914000114

R. Kocourek. Textes et termes. *Meta*, 36(1), 1991. doi:10.7202/003330ar

P. Koehn and K. Knight. Empirical methods for compound splitting. In *Proceedings of Eleventh Conference of the European Chapter of the Association for Computational Linguistics (EACL 2003)*, pages 187–193, 2003.

M. Kraft. Compositionality: The very idea. *Research on Language and Computation*, 5 (3):287–308, 2007. doi:10.1007/s11168-007-9031-5

O. Kraif. Exploration des cognats pour l'alignement. *Traitement automatique des langues (TAL)*, 42(3):2–35, 2002.

G. Kremer, K. Erk, S. Padó, and S. Thater. What substitutes tell us – analysis of an "all-words" lexical substitution corpus. In *Proceedings of the 14th Conference of the European Chapter of the Association for Computational Linguistics (EACL 2014)*, pages 540–549, 2014. doi:10.3115/v1/E14-1057

A. Lehmann and F. Martin-Berthet. *Introduction à la lexicologie : sémantique et morphologie*. Armand Colin, Paris, 2008.

P. Lerat. *Les langues spécialisées*. Presses Universitaires de France, Paris, 1995.

J. Lethuillier. La synonymie en langue de spécialité. *META*, 34(3):443–449, 1989. doi:10.7202/003498ar

J. Levi. *The Syntax and the Semantics of Complex Nominals*. Academic Press, London, 1978.

M.-C. L'Homme. *La terminologie : principes et techniques*. Presses de l'Université de Montréal, Montréal, 2004.

M.-C. L'Homme. Sur la notion de "terme". *META*, 4:1112–1131, 2005. doi:10.7202/012064ar

D. Lin. Automatic retrieval and clustering of similar words. In *Proceedings of the 36th Annual Meeting of the Association for Computational Linguistics and 17th International Conference on Computational Linguistics (ACL-COLING 1998)*, pages 768–774, 1998. doi:10.3115/980691.980696

D. Lin, S. Zhao, L. Qin, and M. Zhou. Identifying synonyms among distributionally similar words. In *Proceedings of the 8th International Joint Conference on Artificial Intelligence (IJCAI 2003)*, 2003.

E. Loginova, A. Gojun, H. Blancafort, M. Guégan, T. Gornostay, and U. Heid. Reference lists for the evaluation of term extraction tools. In *Proceedings of the 10th International Congress of Terminology and Knowledge Engineering (TKE 2012)*, 2012.

E. Loginova Clouet and B. Daille. Splitting of Compound Terms in non-Prototypical Compounding Languages. In *Proceedings of the Workshop on Computational Approaches to Compound Analysis associated to the 25th International Conference on Computational Linguistics (COLING 2014)*, pages 11–19, Dublin, Ireland, Aug. 2014.

A. Ludeling. *Neoclassical word-formation*. Humboldt-Universität Berlin, Berlin, 2012.

J. Léon. Lexies, synapsies, synthèmes : le renouveau des études lexicales en France au début des années 1960. In S. Scalise and I. Vogel, editors, *History of Linguistics in Texts and Concepts*, pages 405–418. Nodus Publikationen, Münster, 2004.

N. Madmani and B. J. Dorr. Generating phrasal and sentential paraphrases: A survey of data-driven methods. *Computational Linguistics*, 36(3):341–387, 2010. doi:10.1162/coli_a_00002

B. Maia. What are comparable corpora? In *Workshop on Multilingual Corpora: Linguistic requirements and technical perspectives at Corpus Linguistics 2003*, pages 27–34, Lancaster, UK, 2003.

D. Malrieu and F. Rastier. Genres et variations morphosyntaxiques. *Texto*, 2002.

C. D. Manning and H. Schütze. *Foundations of Statistical Natural Language Processing*. MIT Press, Cambridge, MA, 1999.

D. C. Manning, P. Raghavan, and H. Schütze. *Introduction to Information Retrieval*. Cambridge University Press, Cambridge, 2008. doi:10.1017/CBO9780511809071

E. Marshman, T. Morgan, and I. Meyer. French patterns for expressing concept relations. *Terminology*, 8(1):1–29, 2002. doi:10.1075/term.8.1.02mar

W. Martin. Remarks on collocations in sublanguages. *Terminology and Traduction (T & T)*, pages 157–164, 1992.

C. Melloni and A. Bisetto. Parasynthetic compounds. In S. Scalise and I. Vogel, editors, *Cross-disciplinary issues in compounding*, volume 311 of *Current issues in linguistic theory*, pages 199–217. John Benjamins, Amsterdam, 2010. doi:10.1075/cilt.311.16mel

I. Mel'čuk, N. Arbatchewsky-Jumarie, L. Elnitsky, L. Iordanskaja, and A. Lessard. *Dictionnaire explicatifet combinatoire du français contemporain*. Presses de L'Université de Montréal, Montréal, 1984.

I. Meyer. Extracting knowledge-rich contexts for terminography: A conceptual and methodological framework. In D. Bourigault, C. Jacquemin, and M.-C. L'Homme, editors, *Recent Advances in Computational Terminology*, pages 279–302. John Benjamins, Amsterdam, 2001. doi:10.1075/nlp.2.15mey

O. Mitrofanova and V. Zakharov. Automatic analysis of terminology in the russian corpus on corpus linguistics. In *Proceedings of the Fifth International Conference on NLP, Corpus Linguistics, Corpus Based Grammar Research (DIALOG 2009)*, pages 249–254, 2009.

M. Montesi and T. Navarrete. Classifying web genres in context: A case study documenting the web genres used by a software engineer. *Information Processing Management*, 44:1410–1430, 2008. doi:10.1016/j.ipm.2008.02.001

M. Morel and J. François. Le dictionnaire électronique des synonymes du CRISCO : un outil de plus en plus interactif. *Revue française de linguistique appliquée*, XX(1): 9–28, 2015.

E. Morin and B. Daille. Revising the compositional method for terminology acquisition from comparable corpora. In *Proceedings of the 24th International Conference on Computational Linguistics (COLING 2012)*, pages 1797–1810, 2012.

F. Morlane-Hondère. *Une approche linguistique de l'évaluation des ressources extraites par l'analyse distributionnelle automatique*. PhD thesis, Université Toulouse II Le Mirail, 2013.

J. Morris and G. Hirst. Non-classical lexical semantic relations. In *Proceeding of the Workshop on Computational Lexical semantics (CLS 2004) associated to Human Language Technologies: The Fifth Annual Conference ofthe North American Chapter of the ACL (HLT-NAACL 2004)*, pages 46–51, 2004.

M. L. Murphy. *Semantic relations and the Lexicon: Antonymy, Synonymy and other Paradigms*. Cambridge University Press, Cambridge, 2003. doi:10.1017/CBO9780511486494

N. Flaux and D. Van del Velde *Les noms en Français, esquisse de classement*. Orphrys, Paris, 2000.

F. Namer. Flemm : un analyseur flexionnel de français à base de règles. *Traitement automatique des langues (TAL)*, 41(2):523–547, 2000.

F. Namer. Automatiser l'analyse morphosémantique non affixale : le système DériF. *Cahiers de Grammaire*, 28:31–48, 2003.

F. Namer and R. H. Baud. Defining and relating biomedical terms: Towards a cross-language morphosemantics-based system. *I. J. Medical Informatics*, pages 226–233, 2007. doi:10.1016/j.ijmedinf.2006.05.001

V. Nastase and S. Szpakowicz. Exploring noun-modifier semantic relations. In *Fifth International Workshop on Computational Semantics (IWCS-5)*, page 285–301, Tilburg, The Netherlands, 2003.

R. Nazar, J. Vivaldi, and L. Wanner. Automatic taxonomy extraction for specialized domains using distributional semantics. *Terminology*, 18(2):188–225, 2012. doi:10.1075/term.18.2.03naz

A. Nazarenko, H. Zargayouna, O. Hamon and J. van Puymbrouck. Evaluation des outils terminologiques : enjeux, difficultés et propositions. *Traitement automatique des langues (TAL)*, 50(1):257–281, 2009.

F. Neveu. *Dictionnaire des sciences du langage*. Armand Colin, Paris, 2004.

A. Névéol, S. Shooshan, J. Mork, and A. Aronson. Fine-grained indexing of teh biomedical literature: Mesh subhading attachment for a medline indexing tool. In *Proceedings of 31th Annual Symposium of the American Medical Informatics Association (AMIA 2007)*, pages 553–557, 2007.

C. Olston and M. Najork. Web Crawling. *Foundations and Trends in Information Retrieval*, 4(3):175–246, 2010. doi:10.1561/1500000017

G. Otman. *Les représentations sémantiques en terminologie*. Masson, Paris, 1996.

M. Pageau. étude descriptive des emprunts à l'anglais dans le domaine de la biologie cellulaire. Master's thesis, Université de Montréal, Faculté des arts et des sciences, Département de linguistique et de traduction, 2003.

A. Panchenko and O. Morozova. A study of hybrid similarity measures for semantic relation extraction. In *Proceedings of the Workshop on Innovative Hybrid Approaches to the Processing of Textual Data (HYBRID 2012) associated to the 13th Conference of the European Chapter of the Association for Computational Linguistics (EACL 2012)*, pages 10–18, 2012.

M. Paquot. *Academic Vocabulary in Learner Writing: From Extraction to Analysis*. Bloomsbury Academic, London, 2010.

B. H. Parnee, A. ter Meulen, and R. E. Wall. *Mathematical Methods in Linguistics*, volume 30. Kluwer, Dordrecht, 1990.

B. Partee. Compositionality. In F. Landman and F. Veltman, editors, *Varieties of Formal Semantics*, pages 281–312. Foris, Dordrecht, 1984.

S. Pavel and D. Nolet. *Précis de terminologie, Terminologie et Normalisation*. Bureau de la traduction, Ministère des travaux publics et services au gouvernement, Canada, 2001.

M. T. Pazienza, M. Pennacchiotti, and F. M. Zanzotto. Terminology extraction: An analysis of linguistic and statistical approaches. In S. Sirmakessis, editor, *Proceedings of the final conference of the Network of Excellence in Text Mining and its applications in Statistics conference (NEMIS 2004)*, volume 185 of *Studies in Fuzziness and Soft Computing*, pages 225–279. Springer Berlin Heidelberg, 2005.

M. Pecman. Variation as a cognitive device: How scientists construct knowledge through term formation. *Terminology*, 20(1):1–24, 2014. doi:10.1075/term.20.1.01pec

S. Pereira, A. Névéol, O. Kerdelhué, E. Serrot, M. Joubert, and S. Darmoni. Using multi-terminology indexing for the assignment of mesh descriptors to health resources in a french online calalogue. In *Proceedings of 32th Annual Symposium of the American Medical Informatics Association (AMIA 2008)*, 2008.

V. Pirrelli, E. Guevara, and M. Baroni. Computational issues in compound processing. In S. Scalise and I. Vogel, editors, *Cross-disciplinary issues in compounding*, volume 311 of *Current issues in linguistic theory*, pages 271–285. John Benjamins, Amsterdam, 2010. doi:10.1075/cilt.311.21pir

A. Polguère. *Lexicologie et sémantique lexicale*. Presses de l'Université de Montréal, Montréal, 2003.

A. Périnet and T. Hamon. Hybrid acquisition of semantic relations based on context normalization in distributional analysis. In *Proceedings of the 10th International Conference on Terminology and Artificial Intelligence (TIA 2013)*, pages 113–122, 2013.

P. Rayson and R. Garside. Comparing corpora using frequency profiling. Presented at Comparing Corpora workshop, held in conjunction with the 38th annual meeting of the Association for Computational Linguistics (ACL 2000), 2000.

P. Resnik. *Selection and Information: A class-based approach to lexical relationships*. PhD thesis, University of Pennsylvania, 1993.

T. Roeper and M. E. A. Siegel. A lexical transformation for verbal compounds. *Linguistic Inquiry*, 9(2):199–260, 1978.

J. Royauté. *Les groupes nominaux complexes et leur propriétés : application à l analyse de l'information*. PhD thesis, Université Nancy 1, 1999.

J. Sager. *A Practical Course in Terminology Processing*. John Benjamins, Amsterdam, 1990. doi:10.1075/z.44

B. Sagot. The Lefff, a freely available and large-coverage morphological and syntactic lexicon for french. In *Proceedings of the Seventh conference on International Language Resources and Evaluation (LREC 2010)*, 2010.

M. Sahlgren. The distributional hypothesis. *Rivista di Linguistica*, 20(1)33–53, 2008.

G. Salton and M. E. Lesk. Computer evaluation of indexing and text processing. *Journal of the Association for Computational Machinery*, 15(1)8–36, 1968. doi:10.1145/321439.321441

E. SanJuan and F. Ibekwe-SanJuan. Text mining without documen context. *Information Processing and Management*, 26(6):1532–1552, 2006. doi:10.1016/j.ipm.2006.03.017

X. Saralegi, I. Vicente, and A. Gurrutxaga. Automatic Extraction of Bilingual Terms from Comparable Corpora in a Popular Science Domain. In *Proceedings of the Workshop on Comparable Corpora associated to the 6th international conference on Language Resources and Evaluation (LREC 2008)*, 2008.

A. Savary. Computational inflection of multi-word units, a contrastive study of lexical approaches. *Linguistic Issues in Language Technology (LiLT) CSLI Publications*, 1(2): 1–55, 2008.

S. Scalise and I. Vogel, editors. *Cross-disciplinary issues in compounding*. John Benjamins, Amsterdam, 2010. doi:10.1075/cilt.311

H. Schmid, A. Fitschen, and U. Heid. Smor: A german computational morphology covering derivation, composition, and inflection. In *Proceedings of the fourth international conference on Language Resources and Evaluation (LREC 2004)*, pages 1263–1266, 2004.

G. Scurtu. Traduire le vocabulaire juridique francais en roumain. *Meta : journal des traducteurs /Meta: Translator's Journal*, 53(4):884–898, 2008. doi:10.7202/019653ar

J. Sinclair. *Preliminary Recommendations on Corpus Typology*. Expert Advisory Group on Language Engineering Standards (EAGLE)), 2003.

G. A. Stephen. *String Searching Algorithms*. World Scientific, Singapore, 1994.

K. Takeuchi, K. Kageura, B. Daille, and L. Romary. Construction of grammar based term extraction model for Japanese. In *Proceedings of the 3rd International Workshop on Computational Terminology (COMPUTERM 2004) associated to the 20th International Conference on Computational Linguistics (COLING 2004)*, pages 91–94, 2004.

A. Tartier. A Method for Observing Terminological Evolution. In G. Angelova, K. Bontcheva, R. Mitkov, N. Nicolov, and N. Nikolov, editors, *Proceedings of the 4th Conference of Recent Advances in Natural Language Processing (RANLP 2003)*, pages 467–471, 2003.

R. Temmerman. *Towards new ways of terminology description. The sociocognitive approach*. John Benjamins, Amsterdam, 2000. doi:10.1075/tlrp.3

P. D. Turney and P. Pantel. From frequency to meaning: Vector space models of semantics. *Journal of Artificial Intelligence Research (JAIR)*, 37:141–188, 2010.

A. Tutin. Autour du lexique et de la phraséologie des écrits scientifiques. *Revue française de linguistique appliquée*, XII(2):5–14, 2007.

K. Uchiyama. A study for identifying domain-specific introductory terms in research papaers. In *Proceedings of the 9th International Conference on Terminology and Artificial Intelligence (TIA 2011)*, pages 147–150, 2011.

L. van der Plas and J. Tiedemann. Finding synonyms using automatic word alignment and measures of distributional similarity. In *Proceedings of the 21st International Conference on Computational Linguistics and 44th Annual Meeting of the Association for Computational Linguistics (ACL 2006)*, pages 866–873, 2006.

F. Ville-Ometz, J. Royauté, and A. Zasadzinski. Enhancing in automatic recognition and extraction of term variants with linguistic features. *Terminology*, 13(1):61–84, 2007. doi:10.1075/term.13.1.03vil

J. Vivaldi and H. Rodriguez. Evaluation of terms and term extraction systems: a practical approach. *Terminology*, 13(2):225–248, 2007. doi:10.1075/term.13.2.06viv

R. A. Wagner and M. J. Fischer. The String-to-String Correction Problem. *Association for Computing Machinery*, 21(1):168–173, Jan. 1974. doi:10.1145/321796.321811

J. . *Measures and Applications of Lexical Distributional Similarity*. PhD thesis, University of Sussex, 2003.

M. Weller, A. Gojun, U. Heid, B. Daille, and R. Harastani. Simple methods for dealing with term variation and term alignment. In *Proceedings of the 9th International Conference on Terminology and Artificial Intelligence (TIA 2011)*, pages 87–93, 2011.

G. C. Williams. *Les réseaux collocationnels dans la construction et l'exploitation d un corpus dans le cadre d'une communauté de discours scientifique*. PhD thesis, Université de Nantes, 1999.

M. Winston, R. Chaffin, and D. Herrmann. A taxonomy of part-whole relations. *Cognitive Science*, 11(4):417–444, 1987. doi:10.1207/s15516709cog1104_2

E. Wüster. *The Machine Tool. An Interlingual Dictionary of Basic Conceps*. Technical Press, London, 1968.

F. Zanettin. Bilingual comparable corpora and the training of translators. *Meta : journal des traducteurs/Meta: Translator's Journal*, 43(4):616–630, 1998. doi:10.7202/004638ar

Q. Zou, W. Chu, C. Morioka, G. Leazer, and H. Kangarloo. IndexFinger: A method of extracting key concepts from clinical texts for indexing. In *Proceedings of 27th Annual Symposium of the American Medical Informatics Association (AMIA 2003)*, pages 763–767, 2003.

APPENDIX A

Notation

A.1 Examples

Examples are in italic.

A.2 Specialised domains

A term exists only in a specialised domain. A specialised domain is systematically associated with terms. The specialised domain is noted between parenthesis.

(AGR)	agriculture
(CAN)	breast cancer, medical domain
(DIA)	diabetes, medical domain
(EOL)	wind energy, energy domain
(MOB)	mobile technologies, technology domain
(SAT)	satellite telecommunication, telecommunication domain

A.3 Specialised corpora

The specialised corpora used in our study are of one specialised domain. Corpora are noted between squares. They are detailed in Section 5.

[CAN]	cancer du sein, domaine médical
[DIA]	diabetes, medical domain
[EOL]	wind energy, energy domain
[MOB]	mobile technologies, technology domain

APPENDIX B

Multext categories

We recall below the main categories used in this document as defined by Multext lexical specifications.

Category	Code
Noun	N
Adjective	A
Preposition	P[1]
Determinant	D
Conjunction	C
Adverb	R
Verb gerund	V:mg
Verb infinitive	V:mn
Verb participle	V:mp
Article	T

For the noun N, they are four attributes:

Position	Attribute	Value	Code
1	Type	common	c
		proper	p
2	Gender	masculine	m
		feminine	f
		neuter	n
3	Number	singular	s
		plural	p
4	Case	nominative	n
		genitive	g
		dative	d
		accusative	a

1. We use P instead of S:p for the sake of simplification and because we do not need the pronoun category (P).

For the adjective A, there are 5 attributes. The second field that characterises the degree is not relevant for terminology extraction.

Position	Attribute	Value	Code
1	Type	qualitative	f
		ordinal	o
		cardinal	c
		indefinite	i
		possessive	s
2	Degree	positive	p
		comparative	c
		superlative	s
3	Gender	masculine	m
		feminine	f
		neuter	n
4	Number	singular	s
		plural	p
5	Case	nominative	n
		genitive	g
		dative	d
		accusative	a

APPENDIX C

Search with Antconc

We detail the use of AntConc[1] in order to obtain n-grams by using corpora studied in Chapter 5. The version we used is 3.2.1.

C.1 Parameters

Main parameters are available in the GLOBAL SETTINGS menu. Parameters to be set are the encoding of characters and the definition of the word. Encoding of characters is available in the LANGUAGE ENCODING SETTINGS menu, choose UTF8. Definition of words is available in the TOKEN (WORD) DEFINITION menu. The hyphen is considered as a word separator by default. Numbers do not belong to characters accepted in words. Therefore it is necessary to change two things:

Letter Token classes choose LETTER
Number Token classes choose NUMBER
Punctuation Token classes choose DASH

C.2 Collection of n-grams

In order to obtain the n-grams with AntConc, choose the CLUSTERS menu and set parameters with the following values for a search of 1-gram about the term (EOL) Fr: *pale* with two spellings *pale* or *pâle*:

Search terms Regex *pale|pâle*
Cluster size Min Size 1
Max Size 1
Min Cluster frequency 1
Sort by frequency

Search in REGEX allows to catch inflections. To catch derivation, input rather a root such as (DIA) *insulin* which should allow to get occurences of *insuline* and its plural inflection *insulines,* but also its derivated element *insulino.* For the n-grams of superior size, for example for the bigrams, it is enough to change CLUSTER SIZE and put the size of exacte cluster 2 at minimum and maximum for the bigrams.

1. antlab.sci.waseda.ac.jp

For the discontinous n-grams, choose the CoNCorDANCES menu and set search by word. For an insertion with the complex term (EOL) Fr: *parc éolien,* input the concordance with the string: *parc#éolien.*

Table C.1 Unigrams of the term (EOL) *blade* for En, Fr, Es.

List of correct unigrams						
1	blade	910	palas	533	pales	287
2	blades	372	pala	277	pale	175
3	three-bladed	28	bipala	21	tripale	29
4	3-blade	25	tripala	20	bipale	14
5	3-bladed	22	monopala	13	tripales	7
6	2-blade	19	multipala	11	bipales	4
7	two-bladed	11	bipalas	8	mono-pale	4
8	two-blade	7	multipalas	7	palettes	4
9	blade-element	5	tripalas	6	pâles	3
10	bladed	5	monopalas	3	mono-pales	2
11	three-blade	3	Multipala	2	multi-pale	2
12	3blade	2	pala-buje	1	multi-pales	2
13	bladeDesign	2	pala-rodamiento	1	multipales	2
14	2-blades	1			monopale	1
15	2blade	1			multipale	1
16	four-bladed	1			Multipale	1
17	multi-bladed	1				
18	Multibladed	1				
19	one-bladed	1				
20	rotor-blades	1				
21	rotorblade	1				
22	single-bladed	1				
23	threebladed	1				
24	turbine-blades	1				
25	Two-bladed	1				
26	twobladed	1				
	26	1424	13	903	16	538
Lists of unigrams with bad hyphens						
1	blade-nearer	1	palabras	12	principalement	60
2	blade-radius	1	Rajagopalan	2	principales	56
3	blade-rotortower-rotor	1			principale	24
4	straight-blade	1			Principales	2
	4 1-grams	4	2 1-grams	14	4 1-grams	142

Search terms Words *parc#éolien|parcs#éoliens*

It should be necessary to renew the search with two # for two insertions, and so on.

C.3 Results of n-grams

Table C.1 shows the list of the valid and non-valid unigrams extracted for English, Spanish and French. Table C.2 shows the list of valid unigrams and Table C.3 shows the list of non-valid unigrams for German. Table C.4 shows the list of valid unigrams for Russian.

Table C.2 Correct unigrams of term *blatt* for WE in De.

List of valid unigrams				
1	Rotorblätter	51	Ncnpn	pale de rotor
2	Rotorblatt	32	Ncnsn	pale de rotor
3	Rotorblättern	19	Ncnpd	pale de rotor
4	Rotorblattes	7	Ncnsg	pale de rotor
5	Rotorblattheizung	5	Ncfsn	chauffage de la pale de rotor
6	Rotorblattvereisung	4	Ncfsn	givrage de la pale de rotor
7	Rotorblattnasenvereisung	2	Ncfsn	givrage du nez de la pale de rotor
8	Rotorblattprofil	2	Ncnsn	profil de la pale de rotor
9	Standortblätter	2	Ncnpn	fiches où se trouvent les pales de rotor
10	Vielblattrotor	2	Ncmsn	'beaucoup de pales de rotor' multipales
11	blatteinstellwinkelgeregelten	1	A	réglage de l'angle des pales du rotor
12	blattgeregelten	1	A	réglé par la pale de rotor
13	Dreiblattrotor	1	Ncmsm	rotor à trois pales
14	Rotorblattaerodynamik	1	Ncfsn	aérodynamique de la pale de rotor
15	Rotorblattfertigung	1	Ncfsn	production de la pale de rotor
16	Rotorblattlasten	1	Ncfpn	charges de la pale de rotor
17	Rotorblattnase	1	Ncfsn	nez de la pale de rotor
18	Rotorblattnasenbeheizung	1	Ncfsn	chauffage du nez de la pale de rotor
19	Rotorblattprofile	1	Ncnpn	profil de la pale de rotor
20	Rotorblattprofilen	1	Ncnpd	profil de la pale de rotor
21	Rotorblattschnitt	1	Ncmsn	section de la pale de rotor
22	Rotorblattschwenkschwingung	1	Ncfsn	mouvement de pivot de la pale de rotor
23	Rotorblattspitze	1	Ncfsn	tête de la pale de rotor
24	Rotorblattvereisungsformen	1	Ncfpn	formes de givrage de la pale de rotor
25	Rotorblattverstellung	1	Ncfsn	changement de position de la pale de rotor
26	Rotorblattvorderkante	1	Ncfsn	bord antérieur de la pale de rotor
	26 unigrams	142		

Table C.3 Bad unigrams of the term *Blatt* 'blade' for WE in De.

List of the unigrams without bad hyphens				
1	Merkblatt	5	Ncnsn	aide-mémoire
2	Formblatt	4	Ncnsn	modèle de document
3	Merkblätter	4	Ncnpn	aide-mémoire
4	Sicherheitsdatenblätter	3	Ncnpn	fiches de caractéristique
5	Ärzteblatt	2	Ncnsn	information pour le patient
6	Datenblätter	2	Ncnpn	fiches de carastéristiques
7	Beiblatt	1	Ncnsn	journal
8	Berichtsblätter	1	Ncnpn	journal
9	Deckblatt	1	Ncnsn	première page
10	Handelsblatt	1	Ncnsn	journal économique
11	Merkblattes	1	Ncnsg	aide-mémoire
12	Sicherheitsdatenblatt	1	Ncnsn	fiche de caractéristique de sécurité
	14 unigrams	26		
List of unigrams with bad hyphens				
1	FMEA-Formblatt	3	Ncnsn	modèle de document FMEA
2	FMEA-Formblättern	1	Ncnpg	modèle de document FMEA
	2 unigrammes	4		

Table C.4 Unigrams of the term (EOL) Ru : лопасти *'blade'.*

List of valid unigrams				
1	лопасти	291	Ncfpn	pale
2	лопастей	276	Ncfpg	pale
3	лопастями	84	Ncfpi	avec pale
4	лопасть	58	Ncfsn	pale
5	лопастях	22	Ncfpv	à pale
6	трехлопастные	6	Afp-pn	tripale
7	лопастного	5	Afpmsg	pale
8	лопастные	4	Afp-pn	pale
9	лопастью	4	Ncfsi	pale
10	лопастям	4	Ncfpi	pale
11	многолопастные	4	Afp-pn	multipale
12	лопастной	3	Afpmns/Afpfsg	pale
13	двухлопастного	2	Afpmsg	bipale
14	двухлопастное	2	Afpnsn	bipale
15	двухлопастные	2	Afp-pn	bipale
16	малолопастные	2	Afp-pn	lit. avec peu de pales
17	многолопастное	2	Afpnsn	multipale
18	многолопастный	2	Afpmsn	multipale

List of valid unigrams				
19	многолопастных	2	Afp-pg	multipale
20	однолопастные	2	Afp-pn	unipale
21	трехлопастного	2	Afpmsg	tripale
22	двухлопастный	1	Afpmsn	bipale
23	двухтрехлопастной	1	Afpmsn	bi ou tripale
24	лопастным	1	Afpmsi	pale
25	лопастных	1	Afp-pg	pale
26	многолопастные	1	Afp-pn	multipale
27	многолопастным	1	Afpmsi	multipale
28	однолопастное	1	Afpnsn	unipale
29	однолопастных	1	Afp-pg	unipale
30	прямолопастных	1	Afp-pg	pale plate
31	трехлопастная	1	Afpfsn	tripale
32	трехлопастное	1	Afpnsn	tripale
33	трехлопастной	1	Afpmsn/Afpfsg	tripale
34	узколопастные	1	Afp-pn	pale étroite
35	четырехлопастное	1	Afpnsn	quadripale
36	четырехлопастный	1	Afpmsn	quadripale
37	четырёхлопастные	1	Afp-pn	quadripale
38	шестилопастного	1	Afpmsg	6-pales
	38 unigrams	788		

APPENDIX D

GGRV

D.1 French

The French GGRV applies to morphological compound and to syntagmatic compounds of N N, N A, N P N, N A A and N A P N patterns.

a. Competing structures

Morphological rules

Op.	Term	Variant
Sg	N/[N_1-N_2]	N_1N_2
	entrée-sortie	*entrée sortie* 'input-output'
PI	N/[EN_1]	N_1 P N_2
	deriv(E, N_2)	
	hormonosensibilité	*sensibilité aux hormones* 'hormone sensibility'

Syntagmatic rules

Op.	Term	Variant
R2	N_1 P N_2	N_1N_2
	panne de réseau	*panne réseau* 'network failure'
R2I	$N_1P_2N_2$	N_1 P N_2
R2D	N_1 P N_2	N_1 A
	deriv(N_2,A)	
	alimentation en électricité	*alimentation électrique* 'power supply'
P	N_1 A_1 A_2	N_1 A_2 A_1
	énergie éolienne propre 'clean wind energy'	*énergie propre éolienne* 'wind clean energy'
P	N_1 A P N_2	N_1 P N_2 A
	coefficient de puissance aérodynamique 'aerodynamic power coefficient'	*coefficient aérodynamique de puissance* 'lit. power aerodynamic coefficient'

b. Augmented/reduced structures

Morphological rules apply to syntagmatic compounds of N A pattern.

Morphological rules

Op.	Term	Variant
PID	$N_1 A_2$ deriv(N_2, A_2) *effet possible* opportune impact	N_2 P N_1 *possibilité d effet* impact opportunity
I	$N_1 A_1$ *énergie électrique* electric power	N_1 A/[EA_1] *énergie hydroélectrique* hydroelectric power'
I	N_1 A [E_1A_1] *diabète insulino-dépendant* 'insulin-dependent diabetes	N_1 A/[E_1RA_1] *diabète insulino-non-dépendant* insulin-non-dependent diabetes
PID	$N_1 A_1 A_2$ deriv(N_2, A_2) *effet secondaire possible* 'potential side effect'	N_2 PN_1 A_1 *possibilité d'effet secondaire* 'potentiality of side effect'

Complex terms taken into account are N N, N A and N P N. The linguistic elements juxtaposed to the term are adjectives and prepositional phrases (P N, P A N, P N A) for N A and N P N. The linguistic elements inserted are adjectives for N A and N P N, and adverbs for N A.

Syntagmatic rules

Op.	Term	Variant
Jr	$N_1 A_1$ *énergie éolien* wind energy	$N_1 A_1$ A *énergie éolien renouvelable* renewable wind energy
Jr	N_1 A *vitesse absolue* 'absolute speed'	N_1 A P N_2 *vitesse absolue de référence* absolute reference speed
Jr	$N_1 A_1$ *aimant permanent* permanent magnet	$N_1 A_1$ P A N *aimant permanent de faible puissance* weak permanent magnet
Jr	$N_1 A_1$ *aimant permanent* permanent magnet	$N_1 A_1$ P N A *aimant permanent de taille moyenne* middle-size permanent magnet
Jr	N_1 P N_2 *abondance des ressources* 'abundance of ressources'	N_1 P N A *abondance des ressources naturelles* 'abundance of natural ressources'
Jr	N_1 P N_2 *vitesse de rotation* rotating speed	N_1 P N_2 P N *vitesse de rotation de référence* reference rotating speed
Jr	N_1 P N_2	N_1 P N_2 P A N
Jr	N_1 P N_2	N_1 P N_2 P N A
Jl	$N_1 A_2$ *rotation rapide* 'spinning'	N P $N_1 A_2$ *éolienne à rotation rapide* 'spinning wind turbine

J1	N_1 P N_2 *médicaments de chimiothérapie* chemotherapy drugs	N P N_1 P N_2 *perfusion de médicaments de chimiothérapie* 'infusion of chemotherapy drugs'
I	N_1 A_1 *caractéristique linéaire* 'linear flow characteristic	N_1 R A_1 *caractéristique non linéaire* 'non linear flow characteristic
I	N_1 $(A\|N_2)$ *accès routier* road access	N_1 P N_3 $(A\|N_2)$ *accès au réseau routier* 'road network access'
I	N_1 P N_2 *prix d achat* 'purchase price	N_1 A P N_2 *prix moyen d achat* 'average purchase price

c. Contextual structures

Contextual rules apply to N A and N P N patterns.

Morphological rules

I	N_1 A/[E_1A_1] *turbine bipale* 'two-bladed wind turbine'	N_1 E_1 C A/[EA_1] *turbine bi- ou tripale* 'two- or three-bladed wind turbine
I	N_1 A_1 *turbine tripale* 'three-bladed wind turbine'	N_1 E C A_1 *turbine bi- ou tripale* 'two- or three-bladed wind turbine'

Syntagmatic rules

Op.	Term	Variant
Jr	N_1 A_1 *rivages marins* 'marine shorelines'	N_1 A_1 C A *rivages marins ou lacustres* 'lake or marine shorelines'
Jr	N_1 A_1 *centrale thermique* 'thermal power plant	N_1 A_1 A, C A *centrale thermique, nucléaire ou fossile* 'thermal, nuclear or fossil power plant'
Jr	N_1 P N_2 *coût de fabrication* 'manufacturing cost'	N_1 P N_2 C P N *coût de fabrication et de production* production and manufacturing cost
Jr	N_1 P N_2 *unités de paysage* landscape units	N_1 P N_2, P N C P N *unités de paysage, des sites et des vues* view, site, and landscape units
Jr	N_1 P N_2 *critère d'accessibilité* 'accessibility criterium	N_1 P N_2 C P N *critère d'accessibilité et de fiabilité* 'accessibility and reliability criterium
J1	N_1 A_1 *isolation acoustique* 'insulation'	N C N_1 A_1 *conception et isolation acoustique*
I	N_1 A_1 *pale rigide* 'rigid blade'	N_1 V A_1 *pale est rigide* 'blade is rigid'
I	N_1 A_1 *rivages lacustres* 'lake shorelines'	N_1 A_1 C A *rivages marins ou lacustres* 'lake or marine shorelines'

IJl	N_1 A_1 *centrale nucléaire* 'nuclear power plant'	N_1 A_1, A C A *centrale thermique, nucléaire ou fossile* 'thermal, nuclear or fossil power plant'
I1	N_1 P_2 N_2 *unités de vues* 'view units'	N_1 P N, P N C P_2 N_2 *unités de paysage, des sites et des vues* 'view, site, and landscape units'
I1Jl	N_1 P_2 N_2 *unités de sites* site units	N_1 P N, P_2 N_2 C N *unités de paysage, des sites et des vues* view, site, and landscape units

D.2 English

The English GGRV applies to morphological compounds and syntagmatic compounds of N N, A N, N P N, A A N, A N N, N N N patterns.

a. Competing structures

Morphological rules apply to morphological compounds of NN or NA patterns.

Morphological rules

Op.	Term	Variant
Sg	N/[$N_1$$N_2$] *windmill* *power-supply*	N_1 N_2 *wind mill* *power supply*
PI	N/[$N_1$$N_2$] *blade-element*	N_2 P N_1 *element of blade*
PID	N/[$N_1$$N_2$] *landowner*	N/[N_2E] P N_1 *ownership of land*

Competing syntagmatic structures apply to terms of A N, N N, N P N, A A N and A N N patterns.

Syntagmatic rules

Op.	Term	Variant
R1Jl	A_1 N_2 deriv(N_1,A_1) *resonance frequency*	N_1 N_2 *resonant frequency*
PI	N_1 N_2 *wind power*	N_2 P N_1 *power of wind*
R2I	N_1 P_2 N_2 *network with users*	N_1 P N_2 *network of users*
P	A_1 A_2 N_1 *negative significant effect*	A_2 A_1 N_1 *significant negative effect*
P	A_1 N_1 N_2 *electronic power converter*	N_1 A_1 N_2 *power electronic converter*

b. Augmented/reduced structures

Morphologically augmented/reduced structures apply to morphological or syntagmatic compounds.

Morphological rules

Op.	Term	Variant
SgD	$A/[(N_1 \mid A_1)V_2]$	$(N_1 \mid A_1)N_2$
	$\mathrm{deriv}(V_2,N_2)$	
	grid-connected	*grid connection*
I	$N/[EN_1]$	$A_1/[E(A_2 \mid N_2)]\ N_1$
	hydropower	*hydroelectric power*
I	$N/[N_1N_2]$	$N_1\ N_2\ N_3$
	airflow	*air mass flow*
I	$N/[A_1N_1]$	$A_1\ (A_2 \mid N_2 \mid R)\ N_1$
	high-risk	*high familial risk*
I2	$(A_3 \mid N_3)\ N_2\ N_1$	$(A_3 \mid N_3)\ N_2\ N/[EN_1]$
	clear cell carcinoma	*clear cell adenocarcinoma*

Terms are those of N N, A N, N P N and A A N patterns. The linguistic elements juxtaposed to terms are the adjective and the noun for all patterns and adverbs for A N pattern. The sole retained preposition for right and left juxtapositions is *of*.

Syntagmatic rules

Op.	Term	Variant
Jr	$(A_1 \mid N_1)N_2$	$(A_1\ \mathrm{l}N_1)\ N_2\ P\ N$
	inflammatory carcinoma	*inflammatory carcinoma of the breast*
Jr	$(N_1 \mid A_1)N_2$	$(N_1\ \mathrm{l}A_1)\ N_2\ N$
	speed wind	*wind speed variation*
Jl	$A_1\ N_1$	$(A \mid N)\ A_1\ N_1$
	ambient value	*extreme ambient value*
Jl	$A_1\ N_1$	$R\ A_1\ N_1$
	excited machine	*electrically excited machine*
Jl	$N_1\ N_2$	$(A \mid N)\ N_1\ N_2$
	axis wind	*horizontal axis wind*
JlD	$N_1\ N_2$	$A\ A_1\ N_2$
	$\mathrm{deriv}(N_1, A_1)$	
	three-blade rotor	*optimum three-bladed rotor*
JlD	$N_1\ N_2$	$R\ A_1\ N_2$
	$\mathrm{deriv}(N_1, A_1)$	
	sensitivity area	*ecologically sensitive area*
PJl	$N_1\ N_2$	$N\ P\ N_2\ N_1$
	speed wind	*variation of wind speed*
Jl	$N_1\ P\ N_2$	$A\ N_1\ P\ N_2$
	screening of project	*preliminary screening of project*
I	$A_1\ N_1$	$A_1\ AN_1$

	large wind	*large offshore wind*
I	A_1 N_1	A_1 A N N_1
	offshore turbine	*offshore floating wind turbine*
I	A_1 N_1	A_1 N N N_1
	offshore technology	*offshore wind energy technology*
I	N_1 N_2	N_1 N N_2
	wind site	*wind turbine site*
PI	N_1 N_2	N_2 P N N_1
	Savonius rotor	*rotor of type Savonius*
I2	N_1 P N_2	N_1 P A N_2
	level of energy	*level of local energy*
I2	A_1 A_2 N_1	A_1 A_2 A N_1
	small additional mortality	*small additive annual mortality*
I2	A_1 A_2 N_1	A_1 A_2 N N_1
	optimum three-bladed turbine	*optimum three-bladed wind turbine*

c. Contextual structures

Contextual rules apply to terms of A N, N N and N P N patterns.

Morphological rules

Op.	Term	Variant
I	N/[$A_1$$N_1$]	A_1 C A N_1
	hydropower	*hydro and nuclear power*
ID	A/[$A_1$$V_1$]	A_1 C A N_1
	deriv(V_1, N_1)	
	left-sided	*left and right side*

Syntagmatic rules

Op.	Term	Variant
Jr	N1 P1 N2	N_1 P_1 N_2 C P N
	provision of ordinance	*provision of ordinance or of license*
Jl	N_1 P N_2	N C N_1 P N_2
	bottom of rotation	*top and bottom of rotation*
Jl	A_1 N_1	A C A_1 N_1
	environmental impact	*social and environmental impact*
PJl		N C N_2 P N_1
	wind decrease	*increase and decrease of wind*
I	A_1 N_1	A_1 C A N_1
	renewable energy	*renewable and sustainable energy*
PI	A_1 N_1	N_1 V A_1
	significant impact	*impact be significant*
PI	N_1 N_2	N_2 C N P N_1
	generator voltage	*voltage and frequency of generator*
I_1	N_1 P_1 N_2	N_1 C N P_1 N_2
	production of energy	*production and storage of energy*
I_1	N_1 P_1 N_2	N_1 P N C P_1 N_2
	provision of licence	*provision of ordinance or of license*

D.3 Spanish

The Spanish GGRV is applied to morphological and syntagmatic compounds of N N, N A, N P N, N A A, N P N A patterns.

a. Competing structures

Competing structures apply to morphological compounds of NN pattern.

Morphological rules

Op.	Term	Variant
Sg	$N/[N_1N_2]$	N_1N_2
	teleservicios	*tele servicios*
P	N_1 $N/[E_1N_2]$	$A/[E_1N_1]N_2$
	carcinoma hepatocellular	*hepatocarcinoma cellular*

The set of syntagmatic rules gathers classical syntactic competing structures, such as the rule involving the term of N P N A pattern. It also includes the substitution of the prepositional group P N by a relational adjective, the deletion or substitution of the preposition for the term of N P N pattern.

Syntagmatic rules

Op.	Term	Variant
R2I	N_1 P_2 N_2	N_1 P N_2
	interconexión en red	*interconexión a la red*
R2D	N_1 P N_2	N_1 A
	deriv(N_2,A)	
	imanes del estator	*imanes estatóricos*
R2	N_1 P_2 N_2 A_1	N_1 N_2 A_1
	aerogenerador de potencia nominal	*aerogenerador potencia nominal*
P	N_1 P_2 N_2 A_1	N_1 P_2 A_1 N_2
	horas de plena carga	*horas de carga plena*

b. Augmented/reduced structures

Morphological juxtaposition applies to syntagmatic compounds of N A and N A A patterns.

Morphological rules

Op.	Term	Variant
I	N_1 A_1	N_1 $A/[EA_1]$
	carcinoma ductal	*carcinoma intraductal*
I	N_1 A_1 A_2	N_1 $A/[EA_1]$ A_2
	carcinoma ductal infiltrante	*carcinoma intraductal infiltrante*

Terms taken into account are those of N N, N A and N P N patterns. The linguistic elements juxtaposed to the term are adjectives and prepositional phrases (P N, P A N, P N A) for N A and N P N. The linguistic elements inserted are adjectives for N A and N P N, and adverbs for N A and N A A.

Syntagmatic rules

Op.	Term	Variant
Jr	N_1 A_1 *impacto ambiental*	N_1 A_1 A *impacto ambiental negativo*
Jr	N_1 A_1 *rotores eólicos*	N_1 A_1 A A *rotores eólicos auxiliar economicos*
Jr	N_1 A_1 *velocidad media*	N_1 A_1 P N *velocidad media/velocidad media del viento*
Jr	N_1 A_1 *turbina eólica*	N_1 A_1 P A N *turbina eólica de directa tracción*
Jr	N_1 A_1 *turbina eólica*	N_1 A_1 P N A *turbina eólica de tracción directa*
Jr	N_1 A_1 *energía eléctrica*	N_1 A_1 R A *energía eléctrica más económica*
Jr	N_1 P_2 N_2 *disminución de capacidad*	N_1 P_2 N_2 A *disminución de capacidad productivo*
Jr	N_1 P_2 N_2 *velocidad de corte*	N_1 P_2 N_2 P N *velocidad de corte del viento*
Jl	N_1 A_1 *pérdida aerodinámica*	N P N_1 A_1 *entrada en pérdida aerodinámica*
Jl	N_1 P_2 N_2 *paso de pala*	N P N_1 P_2 N_2 *control de paso de pala*
I	N_1 A_1 *agua profundo*	N_1 A A_1 *agua poco profundo*
I	N_1 A_1 *carcinoma alveolar*	N_1 P N A_1 *carcinoma de células alveolares*
I	N_1 A_1 *condición favorable*	N_1 R A_1 *condición más favorable*
I	N_1 N_2 *turbina velocidad*	N_1 P A N_2 *turbinas de alta velocidad*
I1	N_1 P N_2 *cambio de aceite*	N_1 A P N_2 *cambio periódico de aceite*
I1	N_1 P_2 N_2 *aerogenerador a barlovento*	N_1 P N P_2 N_2 *aerogenerador con rotor a barlovento*
I2	N_1 P N_2 *aerogeneradores de potencia*	N_1 P A N_2 *aerogeneradores de baja potencia*

c. Contextual structures

Contextual structures apply to terms of A N, N A, N P N, N P N A patterns.

Syntagmatic rules

Op.	Term	Variant
Jr	$N_1\ A_1$	$N_1\ A_1\ C\ A_2$
	factores físicos	*factores físicos y geográficos*
Jr	$N_1\ P_2\ N_2$	$N_1\ P_2\ N_2\ C\ N$
	efectos del túnel	*efectos del túnel y la colina*
Jr	$N_1\ P_2\ N_2$	$N_1\ P_2\ N_2\ C\ P\ N$
	fragmento de roca	*fragmento de roca o de bolos*
Jr	$N_1\ P_2\ N_2$	$N_1\ P_2\ N_2\ C\ P\ N\ A$
	efectos de la estela	*efectos de la estela y del parque generador*
J1	$A_1\ N_1$	$A\ C\ A_1\ N_1$
	mediana tensión	*baja o mediana tensión*
J1	$N_1\ P_2\ N_2$	$N\ C\ N_1\ P_2\ N_2\ N_1$
	longitudes de rugosidad	*clases y longitudes de rugosidad*
Jl	$N_1\ P_2\ N_2\ A_1$	$N\ C\ N_1\ P_2\ N_2\ A_1$
	construcción de turbinas eólicas	*diseño y construcción de turbinas eólicas*
I	$A_1\ N_1$	$A_1\ C\ A\ N_1$
	baja tensión	*baja o mediana tensión*
I	$N_1\ A_1$	$N_1\ V\ A_1$
	colina escarpada	*colina es escarpada*
I	$N_1\ A_1$	$N_1\ A_1\ C\ A_2$
	factores geográficos	*factores físicos y geográficos*
I1	$N_1\ P_2\ N_2$	$N_1\ C\ N\ P_2\ N_2$
	clases de rugosidad	*clases y longitudes de rugosidad*
I1	$N_1\ P_2\ N_2$	$N_1\ P_3\ N_3\ C\ P_2\ N_2$
	emplazamiento de subestación	*emplazamiento de aerogeneradores y de subestación*
I2	$N_1\ P_2\ N_2$	$N_1\ P_2\ N\ C\ N_2$
	Efectos de la Colina	*Efectos del Túnel y la Colina*
I1	$N_1\ P_2\ N_2\ A_1$	$N_1\ C\ N\ P_2\ N_2\ A_1$
	diseño de turbinas eólicas	*diseño y construcción de turbinas eólicas*
I_1	$N_1\ P_2\ N_2\ A_1$	$N_1\ P\ N\ C\ P_2\ N_2\ A_1$
	efectos del parque generador	*efectos de la estela y del parque generador*

D.4 German

The German GGRV applies to adjectival or nominal morphological compounds and to syntag-matic compounds of N N, A N and N P N patterns.

a. Competing structures

Morphological rules

Op.	Term	Variant
Sg	$N/[(N_1 \mid A_1)N_2]$	$(N_1 \mid A_1)\ N_2$
	Magnetfeld	*magnetische Feld*
PI	$N/[N_1N_2]$	$N_2\ P\ N_1$
	Krebsrisiko	*Risiko von Krebs*
PI	$A/[N_1A_1]\ N_2$	$N_2\ P\ A_1\ N_1$
	drehzahlvariabler Antrieb	*Antrieb mit variabler Drehzahl*

Main syntagmatic competing structures apply to terms of N P N pattern. We encode the substitution of preposition and the denominal derivation that comes along with the permutation of the adjective.

Syntagmatic rules

Op.	Term	Variant
R2	$N_1\ P\ N_2$	$N_1\ N_2$
	potenziale die Windenergie	*potenzials von Windenergie*
PR2D	$N_1\ P\ N_2$	$A_1\ N_2$
	$deriv(N_1, A_1)$	$A_1\ N_2$
	Stromerzeugung aus Regenerativen	*regenerativer Stromerzeugung*

b. Augmented/reduced structures

Morphologically augmented structures take into account the insertion of a component in the scope of morphological compound.

Morphological rules

Op.	Term	Variant
I	$N/[E_1N_2]$	$(A \mid N)/[E_1\ (A \mid N)]\ N_2$
	Biokraftstoffe	*biogene Kraftstoffe*
I	$N/[N_1N_2]$	$N_1\ N\ N_2]$
	Primärtherapie	*primäre endokrine Therapie*
PI	$N/[N_1N_2]$	$N_2\ A\ N_1]$
	Energienutzung	*Nutzung erneuerbarer Energien*
PI	$N/[N_1\ N_2]$	$N_2\ A\ N/[EN_1]$
	Krebsrisiko	*Risiko erbliches Darmkrebs*
PI	$N/[N_1\ N_2]$	$N_2\ P\ N/[NN_1]$
	Effizienzsteigerung	*Steigerung der Energieeffizienz*
PI	$N/[N_1\ N_2]$	$N_2\ P\ A\ N_1$
	Mammakarzinompatientin	*Patientin mit kleinen Mammakarzinomen*

Terms taken into account are those of N N, A N and N P N patterns. The linguistic elements juxtaposed to the term are adjectives for A N, N N and N P N, prepositional phrases for N N and N P N, and adverbs for A N.

Syntagmatic rules

Op.	Term	Variant
Jr	N_1 N_2	N N_2 P N
	Ausbau der Windkraftnutzung	*Ausbau der Windkraftnutzung im Offshorebereich*
Jr	N_1 P_2 N_2	N P_2 N_2 P N
	Vorrangigkeit von Biogas	*Vorrangigkeit von Biogas in Erdgasnetz*
Jl	A_1 N_1	A A_1 N_1
	konventionell Kraftwerk	*wirtschaftlich konventionell Kraftwerk*
Jl	A_1 N_1	RA_1 N_1
	eingeführt Windenergienutzung	*zwangsweise eingeführt Windenergienutzung*
Jl	N_1 N_2	A N_1 N_2
	potenzial der Windenergienutzung	*technische potenzial der Windenergienutzung*
Jl	N_1 P_2 N_2	A N_1 P_2 N_2
	Strategie für Komponententausch	*kostenoptimal Strategie für Komponententausch*
I	A_1 N_1	A_1 A N_1
	zukünftig Anforderung	*zukünftig erhöht Anforderung*
I	N_1 P_2 N_2	N_1 P_2 A N_2
	Einspeisung ins Netz	*Einspeisung ins öffentliche Netz*

c. Contextual structures

Contextual rules apply to terms of A N, N N and N P N patterns.

Syntagmatic rules

Op.	Term	Variant
Jr	A_1 N_1	A_1 N_1 C N
	messtechnische Untersuchungen	*messtechnische Untersuchungen und Analysen*
Jr	N_1 N_2	N_1 N_2 C N
	änderung einer Anlage	*änderung der Anlage oder Betreiberwechse*
Jr	N_1 P_1 N_2	N_1 P_1 N_2 C N
	Kraftstoffalternative zu Benzin	*Kraftstoffalternative zu Benzin und Diesel*
Jl	A_1 N_1	A C A_1 N_1
	vertikal Achse	*horizontal und vertikal Achse*
Jl	N_1 N_2	N C N_1 N_2
	Flexibilität der Energieversorgung	*Reaktionsfähigkeit und Flexibilität der Energieversorgung*
I	A_1 N_1	A_1 C A N_1
	horizontal Achse	*horizontal und vertikal Achse*
I	A_1 N_2	A_1 N C N_2
	systematisch Analysis	*systematisch Aufbereitung und Analyse*
PI	A_1 N_1	N_1 V A_1
	erforderliche Genehmigung	*Genehmigung ist erforderlich*

I	N_1 N_2 *Verschärfung der En-ergieeinsparverordnung*	N_1 C N N_2 *Verschärfung und Kontrolle der Energieeinsparverordnung*
I	N_1 N_2 *Erhöhung der Verfügbarkeit*	N_1 N C N_2 *Erhöhung der Zuverlässigkeit und Verfügbarkeit*
I_2	N_1 P_2 N_2 *Versteigerungsverfahren für Lizenzen*	N_1 P_2 N C N_2 *Versteigerungsverfahren für Funkfrequenzen und Lizenzen*

D.5 Russian

The Russian GGRV applies to nominal morphological and syntagmatic compounds of N N, A N and N P N patterns.

a. Competing structures

Morphological rules

Op.	Term	Variant
Sg	N/[A_1N_1] ветроресурс	A_1 N_1 ветровой ресурс
Sg	N/[N_1N_2] электрогенератор	N_1 N_2 электро генератор
P	N/[N_1N_2] энергобаланс	N_2 N_1 баланс энергии
PI	N/[N_1N_2] инсулино резистентность	N_2 P N_1 резистентность к инсулину

Syntagmatic competing structures apply to terms of A N N pattern where the adjective permutes with the expansion noun.

Syntagmatic rules

Op.	Term	Variant
P	A_1 N_1 N_2 альтернативный источник энергии	N_1 A_1 N_2 источник альтернативной энергии

b. Augmented/reduced structures

Morphological rules

Op.	Term	Variant
I	N/[E_1N_2] ветроресурс	A/[E_1(A|N)] N_2 ветроэнергетический ресурс
I	N/[N_1N_2] водоподъем	N_2 (A|N) N_1 подъем уровня воды

Terms taken into account are those of N N and A N patterns. Linguistic elements juxtaposed to the term or inserted are adjectives for A N and N N patterns.

Syntagmatic rules

Op.	Term	Variant
PJr	A_1 N_1 энергоснабжение автономный потребитель	N_1 A_1 N автономное энергоснабжение
Jl	A_1 N_1 солнечный излучение	A A_1 N_1 рассеянное солнечное излучение
Jl	N_1 N_2 энергия ветер	A N_1 N_2 механическая энергия ветра
I	N_1 N_2 аккумулирование энергия	N_1 N N_2 аккумулирование избытка энергии
I	A_1 N_1 международный организация	A_1 A N_1 международная экологическая организация

c. Contextual structures

Contextual rules apply to terms of A N and N N patterns.

Syntagmatic rules

Op.	Term	Variant
Jl	A_1 N_1 автономный сеть	A C A_1 N_1 изолированная и автономная сеть
Jl	A_1 N_1 атомный электростанция	A A C A_1 N_1 мощная тепловая и атомная электростанция
JlI	A_1 N_1 бытовой отход	A A_1 C A N_1 различные бытовые и промышленные отходы
I	A_1 N_1 тепловой энергия	A_1 C A N_1 тепловая и электрическая энергия

Index